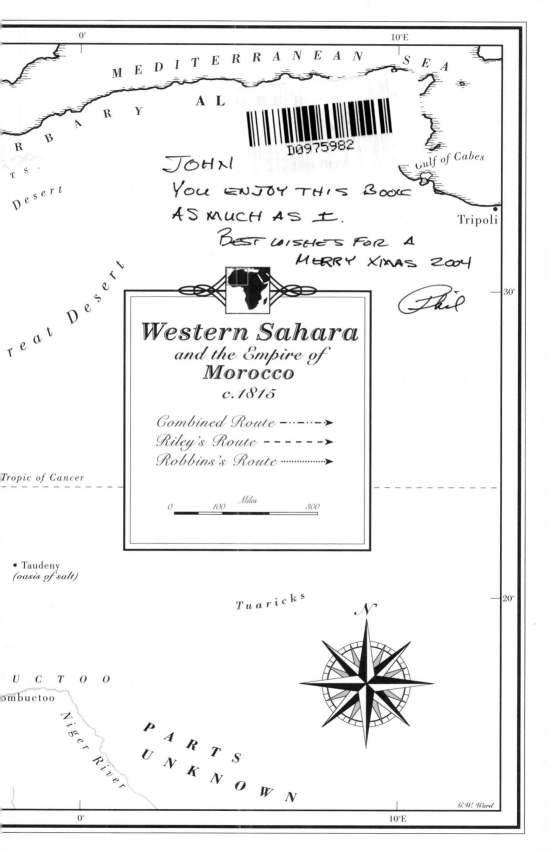

MEDITERRANEAN SEA

BARBARY

AL

Gulf of Cabes

Tripoli

TS.

Desert

reat Desert

JOHN
YOU ENJOY THIS BOOK
AS MUCH AS I.
BEST WISHES FOR A
MERRY XMAS 2004

Phil

D0975982

30°

Western Sahara
and the Empire of
Morocco
c.1815

Combined Route —··—··—→
Riley's Route — — — — →
Robbins's Route ················→

Tropic of Cancer

Miles
0   100   300

• Taudeny
(oasis of salt)

Tuaricks

20°

UCTOO

ombuctoo

Niger River

PARTS
UNKNOWN

N

G.W. Ward

0°   10°E

Skeletons
on the Zahara

also by **Dean King**

AUTHOR

Patrick O'Brian: A Life Revealed
A Sea of Words
Harbors and High Seas

EDITOR

Every Man Will Do His Duty: An Anthology of Firsthand
Accounts from the Age of Nelson, 1793-1815

Skeletons
on the Zahara

A True Story of Survival

Dean King

LITTLE, BROWN AND COMPANY
New York Boston

Little, Brown and Company
Time Warner Book Group
1271 Avenue of the Americas, New York, NY 10020
Visit our Web site at www.twbookmark.com

FIRST EDITION

Maps by G. W. Ward

Library of Congress Cataloging-in-Publication Data
King, Dean.
    Skeletons on the Zahara : a true story of survival / Dean King. — 1st ed.
        p.   cm.
    Includes index.
    ISBN 0-316-83514-5
    1. Africa, North—Description and travel.   2. Sahara—Description and
travel.   3. Commerce (Brig)   4. Slavery—Africa, North.   I. Title.
DT189.K56 2004
916.4804'1—dc22   2003059380

10 9 8 7 6 5 4 3

Q-FF

Book design by Fearn Cutler de Vicq

Printed in the United States of America

∽ Contents ∾

Part Three: Journeys and Sandstorms

Part Four: A Slow Rush to Swearah

✑ Foreword ✑

✑ While researching a book in the library of the New York Yacht Club in Manhattan in the fall of 1995, I spotted an old leather tome with an intriguing title. It said simply *Sufferings in Africa*. I pulled this volume down and soon found myself lost in its musty pages. Though written in language and sentiment not far removed from the Puritan roots of its author, Connecticut sea captain James Riley, this true story of survival — of shipwreck, captivity on the Sahara, and a long journey — was powerful, touching, and extreme.

The year was 1815. The War of 1812 had just come to an end, and the merchant brig *Commerce* set out with a crew of eleven, who held great hopes of restoring fortunes that had suffered during the war. The *Commerce* lost its way in fog and wrecked on the west coast of Africa, on the edge of the continent's Great Desert, a vast uncharted place said to be inhabited by cannibals. Instead, it was camel-riding Arab nomads who captured the starving sailors and introduced them to the strange and rigorous world of the bedouin, traveling from well to well in sweltering heat and sandstorms and living on camel milk. Despised and working as slaves, the sailors faced unimaginable hardships while trying to figure out how to get themselves off the desert and back to their families.

Since at least Homer's day, such accounts of distant voyages, especially voyages gone bad, have mesmerized their audiences, reawakening them from domestic slumber to the world's wonders: its raging elements, its exotic and unyielding geography, its isolated

peoples. The best of these accounts demonstrate anew man's inge-
nuity in the face of adversity, his will to survive, and, in the end, his
intense desire to go home again.

Riley's story did this and more. Like Richard Henry Dana Jr., in
his American classic *Two Years Before the Mast*, Riley recounted his
voyage with the candor of a man who had nothing to prove. Riley
and his men were not professional explorers, like Cook and Banks or
Shackleton. They were not sent to the desert like T. E. Lawrence or
drawn to explore it like Wilfred Thesiger or Michel Vieuchange.
The men of the *Commerce* were just going about the business of being
merchant seamen when they were suddenly thrust onto the Sahara.
Many of the crew left wives and children at home, who expected
them to be back soon with wages much needed to right overdue
accounts.

Not burdened with the need to make history or fulfill the inflated
expectations of a waiting public, Riley, like Dana, reflected a historical time and place with the greater clarity.

Riley's story, published in New York in 1817, gained considerable notoriety, attracting such devotees as Henry David Thoreau,
James Fenimore Cooper, and Abraham Lincoln. Lincoln held up
Riley's narrative as one of the half dozen most influential books of
his youth. But Riley's account had its detractors, skeptics who did
not believe that what he wrote could possibly be true.

Likewise intrigued and curious, I tracked down the memoir of
another survivor of the ordeal, able seaman Archibald Robbins,
whose 1818 account, though briefer, covered an even longer period
of captivity. My own quest had begun. In *Skeletons on the Zahara*
these two firsthand accounts have finally come together for the first
time to tell the story of the wreck of the *Commerce* and the fate of
her captain and crew. But I also felt compelled to go to the Sahara
myself to help bring life to their amazing story after so many decades.
Due to political conditions, unfortunate timing — I arrived three
weeks after 9/11 — and the presence of land mines in Western
Sahara, the former Spanish colony now controlled by Morocco, I was
prevented from reaching many points of interest; however, what I

found during my eight-hundred-mile trek on camels and in Land Rovers retracing Riley's route as best as I could through remote coastal desert was that a great many of Riley's and Robbins's descriptions of the people and conditions hold true today.

In fact, the region remains so little explored and so little changed by modernity that scholars still cite Riley's observations — accurate, with a few notable exceptions — regarding the lives of the nomadic Sahrawis, their customs and beliefs, and the grueling nature of the western Sahara. Riley's is the rare case where disaster begat discovery, instead of the other way around.

In Lincoln's day, Riley's account also spoke to a burning issue: the troubling institution of slavery. Inverting the American paradigm, it provided a useful perspective and helped expose the brutality of that abysmal practice. In our time, when one of the great challenges we face is to find common ground for Muslims, Christians, and Jews, the plight of the crew of the *Commerce* achieves a new relevance. It is my hope that the poignant story of the wreck of the *Commerce* and the journey to redemption of part of her crew will open our eyes anew, at least in some small part, to possibilities.

The Officers and Crew of the Connecticut Merchant Brig *Commerce*, August 1815

Officers
James Riley, age 37, of Middletown, master
George Williams, age 48, of Wethersfield, first mate
Aaron R. Savage, age 20, of Middletown, second mate

Able Seamen
Thomas Burns, age 41, of Hadlyme
James Clark, age 24, of Hartford
William Porter, age 31, of Windsor
Archibald Robbins, age 22, of Stepney

Ordinary Seamen
James Barrett, of Portland, Massachusetts
joined ship in New Orleans
John Hogan, of Portland, Massachusetts
joined ship in New Orleans

Richard Deslisle, of Hartford, cook
Horace Savage, age 15, of Hartford, cabin boy
Antonio Michel, of New Orleans, working passenger;
joined ship in Gibraltar

Places

1815	**Today**

Connecticut

1815	Today
Chatham	Portland
Middletown Upper Houses	Cromwell
Potapaug	Essex
Stepney	Rocky Hill

Northwestern Africa

1815	Today
Agadir, Santa Cruz (Westerners' name)	Agadir
Cape Bajador, Cape Bojador	Cape Bojador, Cap Boujdor
Cape Mirik	Cap Timris
Cape Noun	Cape Draa
Morocco or Marocksh (city)	Marrakech or Marrakesh
Shtuka	Echtouka or Aït Baha
Soudan	Mali
Swearah or Mogadore, Mogador (Westerners' name)	Essaouira (al-Suwaira)
Tombuctoo	Timbuktu or Tombouctou
Wednoon, Wedinoon, Widnoon, Wadinoon	Goulimine or Goulmime
Zahara, Zahahrah, Sahara (from *çahra*, Arabic for "desert"), or the Great Desert	Sahara

For Jessica

Skeletons
on the Zahara

The crew of the *Commerce* seem to have been designed to suffer themselves, that the world, through them, might learn.

—Archibald Robbins, *A Journal Comprising an Account of the Loss of the Brig* Commerce

∾ Prologue: 1812 ∾

∾ In his five crossings of the Sahara, Sidi Hamet had never seen worse conditions. Forty days out of Wednoon, the sand had turned as fine as house dust and as hot as coals of fire. With their heavy loads, the camels labored up shifting dunes in spine-buckling bursts, then stumbled down the other side. With each step, the dromedaries thrust in to their knees, their wide, padded feet, designed by Allah to skim over sand, sinking like stones.

Despite his experience on the desert, Hamet had had no say in choosing this, the most direct route to Tombuctoo, about twelve-hundred miles in all, one that would take many months to travel. Having dropped south from Wednoon, then east around the Anti-Atlas Mountains in six days, the caravan of a thousand men had halted on the edge of the desert, collecting many tons of the date-size argan fruit. The men had extracted oil from the argan pits to fortify their food. They had roasted the meat of the pits, rolled it into balls, and packed these in tent-cloth sacks to serve as camel fodder and fuel for their fires.[1] After ten days of preparations, the caravan headed southeast, navigating the trackless waste by moon, sun, and stars.

Hamet and his younger brother Seid, merchants from the north, near the city of Morocco, had only ten camels. Eight were their own and were richly loaded. The other two belonged to Hamet's father-in-law, Sheik Ali, and they carried barley. There were four thousand other camels in the caravan, many of them milk camels to feed the men en route and four hundred to bear the provisions and water. About half belonged to a powerful warlord who was a friend of the caravan's chief, Sidi Ishrel.

Like all successful caravan drivers, Ishrel was tough but just. Imposing and erect of bearing, the Arab leader had flashing eyes beneath an ample turban and a thick beard to his chest. He wore a long white haik of good cloth, befitting his status, drawn tight around his body and crisscrossed by red belts carrying his essentials: a large powder horn, flints, a leather pouch with musket balls, and his scabbard with a broad and burnished scimitar. He carried his musket night and day, always prepared for a sudden attack from the wild bedouins of the desert. His constant nemeses, however, were the terrain and the sun.

For six days, Ishrel's caravan weltered in the deep drifts, the cameleers alternately singing to their camels and goading them with clubs, constantly dashing on foot here and there to square the loads. They gave violent shoves to bulges in woven sacks and tugged on ropes with the full weight of their bodies. For all their efforts, uneven loads were inevitable, causing strains to the camels' joints and bones. It did not take long for an inattentive master to lame a camel, and a lame camel was a dead camel, a communal feast. In that way, Allah provided for them all. It was his will, and there was no compensation for the camel's owner in this world. "We only feed you for Allah's sake," says the Quran. "We desire from you neither reward nor thanks."

On the seventh day, the *irifi* roared in from the southeast, and the sand swirled. Sidi Ishrel ordered the camels to be unloaded and camp made. In a hurry, the Arabs stacked their goods — iron, lumber, amber, shotguns, knives, scimitars, bundles of haiks, white cloth and blue cloth, blocks of salt, sacks of tobacco and spices — in a great pile. They circled up the camels and made them lie down.

All around them the sand blew so hard that the men could not open their eyes, and if they did, they could not see their companions or their camels even if they were nearly touching them. It was all they could do to breathe. Lying on their stomachs, Hamet and

Seid inhaled through the *sheshes* wrapped around their heads and across their faces, which they pressed into the sand.

They did not fear much for their camels, which have their own defenses: deep-set, hirsute ears and long eyelashes that protect against flying grit, collapsible nostrils that add moisture to the searing air they breathe, and eyes with lids so thin that they can close them during a sandstorm and still see. They did not worry about them overheating either, for camels have a unique ability to absorb heat in their bodies while their brains remain insulated and stable. They conserve their body water by not sweating or panting, instead retaining the heat during the day and releasing it later. On bitterly cold nights, their owners often took refuge in their warmth. As all good cameleers knew, these prized beasts were as impervious to the abuse of the desert as it was possible to be, and they were as long-lived as they were ornery, some reaching half a century in age. Many would outlive their masters.

During the long hours of howling wind, Hamet recalled his reluctance to join Ishrel's caravan. After he had returned to Wednoon from a previous Tombuctoo caravan, which had lasted eighteen moons, his father-in-law had punished him severely for not bringing him a suitable return on the goods he had sent. The caravan, nearly as large as this one, had traveled south on a western route, near the sea, where the poor coastal tribes were too weak to attack them. They had fed, watered, and rested the camels before leaving the north. Only three hundred camels of the three thousand died of thirst and fatigue on the journey, but Hamet and Seid lost two of their four. They returned with two slaves, gold dust worth six camels, and jewelry for their wives. Hamet's father-in-law, Sheik Ali, had demanded both slaves as part of his share. When Hamet refused, Ali destroyed his home and took back his wife along with their children.

Hamet had then fled back to his tribal home near Morocco, a depressed city still feeling the devastation of the Great Plague of 1800. He had sworn off the risky life of a caravan merchant and had begun accumulating livestock. A year later, Ali returned his family to him, but Hamet stayed in the north. Then, after another two years, a friend who had been with them on the caravan persuaded the two brothers to try again. Time had washed away the memory of the cuffing sands and the sting of Ali's unjust demand and swift reprisal. Drawn by an unnameable urge to return to the desert and counting on better luck this time, Seid and Hamet had sold their cattle and sheep, bought merchandise to trade, and joined this caravan.

And now this. For two days, sand filled their long-sleeved, hooded wool djellabas and formed piles on their backs until they shifted to ease the weight. Hamet and Seid and the rest of the traders and cameleers beseeched, "Great and merciful Allah, spare our lives!"

When the wind at last halted and the sand fell to the ground, three hundred men lay dead on the desert. Hamet and Seid, who were strong, rose and joined the rest of the survivors in prayers of thanksgiving to Allah for saving them. They spent two more days burying the dead men, always on their sides, facing east toward Mecca, and topping their graves with thorny brush to keep the jackals away. All but two hundred of the camels had been spared. As the men dug them out, the beasts rose, grunting and snapping madly, weak-kneed, snorting out the beetlelike parasites that grew in their nostrils. There were no plants for the camels to eat where they had stopped, so the men watered and fed them from the dwindling provisions.

For twenty-four more days they racked through deep, hot sand. To keep the camels from flagging under their loads, they gradually dumped tons of the salt they carried for trading. Although they encountered no more sandstorms, they found little forage for the suffering camels, whose humps grew flaccid and sagged. Before they had even reached Haherah, a celebrated watering place perhaps two-thirds of the way to Tombuctoo, they had lost three hundred more camels.

As they neared the oasis, those who had been there before described its verdure and big wells to those who had not. From the lush oasis they would, replenished, continue on to Tombuctoo and its great riches. They would return to the north with elephants' tusks, gold dust and jewelry, gum senegal, ostrich feathers, and many slaves. A fine male slave could be bought for a two-dollar haik and sold back home for a hundred dollars. Yet now thirst coursed so deeply through their veins that greed for Tombuctoo's treasures no longer motivated them. They dreamed not of gold dust but only of purging their cracked throats of dust. To encourage them, Sidi Ishrel let it be known that they would rest the caravan there for twenty days.

When they arrived in Haherah, the news spread like flying sand to the back of the caravan, reaching many of the men before they had even set foot in the much-anticipated valley: There had been no rain in over a year. Haherah's famous wells were dry.

The cameleers panicked. For many, like Hamet and Seid, the camels and goods with them represented their whole fortune, all they possessed for the future support of their wives and children. The caravan disintegrated as men abandoned their stations and set out on their own, frantically scouring the brown valley for water.

After two fruitless days of searching, they realized that such an effort was hopeless. The despondent men made their way back to the caravan, where Sidi Ishrel marshaled them together in teams to remove sand and stones from the old dry wells and mine them deeper. For five days, the teams dug in unison but still found no water. Sidi Ishrel concluded that they had no hope of salvaging the caravan. They could only try to save themselves, so he ordered all but three hundred of the best camels to be slaughtered. They would drink their blood and the fluid stored in their rumens, and they would eat and dry as much of the meat as they needed.

Though aggrieved at what his losses would be, Hamet believed that this was, truthfully, their only choice. Thirty elders selected the camels to be spared, and the slaughter of the rest began. In the heat of the moment, with blood spilling from bellowing beasts and swirling dung dust burning the men's eyes, coating their tongues, and inflaming their minds, they began to quarrel. At first they only brandished their scimitars threateningly, but it was as if death must beget death. Once the crescent-shaped blades clashed, friends joined friends. There was no escaping the feverish battle that resulted. It engulfed the men like a fire sucking in oxygen, leaping from one pocket to the next. Some maimed and killed to slake their helpless frustration; others fought back in self-defense. Seid was stabbed in the arm with a dagger and badly wounded. In their fury, some of the men murdered Sidi Ishrel. More than two hundred others died that day. The survivors drank their blood and butchered five hundred camels for their fluid.

Early that evening, in the exhaustion and despair after the bloodbath, Hamet decided to gather his friends and leave Haherah on his own. He had been made a captain in his previous caravan and knew how to navigate the desert. He and his wounded brother spread the word among their allies to quietly prepare to depart that night. Hamet and Seid killed four of their six remaining camels and fed their blood and water to the two strongest. Hamet packed as much of their barley and merchandise as they could reasonably carry, for they could not arrive at Tombuctoo empty-handed.

Around midnight, Hamet led thirty men and thirty-two camels silently out of the valley into the inky, cloud-dark night. The plain roared with Allah's thunder as they went, but no rain fell.

North of the Niger River in the land Seid and Hamet called Soudan (now Mali), the merchants of Tombuctoo searched the horizon anxiously for the season's caravan. The famous walled city brimmed with fresh stores of gold and slaves to be exchanged for the goods they coveted from the far side of the great void. Once a seasonal camp of the central-Saharan Tuareg nomads, Tombuctoo had risen to prominence in the fourteenth century as the continent's chief marketplace and a locus of African Islam, with learned men and fine books. But its riches also made it a target, and it was sacked by Moroccan invaders in 1591, precipitating a slow but steady decline. Nonetheless, two centuries later, the caravans still came and were sometimes even larger than the one Hamet and Seid had set out in. When the brothers' small company finally limped into Tombuctoo, a total of twenty-one men and twelve camels had survived. They were weary, starving, broke, and alone. No one from their once mighty caravan had preceded them and no one followed.

It was a land of much hardship, and there was little remorse to spare for lost foreigners and even less sympathy for those who had had the fortune to be spared by Allah. The king of Tombuctoo conscripted Hamet, Seid, and ten of their companions and dispatched them in a caravan into the interior. They worked for nearly a year, each earning two haiks and some gold, and then joined a caravan of merchants from Algiers, Tunis, Tripoli, and Fez, returning to the north with turbans, ivory, gum, gold, and two thousand slaves.

On the deep desert, a large party of Tuareg, the Sahara's most feared raiders, armed with muskets, spears, and scimitars, had lain waiting for them for months. They attacked quietly at night, holding their fire until the last minute and then pouring a furious storm of musket balls into the circled-up caravan. Hamet took one in the thigh. One of the Tuareg stabbed Seid in the chest with a dagger. The caravaneers fought for their lives. The raiders killed 230 men and wounded many more before being repulsed, but both brothers survived. Seid assuaged his anger by helping himself to one dead raider's fine musket.

Two years after they had set out in Sidi Ishrel's grand caravan, Hamet and Seid returned to Wednoon with one camel and a trifling amount of merchandise. Sheik Ali had once again failed to profit. This time, he cast Hamet and his brother out onto the Sahara with bundles of haiks and blue cloth to trade with the fierce Kabyles, the desert tribes who raised and raided for camels, hunted ostrich, and on occasion salvaged shipwrecks. Ali had instructed the brothers to trade for ostrich feathers to sell in Swearah or Morocco.

Hamet and Seid wandered south some three hundred miles. One sweltering late-September afternoon in 1815, they spied a cluster of worn-out tents and decided to seek shelter from the sun. They rode into the camp, where to their surprise, they discovered among some Arab women two Christian sailors. One of them was the captain of a merchant ship that had wrecked on the shores of Cape Bojador.

Through his deference to them and his overriding concern for his men, the captain quickly demonstrated that he was a brave and worthy man, no matter how diminished by the Sahara. He approached them with a proposition: He would pay them many pieces of silver if they would render him and his crew, who were scattered nearby among the nomads, a service. But, the brothers knew, the service was as risky as a donkey's trek through a lion's den. It would require that they invest all their goods and then travel across hundreds of miles of *hammada,* dunes, and Atlas foothills. The sailors, frail from thirst, starved, and flayed by the sun, might all die or be stolen before they could be ransomed.

Most of all, Hamet and Seid worried about being cheated in the end. Could they trust a *kelb en-Nasrani* — a Christian dog? Did they dare risk disappointing Sheik Ali again?

Sidi Hamet prayed to Allah for guidance.

PART ONE

Acts of God

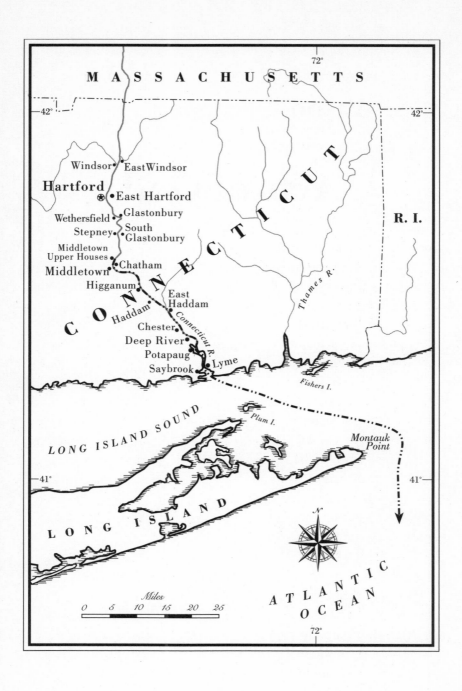

MASSACHUSETTS

72°

42°   42°

Windsor • • EastWindsor

Hartford
⊛ • East Hartford

Wethersfield •   Glastonbury
Stepney •   South
           Glastonbury

Middletown
Upper Houses •
Middletown • Chatham

Higganum •
                     East
                     Haddam
         Haddam •
              Chester •
         Deep River •
         Potapaug •
         Saybrook • • Lyme

C O N N E C T I C U T

R. I.

Thames R.

Connecticut R.

Fishers I.

LONG ISLAND SOUND

Plum I.

Montauk
Point

41°   41°

LONG ISLAND

ATLANTIC
OCEAN

Miles
0   5   10   15   20   25

72°

A Good Yankee Crew

ℜ On a brisk early-May morning in 1815, when Captain James Riley gave the order to cast off from Savage's wharf in the Upper Houses section of Middletown, Connecticut, he had ten men attuned to his every word. "Jemmy Madison's War," a war that New Englanders had bitterly opposed and that had ruined many merchants and left the majority of sailors stranded on shore, was over at last. It was time to get back to work.

Clad in the Connecticut seaman's traditional garb — linsey-woolsey or canvas duck trousers and shirts and snug-fitting round-brimmed hats of tarred canvas or leather — the crew of the 220-ton brig *Commerce* set sail. As those aloft balanced on "horses," the tarred ropes running beneath the yards, they unfastened buntlines, sending the canvas cascading into place. Those on deck hauled and coiled lines. Gruff voices and hammer taps from the now-busy shipyards followed them out on the chilly Connecticut River. The *Commerce* swung around into the channel, and the current, swollen by New Hampshire and Vermont snowmelt, swept them along at five knots back to sea. Now they could look wistfully at the banks they were so desperate to leave. The voyage would take them first to New Orleans and then, if the peace held, across the Atlantic to Gibraltar and partway down the west coast of Africa to the Cape Verde Islands for salt to bring back to Connecticut. If all went well, they would be home before the end of the fall harvest. The wages they earned would help settle overdue accounts.

Captain James Riley
(from *An Authentic Narrative of the Loss of
the American Brig* Commerce, 1817)

The Connecticut — "long tidal river" in the Algonquian tongue — stretches 410 miles from Canada to the Long Island Sound. The river's final 64 miles, from the fall line at Windsor to its mouth at Saybrook, constitute the Lower Valley, a center of shipbuilding and commerce with the West Indies since the Puritans had settled there almost two centuries earlier. But throughout the recent war, it had been bottled up tight.

Lifelong sailors like the *Commerce*'s first mate, George Williams, who hailed from a steady line of sea captains, had chosen to cast about on shore for odd jobs while waiting out the war. The youthful able seaman Archie Robbins, on the other hand, had taken his chances against the Royal Navy, and as a result had turned twenty-one and twenty-two in a Halifax prison. Second mate Aaron Savage, twenty, was the son of a prominent merchant and part-owner of the *Commerce*. Like Williams, Savage had worked on shore, forfeiting crucial years of sea experience. By the time he was that age, Riley had already risen through the ranks in Lower Valley shipping and moved to New York to take command of a vessel in the trans-Atlantic trade.

Now a bearish man of thirty-seven, Riley had been a mariner for twenty-two years. When he was only eight years old, he had been hired out by his father, a poor and ailing farmer, to a neighbor to earn his keep helping with the crops and tending livestock, chores he found especially miserable on frigid winter mornings before the sun rose. At fifteen he escaped to sea. Determined never to return to the farm, he had quickly learned to reef, steer, and navigate. Riley had risen to captain in just five years.

He had most recently been captain not of a ship but of a volunteer company of artillerists, composed mostly of merchant sailors and officers, who had elected him their leader. Riley and his volunteers had grown tired of the British harassing American vessels and impressing her sailors, which had gone on sporadically for more than a decade. But President Jefferson's ill-conceived retaliation in 1808, the Embargo Act, prohibiting exports from the United States and stopping U.S. ships from entering foreign ports, had backfired. American seamen had been cast ashore. Many merchants had failed.

Other missteps had followed, and President Madison had nearly finished off the Yankee merchantman when he declared war on Britain in 1812, bringing on the Royal Navy blockade of the U.S. coast. The value of American exports had plummeted from $60 million in 1811 to $7 million in 1814. Between 1808 and 1813, one Connecticut merchant, John Williams of Wethersfield, had lost five vessels, including his sloop *Merino,* which the British took off Saybrook in 1812 and burned at New London.

In 1814, after the British had torched twenty-eight vessels at Potapaug (now Essex), near the mouth of the Connecticut, and gone on to sack Washington, burning the Capitol, the White House, and many other public buildings, and then, as Riley put it, "loudly threatened to destroy every assailable place on the seaboard," Riley had felt the call to defend his country. He helped form the artillery company, which had forty-four members and, if needed, could muster half that number again within two days.

However, in January 1815, before his company could be deployed, news of the Treaty of Ghent had arrived, putting an end to the conflict if not exactly achieving America's goals of "sailors' rights and free trade." For himself, Riley hoped, it had also put an end to a run of bitter luck.

At eighty-six feet long and twenty-six feet in the beam, the *Commerce* was designed not for river traffic but for the sea. Her two masts of resilient Valley pine towered over the brig's single-decked oak hull. She was square-rigged on both masts but instead of carrying a course on the mainyard had a large fore-and-aft sail rigged out on a boom, making her a more versatile sailor than pure square-riggers. Her dark-painted hull was a bit more than eleven feet deep and roomy enough to hold sixteen hundred barrels. In addition to a crew of eleven, she currently carried what Archibald Robbins called "a small cargo" — twenty tons of hay — though she was also ballasted with 25,000 bricks, which would be sold in New Orleans.

In the early morning light, as a wake formed behind the brig on the surface of the ten-foot-deep pool, the men took a last look at Upper Houses, a prosperous mariner's village of eight hundred, which was technically a section of Middletown but was separated from it by marshland and the Sebethe River. The illustrious Savage family, among others, had built and dispatched merchant ships here for decades. Two new vessels, a brig and a sloop, sat on the stocks nearly ready for launching.

The crew bade farewells to no one but a few hands from the

stores and wharves of Josiah Savage, one of the brig's owners. Savage also owned or had interests in a smithy, a ropewalk, and a slaughterhouse. His men butchered and salted hogs and cattle, packed them in barrels made at his cooperage, and rolled them onto his merchant vessels. The *Commerce* slid past the row of sea captains' silent clapboard houses, many built for various Savage brothers, a testament to the village's seafaring success.

In the *Commerce* and other endeavors, Josiah Savage and his brother Luther were partners with Captain Riley's uncle Justus Riley, of Wethersfield, at seventy-five still an active merchant. Josiah and Justus had prospered together ever since Josiah, now fifty-five, had commanded several of Justus's West Indies vessels and then bought shares in others. The two were cut from the same steel. Shrewd and resourceful, they had been tempered in the Revolutionary War. Justus had captained a privateer and fought alongside half a dozen other Rileys, all adept at that opportunistic, nettlesome mode of warfare. For his part, Josiah had enlisted in the Continental Army as a teen and, alongside his brothers and father, seen plenty of action. After one fight that killed most of his company, Josiah had been stripped of his clothes and forced to run a Mohawk gauntlet, where he had been kicked, clubbed, and beaten in a ritual meant to punish strong men and kill the weak. Josiah was not weak.

Neither was James Riley. Both Justus and Josiah knew a trustworthy man when they saw — or hired — one. They had great faith in Justus's nephew. They liked his intelligence, his industry, his nononsense attitude, and — not least — his massive frame. At six foot one and 240 pounds, James Riley was a good man to have on your side. He was athletically built and powerful by nature, augmented by years of hauling hay and hoeing fields as a youth. Having worked his way up through the ranks, he understood not only his vessel but also the hearts and minds of sailors.

At forty-eight, first mate George Williams was the most experienced seaman on board, a man who could navigate and stand a watch, giving the captain time below in complete security. Williams, whose aunt had married a Riley, had a wife and family in nearby Wethersfield. He was the dependable grandpappy of the crew, linked to the men by family ties, loyalty to their captain, and a shared faith in the sea.

Josiah Savage figured that his third son, Aaron, could learn much by sailing with Riley and Williams, and he had a knack for putting his sons in a position to succeed. His eldest would go on to help found the Aetna insurance company. Another grew immensely wealthy financing the railroads, and his next-to-youngest, a Yale-educated priest and the first Episcopal missionary to Africa, was later credited with discovering the gorilla. Aaron would learn his father's business from the water up.

Captain Riley had taken another Savage on board as well: Horace, the son of William Savage, Josiah's youngest brother and a close friend of Riley's. William had gone to sea in a coasting schooner in November 1799, the year Horace, his second son, was born, and never returned. Ever since, Riley had felt a responsibility to protect the boy and ensure his success. On this trip, the fifteen-year-old would be his cabin boy.

From the brig's flush quarterdeck, Riley could see his former home on Prospect Hill at the top of Main Street. It looked down on Upper Houses and as far as Lamentation Mountain and Mount Higby to the west and southwest. On a tour of the Valley in 1771, John Adams had stood on what would become Riley's property and taken in the view. "Middletown, I think, is the most beautiful town of all," he later wrote in his diary. "When I first came into the town, which was upon the top of a hill, there opened before me the most beautiful prospect of the river, and the intervals and the improvements on each side of it, and the mountains, at about ten miles distant." Adams admired the surrounding fields and small farms with loam "as rich as the soils of Egypt."

In 1807, when everything was going his way, Riley had bought No. 33 Prospect Hill Road, built half a century earlier by Deacon

Ranney. The large two-and-a-half-story clapboard house on a foundation of cut brownstone came with fifteen acres of land and gave his growing family plenty of elbow room.

But hard times had forced Riley out of that house and into humbler lodgings. He could picture his pregnant wife, Phoebe, still asleep in their warm bed there. He was disappointed that their fifth child had not arrived before he sailed, but unfortunate timing was often the lot of the sailor, and there could be no delay. Three long years had passed since he had last set sail, and more than twice as many since a run of profitable voyages had made him temporarily wealthy. There was no more time to lose, not even a day.

Phoebe, the daughter of Hosea Miller, a local Revolutionary War veteran, bore her fate well. She had watched her husband, a passionate man with wide-set eyes and thick dark eyebrows, struggle and brood ever since returning home at the beginning of this recent war. He had been unable to find a position in the Navy. He had no funds to outfit a privateer vessel, and he refused to engage in the lucrative illicit trade with the enemy in Canada or the West Indies, unlike many sailors in New England, a region that opposed the war. Nor would he conduct trade under false colors, trade that necessarily evaded the authorities on both sides of the conflict and was thus against the law.

While he was away, Phoebe would have her hands full with their children — ten-year-old James, Amelia, six, Phoebe, two, Horatio, thirteen months, and a newborn — but she would have help.[1] Upper Houses was a tight-knit community, and James's two spinster cousins, Ann and Eleanor, lived nearby. When their brother, Julius Riley, had sold the place on Main Street in 1784, the new owner agreed to allow the sisters to stay on the third floor until they married. In what was perhaps a case of extreme Yankee thrift, not only did neither ever marry, they both lived to be more than a hundred.

One of the Middletown newspapers, the *Middlesex Gazette*, recorded the *Commerce*'s departure from Middletown on May 2, under a clear sky, with winds blowing providentially from the northwest, and the temperature rising in the afternoon to sixty-two degrees. Two miles south of Savage's wharf, the *Commerce* slipped past the shipbuilding center Chatham on the east bank, which along with Upper Houses was considered part of greater Middletown.

To the north, through fifteen miles of wide floodplains, the river was regularly dredged to Hartford for sloop navigation — vessels drawing eight feet of water or less. Larger vessels drawing up to ten feet of water could reach only as far inland as Middletown, where the federal government, in 1784, had established one of the state's four customs houses to track the profitable sea trade. While Valley ships often ventured across the Atlantic, as the *Commerce* was about to do, trade with the West Indies prevailed.

The Valley's merchants, shipbuilders, and farmers worked together in a lucrative partnership, the farmers raising livestock on fields of clover, timothy, and other grasses and shipping to the West Indies butter, cheese, beef, and pork, along with such crops as corn, rye, oats, and potatoes. They also sent horses, which were tethered on the decks of vessels nicknamed "horse jockeys," and lumber, especially oak barrel staves, which were essential for transporting the islands' sugar. Their ships returned from the islands carrying sugar, salt, coffee, indigo, and rum, as well as manufactured and luxury items from Europe. Until 1790, when it was outlawed, some Connecticut vessels also came home with slaves, who in this part of the country mostly worked as domestic servants.

All of this trade fueled the shipbuilding and maritime industries, and made the lower Connecticut a busy stream. Blessed not only with productive farms but with hardwoods that in colonial days had made Royal Navy shipbuilders drool, it was the most important commercial shipbuilding center between New York and Boston. Over the decades, thousands of small craft and large merchant vessels had rolled off the stocks here. Often painted dark with a single red, white, or blue stripe on the side, the sloops and square-riggers tended to be somewhat rounded in the bow and were admired more for their sturdiness than their speed. By 1815, the wooded banks and hillsides along the lower Connecticut had been largely clear-cut by farmers and shipbuilders. Loggers floated timber for shipbuilding downriver from ever-northerly stands. The demand for new vessels grew steadily, and builders tried to keep up.

Aspiring seamen rose just as quickly to fill the vessels. The *Commerce* had a choice crew, commensurate with its reputable owners and well-regarded captain. Bill Porter, a powerful and friendly man of thirty-one, hailed from Windsor, the inland-most port of the Lower Valley. James Clark of Hartford was a veteran of war-hero Daniel Ketchum's company of the Twenty-fifth Regiment of U.S. Infantry, which had distinguished itself in the 1814 campaign on the Niagara Peninsula. The five-foot-ten-inch Clark, who had enlisted as a private and been appointed sergeant, had dark hair, pale eyes, and a cross tattooed on his arm. The *Commerce's* cook, Dick Deslisle, a free black man, was Ketchum's former servant.

Tommy Burns, who at forty-one was one of the elders of the crew, came from Hadlyme downriver. Burns had served as a fifer in the Sixth Company of the Thirty-third Regiment of Connecticut militia under Captain Calvin Comstock in New London in 1813. Afterward, he had returned to his work on his in-laws' Mount Parnassus farm. In the spring of 1814, his wife, Lillis, had become ill and died suddenly. Grieving, Burns soon left the farm and moved to Hadlyme. He was called up again by the militia in August. At the war's end, he had decided that rather than return to the farm and its painful memories, he would go to sea.

Ordinary seamen Francis Bliss and James Carrington rounded out the regulars, the men who stand a watch. Able seamen such as Porter, Clark, Robbins, and Burns could hand, reef, and steer and could scurry out on the yards in a pitching sea to set or shorten sail as easily as most people walk down a sidewalk. Ordinary seamen, still learning their trade or incapable of advancing, looked after the less technically demanding tasks, mostly on deck or below, heaving, hauling, and swabbing as needed.

They all knew every foot of this last pitch of New England's longest river. Rock ledges, islands, eddies, sediment banks, submerged trees, and creek mouths, as well as wooden posts marking the channel, were the sailors' road signs. The spring freshet always brought changes, sometimes subtle, sometimes dramatic. The officers and seamen kept a keen eye out for these as well as for the river's complex traffic. Fishermen, loggers, brownstoners from the quarries, and merchantmen — mostly sloops and schooners smaller than the *Commerce* — plied the navigable channels. Ferrymen's flat-bottomed scows, each powered by a sweeping oar, crossed from bank to bank carrying horses and wagons, as they had been doing for nearly two centuries.

That evening, spring showers arrived in the Lower Valley. Rain fell all the next day, May 3. One of the sailors, twenty-four-year-old James Clark, who had been released from the military and reunited with his wife, Ruth, and their two young children just six weeks earlier, celebrated his fourth wedding anniversary that day. Back in Upper Houses, Phoebe Riley gave birth to a boy, whom she and the captain had previously agreed to call Asher, after James's father. Barring any unforeseen delays, the captain would meet his son before he was six months old.

From Middle Haddam, where they steered hard astarboard at the end of the Middletown Gorge, the river tugged them south and then steadily southeast. Salt water reached sixteen miles up the river, as far as East Haddam. Here the Salmon River joined in, broadening the Connecticut, at no place more magnificent than in its estuary, where the life of the river commingled with that of the sea. Hardly a Valley mariner could hit this stretch of the river without his heart quickening at the sound of seabirds squawking overhead and the smell of salt air filling his lungs. The Commerces, as the sailors of the *Commerce* would have been called — as if they were simply the living parts of their vessel — were no exception.

In rising high spirits, they chattered and hummed ditties. Yet departing the Lower Valley was always bittersweet. To them, no landscape was as green and salubrious, or as filled with friendly faces, as this one. Some were leaving behind young belles, others would return to a new child in the family. Or, like Horace's father, they might not return at all. Few seafaring families in the Valley had not been touched in this way. Fever took many in the West Indies. All too often a vessel found an unmarked shoal or a sudden squall and was never heard from again. Hostile tribes, cutthroat "salvagers," and pirates held sway in secluded pockets around the globe.

Still, right now departure was more sweet than bitter. Over the years, the sailors had grown used to making two or three round-trips a year to the West Indies. This voyage and the bracing damp chill of the North Atlantic — not to mention a turn of good luck — were long overdue. Activity, conversation, and fresh sights kept their minds in the present while the familiar blue tang of burning Connecticut hardwood still reached out from the riverbanks.

Though young, Archie Robbins, whose father, Jason, was a Wethersfield sea captain, had known almost nothing but hard times at sea and had plenty of stories to tell. In six years, Robbins had been detained or imprisoned by the British three times. In February 1813, the frigate *Surprise* had swooped down and captured the merchant craft in which he was bound for St. Bartholomew, a Swedish territory in the Leeward Islands of the West Indies. He returned on board a cartel ship to New York. In the fall of that year, again in a merchantman bound for St. Bartholomew, he was taken by the blockade off New London. This time he was sent to Halifax, where he was detained for two months. On a third attempt to reach St. Bartholomew, Robbins, who was charged with business from a New York merchant, wisely boarded a neutral Swedish vessel and succeeded, but returning north on board an American vessel, he was taken by the brig *Borer*.

By any standard, Robbins had suffered an impressive run of bad luck, culminating in eighteen months spent in a British prison on Melville Island, Halifax. Now he felt sure that blue skies lay ahead. He called the *Commerce* "a fine stout-built new vessel" and the owners the most respectable merchants. He knew Captain Riley to be an experienced and well-liked commander, and Robbins, whose mother, Honor, was a Riley, also had family ties to the first mate, whose aunts had married Robbins's uncles.

Captain Riley, too, was on the rebound. He had fallen afoul of the international political maneuvering that had oppressed merchant vessels of neutral nations during the Napoleonic Wars. On Christmas Day, he had sailed from New York in the merchantman the *Two Marys* bound for Nantes, at the mouth of the Loire River in France, a port from which he had recently returned. While Riley was at sea, Napoleon had issued the infamous Milan Decree, giving the French any number of pretenses for seizing neutral ships.

On the high seas, Riley had been stopped by two British cruisers. The first was the *Agincourt*, which chased and fired at the *Two Marys* on January 14, 1808. A condescending Royal Navy captain had boarded the merchant ship, admonished Riley not to enter any French or French-controlled port, and recorded the warning in the *Two Marys'* register. Indignant, Riley had demanded to know by what right the captain had barged onto the quarterdeck of a vessel from a neutral nation and made such a rebuke, but he received no answer. Five days later, the schooner *Pilchard* played out a similar scene in the Bay of Biscay. When a third British warship opened fire, Riley sailed into the French port of Belle-Ile. There, officials examined his register, which showed that he had allowed a British officer to board his vessel. They used this excuse to seize the brig and her cargo as a prize of war while Riley watched in impotent fury. He spent the better part of two years traveling around the Continent trying to straighten out his affairs, but in the end the labyrinthine bureaucracy for which the French even then were famous defeated him. When he returned home to his wife and two children in 1809, he was broke.

As Riley later stated in a petition to Congress, he found his nation's commerce "languishing and restricted; many of her mercantile establishments ruined; and individual capital, credit, and resources quite exhausted or paralyzed by the continual hostility of the powers at war, and by measures resorted to by the United States to counteract the English and French policy."[2] Legitimate trade was impossible.

As Riley's debts piled up, Josiah Savage lent him $500 against his

Prospect Hill property and house. Riley owed New York merchants N & D Talcott $2,200 and Middletown merchants Eells Child Co. and other creditors hundreds of dollars more. All took him to court and had judgments passed against him. He was under constant threat of having his house foreclosed on. The sheriff of Middlesex County delivered the judgments to his door and threatened to take him to debtors' jail in Hartford.

Riley scrambled to find a way to make money and to keep his prized home. Having sent mineral water from a spring at the base of his property to the renowned Yale chemistry professor Benjamin Silliman to gauge its restorative qualities, he had laid out on paper his vision of a grand spa with a bathhouse. He had confidently planted forty-two poplar trees to adorn his future establishment, which he imagined would rival the famous Stafford Springs Hotel on the Willimantic. But it was not to be. He could not get ahead of his debts. He leveraged his home and his property until he lost them. Riley had since rebuilt some of his credibility, but he remained haunted by his earlier failure.

On Wednesday, May 4, the rain let up and the clouds lifted, but the wind came from the south, heading the *Commerce*'s square-rigged sails. They were near Potapaug, a shipbuilding center that was still reeling from the so-called Good Friday blaze set by the British in 1814. Two hundred thousand dollars' worth of vessels had incinerated, by some estimates the worst financial loss of the war. The charred spine and ribs of the massive 344-ton *Osage* still jutted out of the mud at Williams Shipyard in North Cove, a grim reminder of the night.

As they passed the renowned Hayden Yard and a slew of smaller yards, it was obvious that the business of building ships from raw materials carried on. Fortified against the spring chill by the customary daily tot of shipyard rum, men worked crosscut pit saws, turning timbers into long planks. They hewed pins with broadaxes and hammered spikes that had been forged by smiths on site. Others stitched canvas in sail lofts and made cordage at ropewalks.

On May 5, the breeze shifted favorably to the northwest, and the next day, the *Commerce* reached the last stretch of the river with the wind gusting over her starboard beam.

At Lyme, the men watched out for the Tilleye's Point ferry as they prepared to pass through the Connecticut's shallow mile-wide mouth. Choked by sandbars, this was the trickiest passage on the river. The *Commerce,* like all deep-bottomed traffic, stuck to the navigable channel on the western side by Saybrook until she passed the wooden lighthouse at Lynde Point, which marked the beginning of the Sound. Once she was clear of the sandbars and in deep water, the brig jogged some forty miles east across the Long Island Sound and rounded Montauk Point into the Atlantic.

Riley was at sea again. He was back in his element, where, like many Rileys before him, he had made his name, where he had garnered a small though temporary fortune, and where he would die.

Riley had made his maiden voyage in the role Horace Savage now filled, cabin boy, on board a West Indies–bound sloop. Since then, few things had been more meaningful to him than the fraternity of seamen and merchants on the Connecticut River. He was pleased that he could stand in for his old friend William Savage and looked forward to giving his son a start in the life his father had loved.

chapter 2

Omens

The year 1815 marked a historical watershed for the burgeoning United States. With the end of the War of 1812, the country entered a phase of transformation fueled by revolutions in transportation and industry. Robert Fulton's steamboat had debuted on the Hudson in 1807. In 1811, the *New Orleans* had steamed from Pittsburgh to New Orleans. Steam would power a new generation of commercial vessels on America's rivers, and industrial workshops would spring up throughout the Connecticut River Valley.

Still, the change would be gradual, and sailing ships would remain in commercial use throughout the century. For the Commerces, whose plight would in many ways symbolize the beginning of the end of the age of the sailing ship, this looming obsolescence was not apparent.

To Riley, sailing on the open sea would always mean freedom and opportunity. As a boy, he had watched his father scratch out a living for his thirteen children on the farm and had helped him and later his neighbor plant and harvest when he should have been in school like other children his age. He would never go back to farming if he could help it. Neither the recent return of Napoleon from his brief exile on the island of Elba, which the newspapers had announced just before the brig's departure, nor the threat of attack by Barbary corsairs off the coast of North Africa would dampen his enthusiasm to voyage across the sea again.

While the Treaty of Ghent had brought the War of 1812 to a close, it had not resolved many of its root issues. American merchant mariners remained wary. The result of the "expensive and bloody" war, complained a February 1815 editorial in the *Connecti-cut Courant,* the Lower Valley's chief voice, was the loss of trading rights to the British colonies in the East and West Indies, which had never been a sure thing anyway since independence. "An American vessel going within a marine league of the coast of any British colony," it warned, "will be liable to be fired on and captured."

Yet during the war, Britain's indisputable rule of the waves had been shaken. Although the United States had had no answer for the blockade that locked up its shores, the heavy frigates of its under-dog navy had won battles that stunned the Royal Navy, and the world. As novelist and naval historian James Fenimore Cooper saw it, "The ablest and bravest captains of the English fleet were ready to admit that a new power was about to appear on the ocean."

The war had given the young nation "a confidence in itself that had been greatly wanted," Cooper allowed, "but which, in the end, perhaps, degenerated to a feeling of self-esteem and security that were not without danger." Britain had built its mercantile empire on the strength of the mightiest navy ever known. What U.S. mer-chants lacked in infrastructure and experience, they made up for by taking advantage of America's wealth of fertile soil, raw materials, and enterprising spirit. But to compete around the world, American commerce had to be protected.

During the War of 1812, the navies of the Barbary states of North Africa — encouraged by the British, who had promised to destroy the fledgling American Navy — had attacked and plundered Yan-kee merchantmen, enslaving their crews. A few weeks after the *Commerce* set sail, Congress dispatched Captain Stephen Decatur at the head of a squadron of warships to subdue the Barbary States: Morocco, Algiers, Tunis, and Tripoli. Before the war, the Americans had reluctantly accepted the Old World system of tributes for peace. Now they were out to change the system.

Two weeks after leaving the mouth of the Connecticut, the *Com-merce* reached the Bahamas, sighting Great Abaco Island and passing Hole in the Wall, a "remarkable perforated rock" at the island's south end, the next day. The blue-water sailing in the Atlantic had been uneventful, the men content to be at peace and at sea again.

The brig now entered the pellucid waters of the Great Bahama Bank, which in places is no deeper than twenty feet. Disarmed by the beautiful view of the bottom, many a ship had run afoul of the area's dangerous crosscurrents and hazardous shoals. As the 1819 *Colombian Navigator* warned mariners, the principal occupations of the region's small craft were coastal trading, fishing, turtling, and searching for wrecks. The locals were licensed by the governor to salvage. They received a percentage of anything they recovered, and quite a few made a living this way.

Riley, who had sailed to New Orleans many times before, crossed the swift-flowing Northwest Providence Channel to the Berry Islands, passing to the leeward of Great Stirrup Cay, the northernmost of this cluster of cays and small islands, and steering west southwest for 36 miles, then south southwest for 120 miles. According to the authoritative *Navigator,* this was more or less a standard route as laid down by a Captain Ferrer in 1800 and appropriate for small vessels. On May 22 the *Commerce* sighted the next landmark, the Orange Cays — a collection of four small bush-covered islands along with two bald rocks — to starboard.

Riley navigated the brig off the bank at about three miles' distance. He now steered west southwest for the Double Headed Shot Cays. The *Navigator* put them at about forty-five miles away and instructed mariners to steer "S.W. by S.," meaning Riley's course was a bit northerly of what the editors recommended.

In the afternoon, the *Commerce* was becalmed at the intersection of the Bahama and Santaren channels, though the day's heat and frustration faded as the breeze picked up toward evening. Riley was intent on taking advantage of this favorable wind and cracked on to make up for lost time. Approaching the Double Headed Shot Cays at night was a dodgy business. These islets south of the Biminis were not well charted. "Should you sail for those kays in the night," the *Navigator* warned, "by all means keep clear of them: there are a

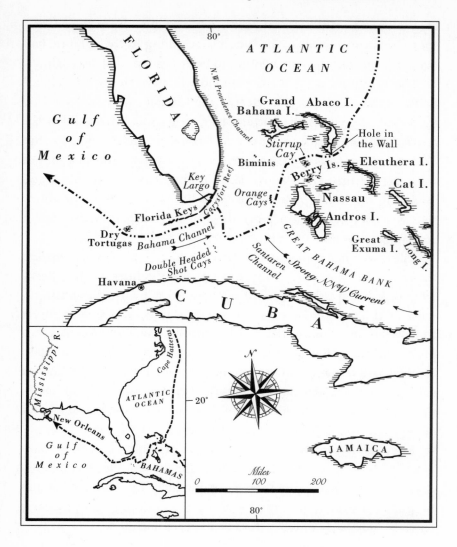

number of bare rocks, perhaps . . . an hundred and twenty, about the size of a vessel, and some less." It recommended delaying an approach until dawn.

But it would be a bright and glorious night. The moon, only a day short of full, rose as the sun set. Riley remained on deck, scanning the horizon all night, anxiously watching, unaware of the extent to which the strong north-northwest current had changed his position that afternoon. He was sure that they should have seen the cays by now. At four in the morning, he concluded that they must have safely passed them. Although he felt a lingering dissatisfaction at not having sighted the flotilla of small islands forming an unpassable trench in the sea, he was dog-tired. Reluctantly, he turned the deck over to George Williams while he went below to get some sleep. Before descending to his cramped private quarters, where his bed held a feather mattress (one of the few indulgences on board), he reminded Williams to keep a careful lookout on all sides for land, breakers, or white water, and he told the watch to look alive.

About an hour later, a shock to the keel awakened Riley from his uneasy slumber. The shriek of wood on coral turned his sweat cold as he flung his legs out of bed. In the next instant, he was up the ladder and rushing onto the deck, where it was now light. "Starboard the helm," he yelled to the man at the wheel. This checked the brig's speed. "All hands on deck," he shouted. With nerves alive and trembling, he took in the crucial data: brig making ten knots to the southwest, land to the north, breakers dead ahead and to the south. He seized the helm and turned it hard to port. At the same time, he commanded the men to let the sails run, in effect turning off the engine, and to ready the anchors for dropping.

Again the coral reef beneath them screeched against the brig's hull and, after an agonizing silence, yet again. The *Commerce* was floating over the reef in about fifteen feet of water. Mercifully, it was calm. In rising and falling seas, her hull would have been slammed against coral heads as hard as stone and as sharp as a razor. "Drop anchor," Riley bellowed. The *Commerce* came to a rest. The men took in her sails. Riley ordered a small boat lowered. In it, he and four men searched for an opening in the reef. Finding greater depth to the reef's leeward side, they sounded out a passage. Riley returned to the brig, ordered her head turned, and got under way again. By seven in the morning, the emergency was over, and the brig was sailing toward New Orleans, but Riley was rattled. In all his long experience at sea, he had never navigated a vessel into such a scrape. Furious, he pored over the chart and the log, astonished to see that the only possible explanation was that the current had forced — as he put it, "horsed" — the brig no less than sixty miles to the lee in sixteen hours, nearly four miles an hour, so far that she was about to be swept onto the menacing Carysfort Reef, a shipping graveyard on the edge of the Gulf Stream, about six miles from Key Largo. Two minutes more, he calculated, and the *Commerce* would have been dashed on the reef's southwest corner.

Yet Riley did not reprimand his crew, nor did he blame himself. "I mention this incident," he later wrote, "to warn the navigator of the danger he is in when his vessel is acted upon by these currents, where no calculation can be depended upon, and where nothing but very frequent castings of the lead, and a good look out, can secure him from their too often fatal consequences." This was the first stroke of bad luck for the men of the *Commerce*.

The brig now ran southwest along the Florida Keys, keeping off them by a dozen or so miles and staying at comfortable depths of some thirty fathoms (180 feet). At noon on May 24, she rounded the Dry Tortugas, the cluster of islets that mark the entrance to the Gulf of Mexico, in sixty feet of water.[1]

Two days later the *Commerce* reached the mouth of the Mississippi River, arriving at Balize, a low, marshy island. Balize was so flat that distant mariners first saw it as an American flag flapping on a pole rising directly out of the sea. Here the brig was met by the pilot boat, which placed her on the official "arrived" list.

Thirty-three miles farther on, Riley presented her papers, as required, to the commanding officer of Fort St. Philip, beside the brackish swamps of the Plaquemine Bend. The *Commerce* proceeded past the tricky shoals seven miles north, where the land was so narrow that at a height of just a few rungs up the shrouds, Riley could see the sea less than a musket-shot away.

Having considerable experience navigating the mighty river, Riley assuaged his ego somewhat on the ninety-five-mile approach to New Orleans. There was an art to swimming against the combined currents of the Ohio, Missouri, Illinois, and dozens of other rivers that formed the Mississippi, especially in the full flow of spring. With a fair wind, the key was to travel from point to point, avoiding the bends as best as possible, and thus not only shortening the distance traveled, but minimizing the effects of the current and avoiding the sunken trees along the murky banks that could puncture a ship's bottom and foul her anchors.

As on the Connecticut River, the bow lookout had to keep a sharp watch for potential hazards. An alert captain took frequent soundings as his vessel approached each point. In light wind, he kept a boat's crew on the ready to carry a hawser, a five-inch-thick rope, to the bank for tying up to trees, which was preferable to anchoring, since it allowed for faster reaction to favorable winds and eliminated the possibility of fouling the anchors.

The crew of the *Commerce* were rivermen, after all, and the Connecticut could be tricky to climb too, requiring towing from the bank at its worst. As the Commerces worked their way up the Mississippi, they passed outward-bound vessels headed for all parts: Mobile, Pensacola, Bay St. Louis, Liverpool. Riley worked the crew hard, out-sailing dozens of vessels heading north and arriving at New Orleans on the first of June.

The city, only recently acquired by the United States from France after four decades under the Spanish flag, bustled with 25,000 people, a population so diverse that the *Navigator* declared no city of its size anywhere in the world had a "greater contrast of national manners, language, and complexion." It also noted that few places could match it for the pursuit of "pleasure or . . . profit."

For three weeks, the Commerces had the run of the waterfront, where sailors bathed at the newly opened Navy Hotel, dined for a dollar at the Irish Coffee House, and for five dollars took home souvenir engravings of General Andrew Jackson, hero of the Battle of New Orleans, the last battle of the war and an unnecessary one since it took place after the signing of the Treaty of Ghent but before the news could cross the Atlantic.[2] They could buy fashionable Cossack boots from Pittsburgh, the latest hats from Leghorn, or old Cognac straight from France. The more reserved Connecticuters could sit back and watch the free-for-all. New Orleans was a magnet for riffraff, drifters, wanted men, and refugees from all over. Two days after they arrived, a *Louisiana Gazette and New-Orleans Mercantile Advertiser* editorial excoriated the city's "wretched police": "The bridges almost at every square are broken, and the accumulated filth in the streets and gutters exceeds any thing of the kind exhibited in [any other] city under the United States government: — In fact, every other part of the police is equally bad," complained the editor. "Licentiousness and riot (if paid for) is granted — and the city guard protects the rioters, by imprisoning all civil citizens who may interfere."

Adding to the city's air of lawlessness were the *Gazette*'s not infrequent advertisements for fugitive slaves and sailors on the lam. The reward for runaway slaves was roughly $30, the reward for Navy deserters $15. Riley might have seen a notice by one plantation owner admonishing captains against shipping a handsome, thickset escaped slave named Shadrack, who could be identified by a small scar on his forehead and burns on the back of his hand. Another of the *Gazette*'s announcements warned that a fugitive mulatto named Tom might pose as a white man.

Slaves could be bought at the auctions that were held frequently at various coffeehouses. Ads, such as one for a "negro house wench, about 19 years of age, and her child about 15 months old" and another, with apparently unintended irony, for a "negro boy named Liberty," alerted potential buyers to public sales.

Riley notified Talcott & Bowers, a well-known merchant house, of his arrival, and two days later the firm placed an advertisement in the part-English, part-French *Louisiana Gazette,* whose banner — "America, Commerce, and Freedom" — exemplified the spirit of the day. The ad, situated in the prime upper-right-hand corner of the newspaper's front page, billed the *Commerce* as a "staunch fast sailing brig" able to stow sixteen hundred barrels and ready to receive cargo in three days.

In the meantime, Riley discharged his hold full of bricks and hay, which Talcott & Bowers also advertised. In New Orleans, captains could fill their vessels with every kind of commodity imaginable, including a batch of two hundred bear skins available when Riley was there. As an experienced supercargo, Riley would have been given loose parameters as to what to carry on the middle passage of his triangular route. He would have been equipped with introductions in New Orleans and a number of European ports, based on the good reputations of Justus Riley and Josiah Savage. Though the owners would rely on Riley's discretion to make the best possible deal here, they presumably gave him more detailed instructions regarding what to bring back for their stores in Hartford and Middletown. Talcott & Bowers lined up a cargo of tobacco and flour for him to carry to Gibraltar, "principally on freight," according to Riley, meaning the brig owners were compensated for hauling the goods and did not share in the risk or profit of selling them at the other end.

Rugged and raw but eminently stylish, half cosmopolitan, half frontier, New Orleans was nothing if not a place of opportunity. The two ordinary seamen, Francis Bliss and James Carrington, asked to be discharged so that they could seek theirs. Archie Robbins recorded only that they "objected to going a voyage to Gibraltar, to which place the vessel was bound." In their stead, John Hogan and James Barrett, two ordinary seamen from Portland, Massachusetts (now Maine), decided to try their luck in the *Commerce*. Riley gave the command to set sail for Gibraltar on June 24, six days after Wellington defeated Napoleon at Waterloo, a fact that had not yet reached America.[3]

On the Atlantic crossing, the men had time to become familiar with one another's habits, quirks, and skills. Porter and Robbins became close friends. Burns put his musical talents to good use. Clark and Deslisle entertained the crew with war stories. At Chippawa, two miles above Niagara Falls, Ketchum's company had held out against three times its number of redcoats in fierce fighting in the woods. At the Battle of Lundy's Lane, the bloodiest battle ever fought on Canadian soil and one that ended the American offensive in the Loyalist British colony, they had laid a trap at Portage Bridge and captured British General Phineas Riall and part of his staff, wounding Riall in the right arm in the process and stunning the enemy.

The old-line Connecticuters had a reserve of family tales to fall back on. Just as the Savages and Rileys had a history of going to sea together, so did the Rileys and Robbinses. One story was always sure to produce hearty laughs. When Frederick Robbins, Archie's uncle, had decided to further serve his country by outfitting and sailing on board a privateer, he asked his neighbor Captain Jabez Riley to take command. Two men more unalike are hard to imagine. A wealthy farmer and veteran of Bunker Hill, Frederick was an erect military man, who in later years took to dressing in a velvet-collared indigo coat and ruffled shirts, riding in fancy carriages, and drinking French wine in crystal goblets. Jabez Riley, a chuff seaman not given to extravagances, buried his savings in an orchard on his property, hidden even from his wife.

To no one's surprise, their partnership was short-lived. Early on their first cruise out of New London, they dropped anchor in a hopeless fog, only to find themselves, when the veil lifted, practically kissing a British frigate. The two had plenty of time to hash out their disappointment on board the infamous death-ship *Old Jersey,* where they rotted for months before being exchanged for Hessians taken by Washington.

The Commerces could further amuse themselves in hearing again the result of Jabez's monetary prudence. During a later storm at sea, certain that his vessel would founder, Jabez put a note with the location of his buried cash in a bottle and threw it overboard, regretting his extreme secrecy and trusting that an honest person would find it and deliver it to his wife. The vessel somehow survived the storm, however, and Jabez rushed home, dug up his money, and deposited it in a chartered bank. When the bank promptly failed, the captain bitterly cursed the fact that he had survived only to make his wife poor.

During quiet times on deck, in the evening or at dawn, Riley had the leisure to reflect on his own experience. He thought back to the debacle of the *Two Marys*. Getting tangled up in the European war had been most unfortunate for him. Chased by one side, he had been robbed by the other and stranded on the Continent. Although he witnessed "many important operations in the science of war" there, his most lasting souvenirs were a facility with French and Spanish and, as he put it, "lessons in the school of adversity, which tended to prepare and discipline my mind for future hardships."

The *Commerce* crossed the Atlantic in good time, about six weeks, and knifed into the Mediterranean through the Strait of Gibraltar, the thirty-six-mile gap that separates two continents and two cultures.[4] At the eastern end of the Strait, the men of the *Commerce* looked upon two mighty promontories, the mythic Pillars of Hercules, which were said to have once been part of the same mountain range until the fabled strongman wrenched them apart, thus joining the two seas. The sailors would have two weeks to explore the fourteen-hundred-foot Rock of Gibraltar on the European side, while they would only view the almost-three-thousand-foot African promontory Jebel Musa from the sea.

On August 13, four days after reaching Gibraltar, the *Commerce* landed her cargo of flour and tobacco. On shore, Riley conducted business with a Gibraltar merchant, Horatio Sprague, who entertained him at his home. Sprague, a bachelor who hailed from Boston, was a stout, vivacious man with wavy, slightly disheveled hair, a broad face, and owlish eyes. He and Riley got on famously. It was a heady time for Americans in the Mediterranean. In June, Decatur's squadron had captured the forty-six-gun frigate *Mashouda*, killing the Algerian admiral who had terrorized the Mediterranean, and prompting the Dey of Algiers to agree to return his American captives, make reparations, and establish normal relations — thus renouncing the right to tributes from the United States. In July, the thirty-six-year-old Decatur gave the Bey of Tunis twelve hours to accept similar terms. Before accepting, the exasperated potentate exclaimed, "Why do they send wild young men to treat for peace with old powers?"

Horatio Sprague, Esq.
(from *Sequel to Riley's Narrative,* 1851)

Decatur's squadron proceeded to Tripoli, where in 1804, as lieutenant, Decatur had made his name in a daring raid to burn the U.S.
frigate *Philadelphia,* which had run aground and fallen into the
hands of the Tripolitans. Then Decatur had saved face for the U.S.
Navy; now he brought the Bashaw of Tripoli to his knees, capping
off a campaign that ushered in a new era of free trade in the
Mediterranean.

The acting U.S. consul in Gibraltar took advantage of the high
spirits generated by these events to beg Riley to accept a passenger,
a penniless old sailor who was anxious to work his passage across
the Atlantic. Antonio Michel, a native of New Orleans, had recently
been wrecked on Tenerife, the largest of the Canary Islands. Riley
agreed, and Michel came on board with little more than the clothes
on his back.

Riley also met Captain Price of the American schooner *Louisa*, which had just arrived from New York City. She was bound for Barcelona and was standing off and on in the bay waiting for Price to return to proceed east. He told Riley that if he accompanied him out to the schooner, he would give him a copy of the New York *Price Current* and some newspapers.

In need of the latest information for gauging his purchases, Riley took the longboat with Porter, Robbins, Barrett, and Hogan out into the bay.[5] It was a windy afternoon, and the schooner was far out, three miles into the Strait, or Gut, as it was then known, where a stiff current ran to the east. By the time Riley retrieved the items Captain Price had promised him, it was dusk, and Price was as eager to proceed to Barcelona as Riley was to return to port.

As Riley and his men prepared to step the longboat's mast and hoist her sail, they were hit by a rogue wave; Riley later called it a "toppling sea." They all jumped overboard in a vain effort to keep the boat from filling. With the light fading and the *Louisa* speeding off and already a mile away, the situation suddenly looked dire. Bobbing in the choppy sea, the sailors shouted and waved their hands in a last-ditch effort to attract the attention of the *Louisa*'s lookout.

By a fortunate stroke, the wind carried their voices. Captain Price heard them and turned the schooner around. In the dark, he sent out a boat. The rescuers hauled up the Commerces and righted their boat. Soaked and shivering but thankful to be alive, Riley and his crew returned to the *Commerce* around ten o'clock.

Following on the near-disaster in the Bahamas, here was another close call, another bad omen. "We were spared," Riley later lamented, "in order to suffer a severer doom."

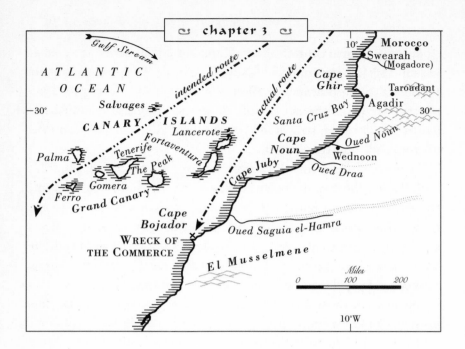

chapter 3

The map shows:

ATLANTIC OCEAN

Gulf Stream

intended route

actual route

-30°

Salvages

CANARY ISLANDS

Lancerote

Palma

Tenerife

Fortaventura

The Peak

Gomera

Ferro

Grand Canary

Cape Bojador

WRECK OF THE COMMERCE

Santa Cruz Bay

Cape Ghir

10°

Morocco

Swearah (Mogadore)

Taroudant

Agadir

30°—

Cape Noun

Oued Noun

Wednoon

Cape Juby

Oued Draa

Oued Saguia el-Hamra

El Musselmene

Miles

0   100   200

10°W

Shipwreck
on Cape Bojador

❧ During the Middle Ages, Cape Bojador on the west coast of Africa, about eight hundred miles south of the Strait of Gibraltar, loomed large in the European imagination. The cape, whose name derives from the Arabic *abu khatar,* "father of danger," marked the southern end of the navigable world, where ships and sailors disappeared without a trace. The source of its infamy lay not in its prominence but in its location — at the south end of the Canary narrows, a rapid south-flowing channel between the Canary Islands and the African coast. Part of the clockwise North Atlantic current, the cold waters of the so-called Canary Current run pell-mell onto Bojador's shallow banks. To add to the cape's ill repute, medieval Europeans believed the coast was inhabited by pagan cannibals.

From the north on a clear day, Cape Bojador appears as a bed of red sand tilting gently to the sea from coastal cliffs that rise to seventy feet. This appearance belies its destructive nature. Fog and foul weather frequent the small bay. Where the northwesterly swells butt heads with the strong land wind, heavy breakers crash on the shallows. At its worst, the low reef ringing the cape becomes a churning death trap for a fog-blind victim.

In 1291, the Vivaldi brothers sailing from Genoa rounded Cape Bojador in hopes of reaching the East Indies. They were never seen again. The Catalan mariner Jaime Ferrer rode a diminutive galley south of the cape to his demise in 1346. Not until the first half of the fifteenth century did the explorers of Henry the Navigator of Portugal, sent out into "the Great Black Sea" to find knowledge, gold, and slaves and "to cause injury to the Moors," finally manage to pass through the Canary Straits and return.

This was no small feat. It expanded the navigable universe for good. Even so, it did not prevent hundreds of sailing ships, each vessel powered by wind and vulnerable to the ripping current, from wrecking on Bojador over the next four centuries. The decades around the start of the nineteenth century were particularly calamitous because of an increase in international shipping.

In his groundbreaking *Account of the Empire of Marocco* (1809), British merchant James Grey Jackson speculated that of the vessels wrecked on the Saharan coast, "many are probably never heard of; and if any of the crew survive their hardships, they are induced, seeing no prospect of emancipation, to become Mohammedans." Among the thirty known wrecks between 1790 and 1806, he tallied seventeen English, five French, five American, and three of various other nationalities. The seamen who were lucky enough to escape from the desert did so with horrific tales.

The French merchant F. Saugnier, on board *Les Deux Amies,* and diplomat Pierre Raymond de Brisson, in the *Ste. Catherine,* had been stranded on Cape Bojador in 1784 and 1785, respectively. In 1800, Judah Paddock, captain of the *Oswego* out of New York, wrecked there, as did New Yorker Robert Adams on board the *Charles* in

1810. Also that year, sixteen-year-old apprentice seaman Alexander Scott of Liverpool, England, began six years of wandering after the Brazil-bound ship *Montezuma,* under Captain Knubley, wrecked north of Cape Bojador. All left accounts of death and bondage on the Sahara and suffering so extreme that the authors begged forgiveness for sounding like liars. And they were among the very, very few survivors.

The *Commerce* had no intention of going near Cape Bojador. Carrying brandy, wine, and Spanish dollars acquired in Gibraltar, as well as Riley's private venture (known as an "adventure") — a chest full of silk lace veils and handkerchiefs — the *Commerce* set sail for the Cape Verde Islands on August 23, after nearly two weeks in Gibraltar.[1]

According to Riley's account, the brig's primary cargo for North America was to be salt, a major export of the dry, windswept tropical archipelago 330 miles west of Africa, which also dealt in ships' provisions and slaves. Riley's plan made sense. The salt trade between the United States and these Portuguese islands had been choked off by the war. Stores would be ample and demand in the States strong.

It is possible that Riley instead intended to buy slaves. He could have done so in the islands, or he may actually have considered landing on the slave coast of Africa. If so, he probably would have planned to sell them in the West Indies, most likely in Cuba, where Connecticut River merchants were well established, and to then take on a cargo of sugarcane, molasses, and rum before returning home. Although the importation of slaves had been illegal in Connecticut since 1790 and in the United States since 1808, some New England vessels, including those of reputable merchants, practiced this lucrative so-called triangular trade well into the nineteenth century.

According to Sherman Adams and Henry Stiles's *History of Ancient Wethersfield,* a rumor later surfaced that the brig was in fact after slaves. This was reported by Charles Williams, a citizen of the town, who reasoned that the *Commerce* was "a long way out of the course she should have sailed," and that "her cargo consisted prin-

cipally of salt beef, potatoes and many casks of fresh water —
circumstances which were suspicious." He believed the stores were
slave provisions. His logic is unconvincing, however. Riley was
already admittedly heading to the Cape Verde Islands, a common
salt-trading destination where slave trading also took place. Veering
off course did not take him nearer to any other slave port. Furthermore, the provisions Williams cited were typical and not indicative
of a slaving ship, which generally served its human cargo corn mush
or rice with palm oil, horsebeans (usually used to feed cattle), cas-
sava, and other inexpensive and easily obtained foods. Slavers
rarely provided the Africans with meat. Finally, at the time of
Riley's voyage, American ships were not officially welcomed in most
of the West Indian colonies. Since the West Indies were both an
important source of salt for the United States and the place where
African slaves were typically taken to be sold, it made perfect sense
for the *Commerce* not to carry slaves to the West Indies but to take
salt back to Connecticut from the Cape Verdes.

On the morning of August 24, the *Commerce* passed through the
Strait of Gibraltar, clearing Cape Spartel, the southern point of the
west end of the strait, by some thirty-five miles. With a fair wind,
Riley set a west-southwesterly course for the Canary Islands,
intending to pass through the narrow channel between the islands
of Tenerife and La Palma. The usual course from Gibraltar to the
Cape Verde Islands, according to Archie Robbins, was more west-
erly, via Madeira, the Portuguese island some four hundred miles
from the coast of Morocco. But, said Robbins, Riley wished to make
the passage "as expeditious as possible."

In the Atlantic, the brig encountered unusually difficult weather.
Along the stretch of coast between Cape Spartel and Dakar, Senegal,
visibility of less than five miles, considered poor, is fairly common,
but the *Commerce* was engulfed in a rare fog. The crew could see
little more than half a mile and could make out no sign of land.

Riley and his mates made noontime observations twice, but they
considered that "neither could be much depended upon." The wind

was fair, and Riley wished to take advantage of it. He held to the course he had set after clearing Cape Spartel. On August 28, using dead reckoning — the courses steered, the brig's speed as determined by heaving the log, and the amount of time the courses were held, but no astronomical observations — he estimated their latitude to be 29° 30′ N, just north of the Canary Islands.

That day the clouds finally parted long enough for him to take "good meridian altitudes" (measurements of the angle the sun makes with the horizon at its zenith, or local noon), which would allow him to determine his latitude. At the same time, Williams and Savage and some of the crew noticed that the water had changed color, suggesting to them that they were nearing land. The mates informed Captain Riley, but he shrugged off the warnings. Judging such signs was tricky here. Along parts of the coast, sand from the desert gives the seafloor a dark olive hue and does not necessarily indicate proximity to the shore. The clouds were a bigger factor, to his mind; any change in the tint of the water here, he assured them, was only an effect of the changing cloud cover.

Riley was more concerned about accurately determining their latitude. What he discovered from his sights and calculations was startling. The brig was in latitude 27° 30′ N — 120 miles to the south of where he thought they were, and past the Canary Islands. Had the *Commerce* sailed eight hundred miles down to the Canaries on one compass setting and then passed blindly through a channel less than fifty miles wide? Had they sailed right by Tenerife, a volcanic island towering twelve thousand feet above the sea, without even a glimpse of it?

It hardly seemed possible, but Riley decided they had, rationalizing that "it was in the night, which was very dark, and black as pitch." Just how unlikely this was would take him some time to grasp.

In reality, the *Commerce* had drifted east and was being swept south by the Canary Current. From Agadir (known then in the West as Santa Cruz) in Morocco, the coast forms a long, shallow bay jutting westward on the south end at Cape Juby. All of this south-flowing water is suddenly forced into the bottleneck formed by

Cape Juby and the Canary Islands, sixty miles west. The Canary Current races around Juby at up to six knots, a pace too strong to row against, one that sweeps even large fish along with it.

It was through this funnel that the *Commerce* had passed on the night of August 27. To the south, the current flows along a south-southwest-sloping face that takes another western turn at Lemsid out to Cape Bojador. Essentially, while the current flows south along the Moroccan coast, the coast steps out to the west. But Riley had no solid evidence to convince him that he was not where he intended to be — only a gnawing feeling that something was not right.

Soon after they took their observations on the 28th and the men mentioned the change in the color of the sea, the weather turned even more menacing. That evening Riley studied his reckoning again and asked Williams and Savage to recheck their own calculations. He certainly knew that, as Saugnier put it, "the currents always set towards the Coast of Africa, that there are long banks of sand which run a great way out to sea, that in the morning and evening it is difficult to distinguish them from the water." But from his calculations and his discussions with his mates, Riley determined that he was not near the coast, that he was indeed correct in assuming the brig had passed between Tenerife and La Palma — through the eye of the needle.

Nevertheless, the crew's opinion and his misgivings made Riley increasingly uneasy. He was confounded by the contradiction between the physical evidence and the ineffable, which had never before "so much prevailed" over his reasoned calculations. He altered the course to the southwest, thinking he was veering toward the easternmost of the Cape Verde Islands.

At 7:20 P.M., the sun set. The moon, Riley knew, would not rise until after midnight. With the weather thickening to the point that they could barely make out their own jibboom, Riley ordered the crew to "round the vessel to," which brought her to the wind, slowing her down. They sounded with 120 fathoms (720 feet) of line. The weight did not touch bottom, indicating to the captain that they were still in the deeps and not approaching the coast. He would not succumb to "his fears," as he put it. He was not paid to be shy. He ordered the helmsman to resume his former course.

Soon they were bowling along again at nine and ten knots, with a strong breeze and a high sea. Riley stayed on deck all evening, looking for signs and mulling over their situation. It bothered him that they had not seen land. He had never passed the Canaries without seeing the islands, even at night and in the fog.

At nine o'clock, he decided that he could not continue on the present course much longer. An hour later, when his sailing log indicated that he should be just thirty miles off the infamous Cape Bojador, he gave the order to Savage, the officer on watch, to haul off to the northwest. He ordered the crew to furl the light sails, the small high ones that give a vessel that much more velocity but make her a little less manageable, and to rig in snug the studding-sail booms, the spars that stick out past the yardarms to add even more canvas power. They had made good time thus far; he was willing to take a few mild precautions.

After the main boom jibed over, Riley heard a roaring sound that stopped him cold. Thinking it was a squall approaching unseen in the dark, he shouted, "All hands on deck!" and ordered Savage to brace up the yards. Under his direction, the men brought the square sails more fore-and-aft. Riley was about to order the sails lowered when he saw foam surging against the lee side of the brig. He was wrong. The roar was not a squall. Even worse, it was the sound of breakers.

Riley kept his head, sizing up the situation and barking out commands almost simultaneously. There was one hopeful sign: he could see no rocks directly ahead. He ordered the men to make the anchors ready, and they cleared away the fourteen-hundred-pound iron and wood behemoth on either bow. Before Riley could order them to be dropped, a ghastly jolt hurled all hands to the deck. Every sailor knew instantly that his worst nightmare — the violent end that had stalked him all his working life, waiting for his vigilance to slacken or his luck to sour — had finally come to pass. Only instead of going to the bottom, the bottom had come to them.

Rising to his feet, Riley commanded the men to drop the best bower, the brig's larger anchor, believing it might prevent them from going further aground. Such was his will and authority that the men obeyed as one. He next ordered them to let the sheet anchor go and then to haul up the sails, to reduce the windage that pinned them against the rocks. They did, but 2,800 pounds of anchor had no effect against the heave of the Atlantic. The thundering surf rammed the *Commerce* onto the rocks again and again, until the brig, facing the beach to the southwest, lodged in a jagged crevice.

Waves broke one after another over the stern and starboard quarter, sweeping the decks. Each deluge of foaming sea sent the men sprawling or scurrying for a handhold to keep from being washed overboard. Riley quickly realized that there was no hope of saving the *Commerce*, which would soon bilge and fill with water. But, carrying only a light cargo, she sat high on the rocks, and her oak timbers could stand the beating for a while.

He ordered part of the crew to bring provisions up from the hold and to draw water from the large casks. They emptied two quarter-casks of wine and began filling them with water. On deck, he and the rest of the crew hauled in the small stern boat, which was being pounded by the waves, and slung it so as to keep it from beating against the side of the brig and staving. They cleared away the larger longboat and hung it in tackles, ready for launching.

The *Commerce* wedged deeper into the mandible-like rocks with each surge of the sea. Water poured into her hold, yet the men remained orderly and calm. Those working below had already brought up half a dozen barrels each of water and wine. Three barrels of bread and four of salt meat were also on deck, ready to be loaded in the boats. They had secured a variety of chests and trunks, including some with clothing and Spanish coin. Riley still had not seen land and had no idea how close they were. Not knowing what his next move would be was the worst part. He had to act decisively — both to save the crew and to convince them he *could* save them. For now, his close ties with his mates and men were paying

off. He could sense their alertness, their sharp determination to follow his orders. But if they saw any wavering, any weakness, on his
part, then their discipline might collapse and all could be lost. As he
considered his next move, Riley instructed the men to load his
books, charts, and navigational instruments.

Around midnight, as the brig settled and the waves broke with
increasing strength over the deck, Riley studied the billowing horizon around them in the dim light of a quarter moon rising to the
north of east. At last he made out the coast, the charting of which to
this day, the Royal Navy's *Africa Pilot* cautions, is "reported to be
inaccurate," primarily because it is constantly changing. The Sahara
abuts the sea in a mutable front of rust- and dun-colored cliffs,
black rock, and slopes of wind-scoured sand. As the sea under-
mines the desert, the rock and sand tumble in, altering the shoreline and creating new hazards. Riley strained to see in the dark.
Catching faint glimpses of reflected moonlight, he determined that
the shore was not far, perhaps two hundred yards. Reaching it was
their only chance.

The crew cut away the port bulwark so that they could launch the
boats with greater ease. Riley had them attach a line to the small boat
and lower it into the calmer water in the lee of the brig with himself
and Porter on board. The two men shoved off. But as soon as they
cleared the brig's bow, the whitecapped sea met them full force, capsizing the boat. Both men were repeatedly swallowed in the churning
surf. As they fought to stay afloat, the current dragged them to the
south and west, then tossed them onto the beach some three hundred
yards away from the brig. The boat washed up beside them.

Riley and Porter caught their breath and vomited salt water into
the sand. After hailing the brig, they seized the boat, emptied it of
water, and dragged it, still attached to the brig by the rope, out of
the surf. They maneuvered it up the beach to a point directly leeward of the wreck and secured it to a number of pieces of driftwood
from the brig, which they then drove into the sand.

The rest of the crew had not been idle. The tide was rising, and
Riley had instructed them to put everything that could float and that
would not fit in the longboat into the water, which was flowing to

shore. They were busy heaving chests, trunks, and barrels of water and wine overboard when Riley signaled to them to toss overboard the end of the hawser that they had fastened their end of the shore line to. Riley and Porter hauled in the shore line, pulling the more massive hawser to the beach, where they secured it. The men then lowered the longboat, packed with their possessions and provisions, including three barrels of bread and a barrel each of salt beef and salt pork.

Robbins and Barrett were chosen to take the longboat to shore. Stationed in the bow and stern, they steadied the craft with lines attached to rings on the bow and stern posts and looped over the hawser. This enabled them to keep the bow to the surf and pull themselves forward. As they neared the shore and the swells lifted and dropped them, they studied the waves to time their run through the surf to the beach. The roller they chose to ride in on picked them up, shot them forward onto the sand, and crashed them down with a thud, staving in the bottom of the boat.

Riley, Porter, Robbins, and Barrett wrestled the heavy barrels up the beach and were relieved to discover that except for a small amount of bread, the food had not been ruined in the landing. Daylight arrived while they gathered the objects floating in from the wreck. According to Robbins, Riley ordered the chest of money sent ashore. The mates unfastened one of the ropes extending from the ship to the shore and secured it around the chest of coins, and the four men hauled it in.

Still firmly in the clutches of the reef, the brig had filled with water but for the moment resisted her inevitable disintegration. Riley signaled to the mates to cut away her masts to ease the strain on the hull. Burns, Clark, and Hogan set to work, and the rigging soon tumbled to starboard, toward the sea, projecting beyond her bow and blocking the waves, which increased her protected lee. Although the brig was free of the top burden, the crew was now more exposed. Waves broke high over the hull, sweeping unimpeded across the bare deck. In danger of being washed off, the men clung to the bowsprit and the fore-chain-wales on the leeward side.

With the longboat smashed and the small boat useless in the rollers, Riley signaled to his men to come to shore by way of the hawser. Hogan was the first to try. He pulled off his jacket, grabbed onto the hawser, and began to shinny toward shore. As he cleared the wreck, each surging black curl of sea swallowed him. Time after time, he clung desperately, emerged from a foaming maelstrom, and crept forward again. Led by Riley, the sailors on shore moved along the hawser into the surf to help.

Finally, a wave broke over Hogan's head and ripped him away. Riley had waded out along the massive rope until he was chin deep, stationing Barrett, Porter, and Robbins behind him, all using the hawser to stabilize themselves against the breakers. When their shipmate came tumbling toward them, they managed to grab him and drag him ashore. They placed Hogan facedown and pumped the seawater from his belly.

Second mate Savage followed Hogan down the hawser. The crew again stationed themselves in the surf and caught him as he approached the beach. Horace followed his cousin. Then came Michel, Williams, Clark, Burns, and Deslisle. A lone pig, a runt of only twenty pounds, had bobbed ashore and came squealing up the beach. It was the only survivor of the *Commerce*'s livestock.

The crew had made it ashore intact, but they had little cause to celebrate. The coast of the Sahara had a reputation that had unnerved many good men. In 1810, when the 280-ton New York brig *Charles*, under Captain John Horton, wrecked here en route from Gibraltar to the Cape Verde Islands, Robert Adams, a seaman on board, commented that "though the captain was a man of courage, he appeared to be utterly deprived of reflection after the vessel struck." Deranged and combative, Horton was murdered by the Arabs. Before that, when the French ship *Les Deux Amies* grounded near Cape Blanco in 1784, Captain Carsin became so distraught at the thought of being eaten by cannibals that he tried to blow up the ship's magazine. When stopped, he put two bullets in his throat.

Riley allowed the men a few minutes to recuperate on the beach before he directed them to haul the boats and chests farther from the surf. Curiously, they had not managed to bring any guns ashore. Neither Riley nor Robbins mentions what became of their weapons. Riley says only that on the beach they "had no fire or side arms," though they did have handspikes, six-foot iron-shod wooden levers for turning the windlass — or, when necessary, for fending off boarders. A merchant brig would certainly have carried at least a chest of small arms and ammunition and quite probably more. For instance, the 171-ton English brig *Thames,* trading in Africa when it was taken by the American privateer *Yankee* in 1813, mounted eight 12-pound carronades, albeit during war. Since, like most mariners of the day, Riley believed that cannibals lived on this coast, one would think that he would have made it a priority to secure the small arms and ammunition.

Perhaps they had been waterlogged or had sunk into the sea during the tumultuous trip to shore. Or maybe the men had been so busy trying to survive the wreck and the surf that they forgot about the threat on land. In any event, Riley had already formulated a rough plan, and it focused on mobility, not force. He hoped they would not encounter the natives at all. He needed only enough time on the beach to repair the boats and, after the surf had calmed, to put to sea. His compass and other navigational tools had made it safely to shore. Using these, he hoped to find a friendly ship to rescue them or to sail down the coast to a European settlement or the Cape Verde Islands. Undoubtedly, this was the best tactic. Christian sailors who refused to disarm on this coast were treated brutally by the Arabs and often slaughtered to a man.

Riley harbored no illusions about their prospects of escape, however, and immediately prepared for the worst. Once they had gathered the important possessions, he opened a chest and produced two bags containing about a thousand Spanish dollars each. Although the money belonged to the brig's owners, he handed it out in the hope that it might be useful if they were captured.

"He told us all to take as much of it as we could conceal," recalled Robbins, who said that he took none because he already had more of his own than he could hide from the "eye of an Arab."

Others were not so bashful. They made themselves richer than they ever had been or ever would be again.

But they had little time to revel in it. As the sun rose over the African dunes and they buried the remaining bag of silver pieces of eight in the sand, they noticed a wild-looking man about half a mile away, walking up the beach toward them.

chapter 4

A Hostile Welcome

∽ After running aground at Cape Noun in 1800, Judah Paddock, captain of the merchant ship *Oswego,* out of Hudson, New York, gained some valuable insights into the mind of the desert Arab from his captor, Ahamed. Ahamed explained to him that the people of the coast "pray earnestly to the Almighty God to send Christians ashore."[1]

A large ship had wrecked there recently, Ahamed elaborated. Three Arab tribes had banded together and slaughtered the defiant crew, not only because the Christian sailors were infidels and interlopers, but because they had failed to submit to the "true believers" and to surrender their property, which the Sahrawis believed now rightfully belonged to them.[2] "There is no confidence to be placed in Christians," he admonished Paddock, "for whenever they come ashore . . . they bury their money in the sand, as you yourself have done, to prevent it from falling into the hands of the true believers."

What they could use and carry from a shipwreck, the Sahrawis took. What they could not take, it was their custom to burn. To the victims who witnessed this destruction of their personal articles and the cargo of their vessel, it was often the last cruel blow before they assumed the life of a slave to some of the poorest people on earth, living in some of the harshest conditions imaginable.

By the time the wild-looking man had come within a hundred yards of the Commerces, they could see that he was old, dark-skinned but not black, and that his hair looked, according to Riley, like "a pitch mop, sticking out every way six or eight inches from his head." He approached them guardedly, poking at the clothing and the wreckage strewn along the beach, seizing anything he wanted. Robbins observed that he seemed "agitated by the mingled operations of joy and fear."[3]

Slowly, Riley began walking toward the stranger. When he got to within ten paces, the man motioned for him to stop.

Riley was now close enough to get a good view of the man Robbins would later call "a slander upon our species." He was about five foot seven and dressed in a crude woolen cloth from his chest to his knees. His red eyes glared out, according to the captain, from a weather-beaten "ourang-outang" face, covered in a matted beard curling to his bare chest. His mouth was wide like a jackal's.

He was possibly an Imraguen, a dark-skinned people who predated the Berbers in the region, having arrived during Neolithic times, but more likely a Berber, whose ancestors first rolled onto the plains of the western Sahara in horse-drawn carts and chariots around 1000 B.C. and with their iron spears began to dislodge the Imraguen. In more recent centuries, waves of Arab invaders had Arabized or vassalized the Saharan Berbers. The Arabized Berbers called themselves Arabs and adopted bedouin life, using the camel to roam and dominate the Saharan plains; they stripped their defeated enemies of camels and firearms and banished them to the coast. In one of the supreme ironies of the Sahara, the shoreline — where it was easiest to sustain life by taking advantage of the rich sea and relatively abundant pasturage — was the domain of the degraded: tributary Imraguen and Berbers who caught fish for their masters.

Portuguese sailors had long claimed that these coastal dwellers ate the livers and drank the blood of dead Europeans, and this belief was still current, at least among seamen. Nonetheless, Riley made signs of peace and friendship to this jackal of an old man. He waved at the wreckage on the beach and invited him to take some. According to Robbins, the Sahrawi helped himself, then quickly retreated with his spoils over the dunes, his intentions still unclear.

Though they had not been attacked, this first encounter with a native was a blow to the sailors. He seemed as primitive and ill-looking as they had feared, and as inhospitable. They had no doubt that he would return with superior numbers. Morosely, they turned to setting up camp, building a tent out of broken spars, oars, and studding sails, and gathering in the salvaged provisions and water, which represented their only means of survival on the godforsaken coast.

They had little time to fret, however, before the jackal returned with others. This time he showed no trace of the fear that Robbins had detected before, only insolence. But it was his two wives who most unnerved the sailors. With protruding eyeteeth, blazing eyes, and wrinkled folds on their faces and bare chests, they looked ancient, reptilian, every bit the primitive flesheaters of the sailors' imaginations. A bevy of frenetic naked youths danced around them, including a shapely, smooth-skinned teenage girl, whose disarming beauty was jarring in such a threatening horde. Among them flashed an ax and an English hammer. Long sheathed knives hung from ropes at their sides.

The sailors were inclined to drive them off with handspikes, but Riley restrained them. He was not optimistic about their chances to escape either by land or by sea. As unlikely as it seemed, these Sahrawis might be their only hope. Besides, he felt sure that if they attacked this motley band, any of the Sahrawis who escaped would call in reinforcements and destroy them. Riley drew a line only at the provisions, the loss of which would mean their doom anyway. Their bread and salt meat, he instructed, their casks of water and wine, should be guarded at all costs.

At first the Sahrawis moved about warily, gathering odds and ends washed up on the beach. As they met no resistance, they grew more audacious, smashing open sea trunks and chests, grabbing the clothing inside, and carrying it up onto the dunes, where they spread it in the sun to dry as if they were doing their laundry.

They secured what was easy first. They found Riley's chest of silk veils and handkerchiefs, and this was most pleasing. They made turbans of the veils and festooned their arms and legs with the colorful handkerchiefs. Not knowing what to make of the feather bed, they slashed it and laughed as the powerful wind carried away the sodden feathers.

Seething and heartsick, the sailors watched as these strange people reveled. Riley tried to convince his humiliated men to attempt to befriend the natives, but it was all he could do to keep them from a violent reprisal. Then one of the plundering youths handed the cold, wet, miserable sailors fire, a good turn that neither Riley nor Robbins tried to explain in their memoirs but that underscores just how differently the Western sailors and the Sahrawis perceived their positions and circumstances. What the sailors saw as robbery, the Sahrawis viewed as accepted, even expected, behavior on the desert. For the moment, this sympathetic act averted a confrontation.

Now that they had abandoned the *Commerce,* Riley privately questioned his legal authority over the crew, though outwardly he remained in full control. By U.S. law, the master of a vessel held the power to command his men as a father would his children. As late as 1880, a Maine court wrote that three classes of people are rightly governed in this manner: children in families and schools, lunatics in asylums, and sailors on ships. However, Riley now had no ship.

While the Sahrawis came and went over the dunes with their booty, Riley calmly turned his attention to repairing the longboat, which had suffered both from neglect and from the beating it had taken in the surf. He found damaged planks on the verge of springing and nails so corroded by rust that they were shearing off. He hesitated even to turn the boat over to work on its bottom, afraid that it would collapse under its own weight.

Some of the crew followed the captain's lead and came to help, while others gave in to despair. Tired of the futile waiting, Porter volunteered to swim out to the brig to get tools and supplies to make repairs. He was a strong swimmer, and when the wind lulled in the afternoon, he made it to the hull and searched around. He returned to shore again with a marlinespike, a foot-long pointed metal rod useful for hammering as well as splicing, and some badly needed nails. Riley and some of the men set to work on the boat. Horace and Savage pitched in, along with, Riley noted laconically, "one or two more," probably Robbins and Porter, who helped turn the boat over and filled the hull's loose seams with oakum.

The rest, apparently including first mate Williams, tended to the fire and tapped a cask of wine and drank to dull their fear. They seemed unconcerned that they were weakening themselves in case of attack. Riley later chose not to identify those who had discredited themselves, perhaps because by that time any further punishment would have been redundant. Riley stationed the drinkers, armed with handspikes, around the camp as much to keep them occupied as to dampen the ardor of the thieving Sahrawis. But the former persisted in guzzling wine and the latter in snatching things and carrying them off. After the Sahrawis took the first of the two sails that composed the makeshift tent and then tried to grab the second, Riley rose to his full six feet and indicated with his hands that they must stop. The jackal and his band unsheathed their weapons and held them up menacingly but Riley refused to be intimidated. He did not flinch, and they backed off, eventually leaving with their haul.

That night, using the dried spars and timbers of previous wrecks for their fire, the sailors roasted a chicken that had drowned in the wreck and washed ashore. Their last hot meal for a while also included salt pork and bread and butter. The jackal had indicated to Riley that he and his band would be back in the morning. The captain set a watch of two men, instructing them to keep a fire burning with the withered debris they had gathered on the beach. The rest of the men fell asleep on the sand.

Except for Riley. To the lament of waves crashing on desert sands, he reflected painfully on the fate of his wife and — by now, God willing — five children. Who or what would prevent them from falling into "indigence, degradation, and ruin"? he wondered. Beneath the resplendent sky, the Milky Way an arc of angels' breath from the southwest to the northeast, he felt a swell of regret at the unfettered pursuit of wealth practiced in his country, "a land called Christian it was true," he later wrote, "but where avarice taking possession of the soul leaves little for the unfortunate widow, the fatherless child, or helpless orphan to expect save a bare existence."[4] And, it went without saying, where men were sent on long and dangerous voyages for the sake of profits.

The night sky was perfect and he wished he could share it with his family, fearing that they might never share another. After midnight, the waning quarter moon rose at the tip of the upper horn of Taurus, near Orion in his eternal dance with the Pleiades. Higher up, red Mars simmered. In the northwest, Vega, Altair, and Deneb glistened brightly like children's eyes. Elegant Cassiopeia crowned the northeast, while Hercules was setting in the west. These were his signposts in the sky, his map of the planet. Shuddering in the cold wind, Riley begrudged them their constancy. He could do nothing for his family now. He was like the lost Pleiad: separated from his family for eternity. He looked over the sleeping crew. "It was a sacred duty assigned me by Providence," he concluded, "to protect and preserve their lives to my very utmost." He could only try to keep himself and his men alive, and pray for a miracle.

Shortly after sunrise, the Sahrawis returned. This time there were no pretenses. Their leader, the jackal, brandished a colossal spear over his shoulder, cocked and ready to throw. Jabbing his free hand at the sea and braying, he demanded that the sailors go to the wreck and bring more things to shore. Then he pointed to a drove of camels and camel riders approaching from the east. The women ran down the beach ululating, stooping to gather sand and tossing it in the air to attract the riders.

The jackal advanced on the tent, thrusting his absurd-looking spear — an iron head on a spliced shank about twelve feet long — at the sailors. Riley ran to the surf and grabbed a long spar. Using his size advantage, he parried the Sahrawi "with the most consummate coolness," according to Robbins. As he did, he ordered the crew to launch the small boat.

The men dragged it into the sea beside the hawser still fastened to the wreck. Riley kept the Sahrawi back as they piled in haphazardly. But before the captain could get in, the nervous men capsized their one seaworthy craft in the crashing surf. The boat filled almost instantly and sank. Spilling out, the men scrambled onto the beach, reassembling behind Riley. Together they shifted farther ashore, stumbling in the sand as they went. The jackal scurried along with them as deftly as a crab, heading them off. He and two armed boys drove the sailors back toward the sea. With grunts and gestures, he threatened them. Despite his crude methods, his message was clear: The men on camels had guns and would kill them.

Riley ordered his crew to ready the longboat for launching. He could only hope that the repairs would allow it to reach the wreck. The sailors ran the boat into the sea and this time, following Riley's instructions, boarded in an orderly way, over the stern one at a time. In their rush, however, they had failed to bring the oars. Grabbing a broken board, they paddled the heavy vessel through the surf.

The boat was half swamped by the time they reached the wreck, but Riley was determined to keep it afloat. He and one of the crew stayed behind while the others climbed on board the *Commerce* and handed down a bucket and a small keg for bailing.

Then came an unexpected arrival. The pig, as loyal as a dog, paddled up to the wreck. The sailors shoved it on board.

On shore, two of the camel riders, probably Arabs, who were armed not with the threatened firearms but with scimitars, reached the sailors' bivouac and joined in the plunder. They made the camels kneel and loaded them with barrels of bread and salt beef, sails, spars, and the other useful items the sailors had hidden in their tent. These discoveries seemed to inflame the Sahrawis' passion. The jackal pranced about feverishly, staving in the casks of water and wine with an ax, defiantly spilling their contents on the sand. The campfire quickly became a bonfire, the Sahrawis zealously piling on everything they could not carry. The sailors watched dejectedly from afar as their trunks, chests, navigational instruments, books, and charts went up in flames. At last, some of the youths drove the loaded camels over the dunes.

Riley conferred with the crew. They had nothing left to feed or comfort themselves with. There was no escape on shore. They would likely be washed off the wreck and drowned at night when the tide came in. And if not, a rising sandbar behind the brig would allow the Sahrawis to approach them at the next low tide. They found a few bottles of wine and some salt pork left on board. With these, they decided to head out to sea in the longboat.

As they shoved off, a wave crashed over the bow. The boat reeled backward, filled, and began to sink. They hit the brig stern-first. Some of the sailors scrambled up onto the deck. Two grabbed the boat's painter and stern line and steadied it, preventing it from smashing against the brig again. Two others bailed furiously.

The Sahrawis watched dumbfounded from the shore. The idea that the sailors would escape in a boat was almost as ridiculous as the possibility that they might run away on the desert. There was no place to go. Nonetheless, they were vexed by the sailors' attempt to flee and began gesticulating to convince Riley to return. The jackal shouted at the youths, who with their weapons hustled over the dunes. The remaining Sahrawis bowed to the ground, rose smiling, and calmly beckoned with their hands. On the brig, the sailors scoffed at them. After a while, the jackal sent the others away. He took up a goatskin filled with water and held it over his head, offering it to the sailors. He then waded with it into the ocean up to his chest.

Judging their chances in the longboat to be slim, Riley had no choice but to try to establish some sort of rapport with the old man and hope for a change of heart. He lowered himself over the side by the hawser and crawled along it to the shore, where the Sahrawi handed him the skin. Riley thanked him and carried it back to the brig. The Sahrawi now indicated that he wanted Riley to return to the shore while he went on board the brig.

Riley explained to his reluctant crew that he thought their only chance lay in befriending the man and submitting to the will of the Sahrawis. He was going to return to the shore and allow him to come out. The jackal's clan hiding behind the dunes now returned to the beach unarmed. The half-naked women and naked youths sat on the sand near the water with pacific expressions. They looked up to heaven to show their kind intentions. The jackal greeted Riley in the Sahrawi way: "Allahu akhbar!" God is great![5] He then made his way out to the brig.

Riley sat down among the family. Grinning, they pulled the hat from his head and passed it around, trying it on one another and laughing. They stroked his trousers, his hands, his hair, and his sodden leather "feet," fascinated by the unfamiliar textures. Some intertwined their fingers with his while others shamelessly rifled his pockets. He could smell their dusty unwashed bodies and matted hair, and he could sense his own fear in his twinging nostrils and knotted intestines. Their sudden change in demeanor did not fool him. Their treachery was palpable. He rose to his feet, waved his arms desperately, and shouted to his men, but the noise of the surf swallowed his words. What he was trying to communicate could not be signed. He wanted them to hold the jackal until he had been allowed to leave the beach.

Meanwhile, the sailors grabbed the jackal's arms and lifted him onto the wreck, where he demanded their guns and money. The sailors denied having either. He rummaged around the cluttered deck and peered into the flooded hold. Finally, finding nothing, he dived back into the sea. As the jackal neared the beach, Riley started to rise to his feet. The two cameleers, who had quietly positioned themselves on either side of him, seized him by the arms. Daggers suddenly appeared in the Sahrawis' hands. To struggle, it was clear, meant death.

Riley did what came naturally to a good captain under stress. He feigned unconcern. "The countenance of everyone around me now assumed the most horrid and malignant expressions," he later wrote. "They gnashed their teeth at me, and struck their daggers within an inch of every part of my head and body."

All at once, the jackal was at his throat. He yanked Riley's head back with his hand and raised a scimitar. At that moment, Riley believed he would be beheaded and suffer the further ignominy of providing a meal for this barbarous gang. The jackal slowly drew the blade across Riley's shirt collar, slicing it and letting him feel the metal on his skin. But he wanted silver, not blood. He let go of Riley's head and ordered him to make his men bring the ship's money to shore.

On the brig, the seamen had watched this scene unfold. When it appeared that their captain would be executed, they had vowed to avenge his death by arming themselves as best they could, rushing to shore in the boat, and killing as many Sahrawis as they could before they paid with their own lives. Now, to their surprise, Riley hailed the brig. His voice did not carry over the surf. Savage lowered himself down to the sea by the hawser and made his way toward the shore.

"Bring the money," Riley called to him, when he was within shouting distance. Savage immediately returned to the brig, not hearing Riley's final words, "Do not give it to them until I am fairly released."

The old man had not found any money on board the *Commerce* because it was still hidden in the sailors' clothes. The men now pulled out roughly a thousand dollars and tossed it into a bucket. Porter made the strenuous trip to shore, pushing the bucket lashed to the hawser along in front of him.

Fearing that the Sahrawis planned to take Porter hostage as well, Riley yelled to him not to come ashore. Porter complied, and one of the cameleers went out into the surf to get the bucket. All the while, the jackal held his scimitar point to Riley's throat.

The bucket was emptied on the end of a blanket in front of the jackal, whose eyes gleamed. The sight of such a treasure made him feel suddenly vulnerable, and he ordered his people to carry it down the beach, away from the brig. With their weapons drawn, the Sahrawi men hustled Riley along with them, followed by the women, who kept the jackal's crude spear homed on their captive's back.

After a short walk, the group sat down, and the old man jubilantly divvied up the coins, pushing stacks of ten into three equal sparkling piles: one for the camel men, one for his wives, and one for himself. As the piles disappeared into their haiks, Riley sensed that in their greed they had momentarily forgotten him. He decided to make a break for it.

As soon as he made a move to rise, however, an alert youth lunged at him with his scimitar. Riley dodged the blow, but the blade drilled his waistcoat before he could roll away from it. The young man prepared to strike again, but the jackal stopped him and gave some commands, which Riley could not understand. The party rose and prepared to leave the beach, and he could see they intended to take him with them. Desperate not to be carried off into the interior, he indicated to the jackal that his crew had more money. This had its intended effect. Instead of leaving, the Sahrawis took him back down the beach and ordered him to hail his men.

What exactly Riley had in mind at this point is hard to tell. "I imagined if I could get Antonio Michel on shore," he later wrote, "I should be able to make my escape." He does not further explain his intentions, claiming that he "knew not how, nor had I formed any plan for effecting it."

Why Antonio Michel, the old sailor on his way home after years at sea? Was he the only man Riley deemed expendable? Did he feel less responsibility for him than for the crew he had hired?

From the brig, the sailors could see that both sides were playing their final cards. The Sahrawis repeatedly threatened Riley with their blades, as he hailed his crew. Of the brave men who shortly before had vowed to go down fighting, not one was now willing to venture ashore. Riley's desperate voice became a croak.

Aaron Savage finally screwed up his courage and hauled himself to shore on the hawser. When he neared the beach, Riley motioned for him to stay in the surf. The jackal, thinking Riley meant to instruct Savage to bring the money ashore, allowed them to talk to each other. Riley told Savage his plan, one that would trouble the captain ever after, though no one ever criticized him for it.

Savage returned to the wreck and told Michel that Riley wanted him on shore. The working passenger from New Orleans dutifully obeyed. The Sahrawis surrounded Michel menacingly as he trudged onto the beach. They expected more money. He had, of course, nothing but the clothes on his back. Enraged, they beat him with their fists and the butts of their daggers. They ripped off his clothes,

Wreck of the brig *Commerce* on the coast of Africa
(from *An Authentic Narrative of the Loss of the American Brig Commerce*, 1817)

and the youths jabbed him with the points of their blades. Forced to his knees, Michel pleaded with them to stop.

Riley instructed Michel to tell them that he knew where the crew had buried money. This was true. Near the tent, they had planted a new spyglass, a saw, and some other useful tools in one hole and a sack containing $400 in another. In a quavering voice, the rattled old sailor made himself understood. With blows, his captors drove him to the spot.

Seated on the sand, Riley watched intently, the jackal's spear poised at his chest and a young brute's scimitar inches from his head. He knew that he was out of ploys. He also knew that when the buried treasure was dug up, greed would get the better of his guards, at least for a moment. Slowly, imperceptibly, he inched his legs up under his body.

When the excited cries came at last, his guards turned reflexively to look, as he had predicted. Riley sprang to his feet and bolted for the sea. Nothing but his own escape filled his brain, but his legs were slow and dumb on the sand. The padding feet of his pursuers closed on him. He dived headfirst into the surf. The jackal followed him in.

Riley swam underwater, holding his breath until he could no longer resist the urge to surface. As he breached, he swiveled to see where the Sahrawis were. No more than ten feet behind him bobbed the head of the jackal. Riley felt the spear plunge near his body. Just then a breaker caught the jackal and knocked him backward. Riley swam as hard as he could. He fought through the cresting waves until he felt the hands of his men grabbing his shirt. They pulled him over the stern of the *Commerce*.

He collapsed on the deck.

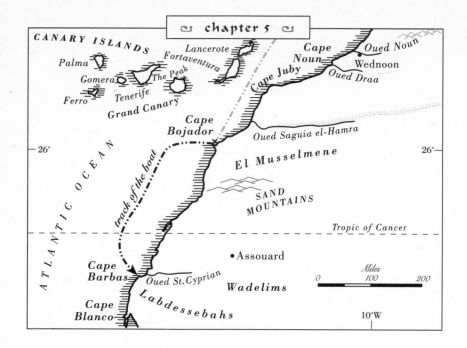

chapter 5

CANARY ISLANDS

Palma   Lancerote   Fortaventura   Cape Noun   Oued Noun

Gomera   The Peak   Cape Juby   Wednoon

Ferro   Tenerife   Oued Draa

Grand Canary

Cape Bojador   Oued Saguia el-Hamra

ATLANTIC OCEAN

—26°   El Musselmene   26°—

track of the boat   SAND MOUNTAINS

Tropic of Cancer

• Assouard   Miles

Cape Barbas   Oued St. Cyprian   Wadelims   0   100   200

Cape Blanco   Labdessebahs   10°W

Misery in an Open Boat

༄ As wind and water swept the *Commerce*'s deck, stinging the sailors' hands and faces, they watched the Sahrawis beat and stab Michel. Finally they loaded his back with their plunder and forced him over the dunes. It was terrible to observe and cast a pall over the men. Not only were they unable to help their brutalized shipmate, but their own helplessness was driven home in the most graphic manner.

Nevertheless, there was no time to dwell on it. Each wave hammered the longboat against the brig's hull, racking the smaller craft and jarring the tenuous deck on which they crouched. They now had to pick from their own dismal options. They could return to the shore and try to negotiate their surrender to the Sahrawis; at best they would be beaten and enslaved, like Michel, and quite possibly murdered if they gave offense. Or they could try their luck at sea in the longboat, gambling that it could weather the twenty-foot waves and stay afloat long enough for them to flag down a passing ship.

According to Robbins, there was "long deliberation" on the question, but this certainly did not amount to more than a matter of minutes. They saw no hope in surrendering to the Sahrawis, whom they bitterly called "barbarians," "savages," and "merciless ruffians." Instead, most of the talk concerned the feasibility of putting to sea in the rudderless, hastily repaired longboat. In Robbins's opinion, it was "shattered." Riley called its condition "crazy," a technical term in his day meaning "in bad shape," and said it "writhed like an old basket." Crammed with eleven men, the sixteen-foot craft would ride dangerously low in the water. They took heart in the one factor that had turned in their favor: The wind had grown more easterly, which would help them get clear of the dangerous coast. While the odds were stacked against an escape at sea, the crew opted for the element they knew best, the natural force they had wrestled with all their lives as opposed to the strange and malevolent human one on shore. They would try their luck in the longboat.

The captain set two hands, probably the ordinary seamen Hogan and Barrett, to bailing out the longboat with buckets. He sent Porter, a strong swimmer, to the momentarily deserted beach to retrieve the two broken oars, which they needed to get through the surf.[1]

Riley instructed the rest of the crew, under the two mates, to lash together some spars and rig them out over the stern of the *Commerce* in its lee. They were to guide the boat there and secure its bow and stern lines to the ends of the spars so that the boat was held clear from the brig. When it came time to cast off, Riley hoped, this would give them headway and prevent them from being smashed by a wave on the hull of the brig.

Riley had much to orchestrate before they left the wreck, but he personally attended to the most important thing: securing fresh water. At the brig's hatchway, he stripped off his shirt and lowered himself into the dark abyss. Guided by touch, he moved through the trapped seawater down through the hold, now on its side, until he surfaced in a pocket of air. As he took in the strange sensations, the odd, muted shifting of the cold water, the echo of the surf, the ominous creaking of the brig's straining timbers, his thoughts inevitably turned to Michel.

The story of Michel's fate was something that the captain, caught up in an insidious cycle of guilt and denial, would never quite get straight. Despite later stating that he did not actually see what happened to Michel, he offers a graphic description in his *Narrative* anyway: The angry Sahrawis, he wrote, plunging "a spear into his body near his left breast downwards, laid him dead at their feet." They dragged Michel's "lifeless trunk across the sand hills" and he felt "an inexpressible pang" at the sudden realization that he alone was responsible for the sailor's "massacre." He was momentarily "bereft . . . of all sensation."

In reality, it did not happen that way. In a letter published in the *Connecticut Courant* predating this account, Riley wrote that the crew escaped the "armed Arabs, all except Antonio Michael [*sic*], whom they seized and kept." Robbins's version concurred with Riley's letter. Perhaps Riley later concluded that it was more reprehensible to have left a captive than a dead man.

Riley certainly knew that he had encountered a moral conundrum.[2] As a captain, a man who was used to bearing total responsibility for his ship and men, he believed that he had done what he had to do to protect his crew. He was correct that the practical effect of his actions had been best for his men, preserving for them an indisputable leader rather than an outsider, and an old man at that. Yet he continued to struggle with the morality of his decision and his lingering guilt.

As his eyes adjusted to the dark hold, Riley sifted through the floating tangle of hammocks, sea chests, and odd planks until he found what he was looking for. Rolling over a large half-full cask, he felt the bung still tight. This good luck encouraged him, and he applied all his strength to maneuvering the barrel through the flooded wreckage and up the hatchway to the surface.

On deck, Savage and Clark helped him stave in the cask and transfer the water to a four-gallon keg that would fit in the boat. There was enough left over for everyone to drink as much as he wanted. It was a moment to savor. Some — the lucky ones — would not fully assuage their thirst again for a long time.

Porter returned with the oars. Of his own accord, he had also dug up and lugged back the sack of silver coins buried the day before. This was apparently the same bag of dollars that Antonio Michel was digging for when Riley made his escape. For this to be the case, Michel must have dug up the instruments that they had buried nearby instead of the silver, and either the silver must have been forgotten after Riley's escape, which seems improbable, or Michel could not find it. Ironically, the Sahrawis would have preferred the dollars, and the sailors could have made much better use of the spyglass and tools. In any case, Riley only shook his head, thinking that either greed had overcome Porter's sense or he was foolishly optimistic. Later he would make Porter bury it again.

"Stow the gear," ordered Riley. Wading through the surf from the brig to the longboat under the mates' direction, the men loaded the small boat's jib and mainsail, the brig's fore-topmast staysail, and a spar for a mast, as well as the few items they had rummaged from what had already been passed over once. In addition to the keg of water and a dozen bottles of wine, which were probably stowed amidship, they had fished out of the sea several pieces of salt pork and a four-pound bag of figs. They loaded the brig's colors, which in that day bore fifteen stars and fifteen stripes, and the lucky if scrawny pig, which had defied the odds and survived. Its pluckiness made it an apt and reassuring mascot — and a potential meal for later.

With a mixture of foreboding and eagerness, the crew positioned themselves in the longboat two by two on the six narrow planks that served as seats. No one recorded the seating arrangement, but given the clearly defined roles of the mariner's profession, it is easy to approximate. Deslisle, the cook, and Horace, the smallest member of the crew, together with the pig, probably sat in the narrow bow. The two ordinary seamen, Hogan and Barrett, would have come next, followed by Burns and Clark, then the two mates in the center. Porter and Robbins, both powerful, skilled seamen, and close friends, would have been positioned aft of center, where the oars could be used to best advantage. Riley would have taken the all-important forward-looking stern seat to steer and to have a commanding view of his men, all of whom, with the possible exception of the bowmen, faced the rear, looking only at him and where they had been. Each man would spend the coming days in a space about two feet by three feet submerged up to his ankles and sometimes higher in salt water.

Riley now did one of the hardest things a captain can be called upon to do. He finally abandoned his sweet, new, now broken-backed ship, the one his uncle Justus had entrusted to him, the one with good enough prospects for Josiah Savage to ship a son and a nephew on board. Climbing into the stern of the longboat, he looked into the grim faces of his men beneath their furrowed hats. Before casting off, he asked them to uncover their heads. Riley begged the "great Creator and preserver of the universe" to spare their lives and to let them pass through the surf to the open sea. "But if we are doomed to perish," he implored, expressing what was on the mind of each of the family men, "oh, universal Father, protect and preserve our widows and children."

Riley examined the heaving sea around them for a clue to their escape. Because they had no means of fashioning a makeshift rudder and no place to lash an oar except the stern ring, which was too unsteady, he would steer with a plank. He saw no possible way to evade the breakers without divine intervention. All he could do was to force the issue. "Haul out the boat!" he ordered. The men released the lines, and they floated free of the *Commerce*. On command, the men heaved to the oars.

And then, the miraculous did happen. The wind died down, and between the giant swells — each one capable of flipping the overloaded longboat like a leaf in a storm — a path suddenly appeared. The men pulled in unison as waves crashed around them and Riley steered toward the open sea. A mile out, he told them to rest. Hearts racing, each took a last look at the dismal coast, the wreck, and the surf they had just evaded. A spontaneous cheer burst from the crew. Robbins recalled that they doffed their hats again, and "Capt. Riley returned thanks to Heaven." Riley had no doubt that an "immediate and merciful act of the Almighty" had saved them from the surf at Bojador. According to him, all of his men believed this too. Later, when a friend advised him to play down this conviction, because skeptics would use it to discredit the rest of his account of the voyage, Riley refused.

As darkness descended on the longboat, the Commerces still faced a current that would throw them back onto another section of Cape Bojador if they could not get to seaward of it. Without a rudder, Riley had no margin for error. He ordered the men to set the mainsail, making their progress now a matter of seamanship and wind. Their good fortune held in one regard. The gusts continued shifting to the east, giving them the needed sea room to weather the cape. The crew rowed and bailed, swapping tasks every half hour, as Riley managed to steer the longboat into the open sea.

Their escape from this hazard only led them to another. That night, the wind increased, reaching gale force, and the growing swells threatened to capsize them. Water streamed in over the sides and through the widening seams between the boat's planks as fast as the crew could bail. Under dense clouds, Riley had no stars to navigate by, and all he could do was keep the boat to the wind by guiding it with one of the broken oars. He desperately fought off exhaustion; nodding his head for a second could cause him to lose control of the boat, and a slight yaw in a trough could cause them to founder.

Dawn the next day, August 31, brought more tumescent, gray clouds, dark, steep seas, and no sight of land. Intending to run south within view of the coast, Riley steered southeasterly through the haze. The crowded boat sat so low in the water that he could not hear or see far. When the crew first heard a roar in front of them, they were confused. By the time they identified the sound as breakers, it was nearly too late. Once again the current was hurtling them toward the shore. On the brink of the surf, Riley managed to tack the boat around. As he searched unsuccessfully over his shoulder for any sight of land through the haze, he realized the futility of his strategy. With its reefs and difficult weather, the shallow, jagged coast was too treacherous to follow. Without a compass, a quadrant, and charts, all lost in the wreck or to the Sahrawis, they would be in constant danger of running aground.

Riley consulted the crew. They could continue to stand down the coast, the risks of which were now unsettlingly clear. Given the deplorable sailing conditions and the distance they had to go — more than five hundred nautical miles — they might easily miss both major landmarks, the British-held French settlement of Saint-Louis, at the mouth of the Senegal River, and the Cape Verde Islands. If they did, they would wind up adrift in the doldrums, the windless open sea near the equator, a region whose torments were well known to sailors. The alternative was to head farther west. The Canary Islands lay close enough for the winds of "the burning plains of Africa," as one period gazetteer put it, to destroy vegetation and induce drought and diseases. But while the Spanish-controlled archipelago was only about sixty miles offshore and about a hundred miles from Cape Bojador, it lay to the northwest, against the Canary Current and northeast trade winds, and would have been nearly impossible to reach in the longboat. Really, their only hope in that direction was to spot and hail a ship by chance. Finally, they could try to make landfall as soon as possible and face the perils of the shore while they still had strength.

The sailors knew as well as anyone how very great an expanse the sea covered, how rarely ships came and went outside the high-traffic lanes, and how hazardous the passage would be for the diminutive longboat. Against this they weighed not only their recent confrontation on the shore but also their collective cultural perception of the Sahara. Tales of cannibalism along the coast of the Great Desert, though untrue, were exchanged in gun rooms and in port alehouses around the world and given much credence. The desert's desolation was legendary, as was its inhabitants' penchant for torturing white men, starving them, and subjecting them to brutal slavery.

When the sailors of the *Commerce* voiced their opinions one by one, the decision was unanimous to head out to sea.

Using the brig's fore-topmast staysail, the men made an apron and attached it to the longboat's gunwale, raising the sides by eight inches. The reward for their labor was nothing but the knowledge that they had done something to improve their plight and the right to an eleventh share of the provisions allotted for that day, which they would have gotten anyway. The mates carefully doled out to each man two briny figs and a withered piece of salt pork, a substance so saline that it was usually soaked in seawater before being served in order to *lower* its salt content. The pig gnawed on canvas and rope.

Ironically, they were floating on the surface of what would be Africa's most fruitful fishing ground in the twentieth century, where schools of sardines swam so thickly that sailors often mistook them for whitewater on reefs. Since it was customary for both merchant and navy ships to supplement their fare with fresh fish, it was likely that the *Commerce* carried fishing tackle. But perhaps the tackle was unreachable or the men simply had not thought to secure it when they ran aground. Like so many victims of shipwreck in the age of sail, including the whalers of the *Essex* and Captain Bligh's Royal Navy men, the lifelong seamen on board the *Commerce* were unprepared to catch fish to feed themselves in an emergency.

Worse than the lack of food was the dwindling supply of anything to drink. To slake their thirst, the men shared one bottle of water and a half bottle of wine in a day. Amounting to several ounces for each man, it was little more than a tease. They could have added some seawater to their fresh water and wine to expand their rations, but drinking seawater — as elegized in Coleridge's classic lines "Water, water, every where, / Nor any drop to drink" — had long been considered deadly. Every sailor had heard tales of the thirst-demented castaway who, despite the warnings of his shipmates, suddenly plunges his head into the sea and gulps down salt water as if it were flowing from a mountain spring. Returning to his feverish delirium, he raves loudly as the imbibed salt extracts more moisture from his cells, driving his pain to an even more agonizing pitch. By the time the sufferer leaps screaming into the sea, convinced that it is an ice bath, his shipmates, on the brink of their own quieter demise, are more relieved than sad.

However, anecdotal evidence and scientific tests have since suggested that consuming a moderate amount of salt water can be beneficial to those lost at sea as long as they have some fresh water to mix with it. In his 1950 classic, *Kon-Tiki,* Norwegian adventurer Thor Heyerdahl noted that on board his raft sailing through the South Pacific, on very hot days when the crew lost a lot of salt by sweating, they added between 20 and 40 percent seawater to their fresh water and found that it quenched their thirst better and had no adverse effects. A few years later another ocean rafter, William Willis, was forced to drink seawater when his water cans corroded through. For seventy days, according to Willis, he consumed no less than two cups of salt water a day against as little as one cup of fresh. He claimed to have suffered no side effects whatsoever. But the Commerces apparently did not dare to experiment with drinking seawater, and thus they missed out on what, judiciously consumed, could have proved a valuable source of hydration.

A strong breeze carried the boat west as flashes of heat lightning illumined the sky. Riley kept the boat close to the northeast wind, perhaps trying to angle northwest toward the Canaries, though he never admitted it in his memoir. Against the current, they made little headway. Immense swells, black firmament, vast remorseless sea: it was a discouraging picture.

Day turned into sleepless night as Riley battled exhaustion. Not surprisingly, his religious upbringing now asserted itself. As a boy, he had been able to recite entire chapters of the Bible. He had known the catechism and creeds by heart and could sing any number of psalms from memory. In trouble, he grasped the spiritual girder and hung on tight. Revisiting in his mind the recent confrontation with the Sahrawis and the escape from Bojador, he convinced himself that God had not saved them from these crises just to watch them go down at sea. He did his best to encourage the men: "It is our duty to God and ourselves to strive to the latest breath to prevent our own destruction," he entreated. "Look alive, and you will be in the bosom of your families once again."

On September 1, their third day at sea, the weather abated enough for the crew to slaughter the pig. It was growing emaciated, and, despite their affection for it, they decided to kill it while it still had some weight. It would have been Dick Deslisle's job to slit its throat and butcher it, but all hands paid careful attention to the process, collecting its blood to drink and dividing and eating its moist liver and intestines to soothe their leathery tongues and dry throats. Working round the clock, it had taken little time for their thirst to become severe. Now that they had a notion of what it might be like to die of thirst, this had surpassed the boat's lack of seaworthiness as their chief fear. As they emptied bottles of wine, blood, or water, the crew filled them with their own urine.

It was a good thing they took in extra nourishment that day. In the afternoon, the weather turned foul again. That night, the worst yet, required all their strength. Thunder squalls blew in from the northeast, whipping the seas into a frenzy and streaking the skies with lightning. In between thunderbolts, it was pitch-black. Unevenly spaced waves staggered the boat with annoying stealth.

By midnight they again rowed and bailed in constant fear that the next swell would swamp them. As the water washed in and back out again, it was sometimes difficult to tell if they were actually afloat. All hands not rowing or steering bailed furiously with buckets, hats, or anything else that would scoop or push water out of the boat. Through the night, the captain and Aaron Savage took turns praying out loud with the crew, which, Robbins reported, "had considerable effect in allaying our fears and encouraging our dying hopes."

As a gloomy dawn broke on September 2, the wet, stiff, haggard sailors continued to perform their tasks in silence. They fumbled in exhaustion, lapsed into delirium, woke again with a jerk to return to bailing, rowing, or stuffing seams with oakum. When low in the water, they heard only the sound of lapping waves; when aloft on a swell, moaning wind; and in between, creaking, as the longboat's timbers rubbed and flexed.

According to Robbins, the boat's incessant rocking had "drawn most of her nails" above the waterline. Those below the waterline, believed Riley, who had hammered many of them in on the beach at Bojador, stayed in place only because of the pressure of the sea. According to both men, the craft could not take the present conditions much longer. It was on the verge of disintegrating when, shortly after dawn, the wind shifted to the north-northwest, the storm relented, and the sun emerged. The wind was now in their face. Any thought of reaching the Canaries had to be abandoned. They resigned themselves to searching the horizon and praying for the sight of a sail. Even if they did see a ship running down the coast, however, it did not mean her lookout would spot the longboat, a low, muted heap of brown and gray adrift in a frothy monotony of gray-green.

The men now joked darkly that Michel had not drawn the short straw after all. At least as a slave, he had water to drink. If anyone, it would be he, not they, who would carry home the news of the brig's disaster. Confronting Riley was the black irony that instead of giving the son of his friend William Savage a chance in life, he would in all likelihood deliver him to the same miserable fate as his father: to end up as a shadowy hope haunting his family for the rest of their days. While others thought of the wives or sweethearts slipping further and further from their grasp, Burns, on his sixteenth wedding anniversary — September 2 — at least had the solace of knowing that he might soon be reunited with his beloved Lillis in death.

The swells flattened out. As the threat of capsizing or swamping receded, sun and tedium took its place. The demanding night had increased to a new degree the men's thirst and the nausea caused by dehydration. That day, they drifted to the south and at some point crossed over the Tropic of Cancer, a signal moment for sailors under normal circumstances, usually celebrated by games, music, dancing, and the ritual initiation of all greenhorns into the mysteries of the sea. Often, a swab-headed Neptune and his lady — seamen in drag — forced those who had not crossed the line before to quaff mugs of bilgewater, to undergo lathering in tar and slush, shaving, rinsing in buckets of seawater, and then to take the sacred oaths: "I will never leave the pump till she sucks . . . never go up the lee-rigging in good weather . . . never desert the ship til she sinks, and . . . never kiss the maid when I can kiss the mistress."[3]

On this voyage, there was no need for a trumped-up initiation into King Poseidon's rites. "The scorching rays of the sun, being within the Torrid Zone, were," according to Robbins, "nearly intolerable." The sailors' dry mouths and throats felt like they were coated with fur, and their breath was foul, both conditions caused by the buildup of waste in their bodies due to dehydration and the rampant growth of bacteria that resulted. Riley by necessity now allowed each man only to wet his mouth twice a day with a few drops of wine and water and twice with their collected urine, hardly enough, given that humans lose a full pint of water each day just through respiration.

It is said that to a thirsty man in a boat, sea spray is a constant torment. It taunts him in its plentitude. It beads on his brow and runs down into his mouth, only to make him thirstier. Inevitably, some of the crew began to crack. A couple of them indulged their increasing fascination with death by leaning over the gunwale and submerging their heads, claiming that they wished to taste what was sure to be their fate.

The stages of dehydration would be categorized a century later by W. J. McGee, a notable amateur thirst-researcher and director of the St. Louis Public Museum. His portrait of the process of human dehydration, which has become the sine qua non of the field, shows five distinct phases: clamorous, cotton-mouth, swollen-tongue, shriveled-tongue, and blood-sweat, each roughly equivalent to a 5 percent decrease in body weight. The Commerces had long since grown clamorous: uncomfortable, irritable, feverish. Their stale throats

cracked when they spoke. Their fat, sore tongues restricted conversation to terse phrases, and they slurred or lost words. Their hearing had grown muffled, due to loss of moisture in the inner ear. In
the cotton-mouth stage, the mind increasingly distorts reality and
desires. Sufferers rashly toss off clothes or possessions or, in the
case of the Commerces, become obsessed with how it would feel to
die in the sea. It is normal for spells of feverish dreams to focus on
the urge to drink, and the Commerces, parched beyond imagination
and penetrated by salt, extolled the lush banks of the Connecticut
River and craved a cup — or a barrel — of the delicious mineral
water from the freshets that filled it. In his head, Riley built and
rebuilt the stately spa he had dreamed of.

That afternoon, Riley gave up any hope of a rescue at sea. To
continue on meant certain death, roasting on the woeful collection
of planks that formed their boat, now an inhuman prison cell that
confined their bodies in cramped agony. They might fight on
another handful of days, but they did not have enough food and
water to maintain their strength. They would soon lose the power to
affect their fate.

Riley had an idea. To motivate the crew, he proposed heading
back to the *Commerce*. The brig, built in Keeney's Cove, Glastonbury, across from Wethersfield, in 1811, was now their lone connec-
tion to the Lower Valley. If part of a shipbuilder's soul goes into his
craft, then master carpenter Horace Fish was a worthy soul; he and
the Glastonbury crew, men the Commerces knew, had produced a
fine vessel. Mothballed during the war, she was still fresh and tight,
smelling of Valley oak and pine. By the "will of Providence," Riley
now suggested, the wreck might have been discovered by civilized
people, who would restore them to their country and families. As
farfetched as it was, this inspired bit of chicanery offered the crew
new hope, and they seized on it. The invocation of family, Riley
noticed, eased his shipmates' agony and even his own. It was as if
they believed they were heading straight to the Valley to see their
wives and children.

Sentimentality was not one of Riley's chief characteristics. In the
past he had begun at least one lengthy voyage on Christmas Day,

and on this trip he had never considered postponing the departure of the *Commerce* to wait out Phoebe's impending childbirth. Yet he surely longed for his home and the embrace of his chestnut-haired wife of thirteen years. The clamor of his children was now a strange, far-off reality, but one that he had not yet given up hope of hearing again.

In a voice vote, the tattered crew all agreed with Riley. They tacked the boat around and, steering by the sun, headed back to the coast. Though more storms followed, the crew remained hopeful. "Dismal as the prospect before us appeared," Robbins explained, "horrid as the recollection of the coast we had left was to our minds, we still felt a kind of desperate satisfaction in returning to it." They needed the resolve that this hope kindled, for starvation had left them weak and listless. For four days they had bailed the longboat incessantly, working two buckets at a time in roughly thirty-minute shifts (though they had no accurate way to tell time). The muscles in their arms, backs, and hands, which were raw and covered with boils from the abrasion of wood and salt, ached from the repetitive motion. While they lost strength, however, the sea did not. Its persistence made the task almost too difficult to bear. They ate the skin and raw flesh of the pig as it was doled out in precious, rancid-sweet bits. Then they ate its bones. They continued to wet their blistered and festering lips twice a day with wine, water, and urine. Their fiery heads and necks radiated heat. Their skin peeled off in sheets, leaving bleeding sores.

Having sailed more than three days back toward the coast, the crew again grew desperate.[4] Riley told them they would see land that day, and they kept a vigilant watch. Each passing hour grew more intolerable. By nightfall, they had not seen even a shadow on the horizon. They began to grumble. It was apparent to all, Riley noted, that they "could not hope to make the boat hold together in any manner above another day." That night, presumably while Riley, Williams, and Savage dozed, some of the crew — perhaps convinced that it was their last night in this world or perhaps to spite the captain whose promises that day had proved false — stole one of the two remaining bottles of wine and drank it.

In the morning, Riley discovered the loss and demanded to know who had taken the bottle. Each man denied it. No one confessed to having drunk any of the wine, and all denounced the theft as "an unpardonable crime," whose perpetrators should be "thrown overboard instantly." In the heated discussion that resulted among the crew, however, it became apparent to Riley who the culprits were, though he never publicly named them. Attempting to identify them today, though difficult, is perhaps worth the exercise. From their rank in the crew, one might doubt that Barrett or Hogan would have dared such an offense. Horace was too young, and Deslisle, being the only black man, probably would not have risked calling attention to himself at a time like this. Savage, Porter, and Robbins had maintained a positive outlook and were among the most helpful in the early stages of the crisis, making them less likely transgressors. Excluding Riley, that leaves first mate Williams, whose subsequent behavior would make him more rather than less probable, Clark, and Burns.

Although capital punishment would have been justified under maritime law, Riley decided the resulting blow to morale would be too severe. The wine was gone. There was nothing he could do about that. Besides, it was likely enough that the culprits would soon have their judgment day. "No remedy remained," he decided, "but patience, and stricter vigilance for the future."

The breach in discipline was perhaps inevitable. That Riley had staved it off for as long as he had and then let it pass without a showdown demonstrated shrewd leadership. Raised in the black-and-white world of New England Protestantism, he was stern and moralistic by nature, so it was difficult for him to ignore the offense. True to that same background, however, he was pragmatic and egalitarian. He now led more by common consent than by divine right. In his manuscript Riley called his leadership role at this stage "advisory." Furthermore, he was human; his struggle to survive had already resulted in the loss of one man, whether intentionally or not, and he did not want to lose any more. Perhaps, too, he had gained an understanding of the depths to which despair could drive a man.

Shortly after this confrontation, the sailors spotted land, far off but fortunately to leeward. Their spirits soared. "Why we should have rejoiced at beholding a coast from which we had so recently escaped with our bare lives is difficult to determine," Robbins later mused. Studying the shimmery ghost of land on the horizon, Riley secretly fretted. Despite his earlier promise that he was aiming to return to the wreck site, he had held out hope that they had traveled far enough south to escape the desert. To his eye, the land was uniformly flat. He guessed that they were looking at the Sahara.

The boat neared the coast around sunset, with the fading rays running along the water behind them and pushing at their backs, like the hand of fate. When they were suddenly hurtled to the southeast like a canoe in rapids, they were rudely reminded of the nature of the current. They could now hear the tremendous influx of sea roaring as it crashed into the towering wall of the continent. The sand and brown cliffs came into clear focus, rising directly from the sea, in, as Robbins deemed it, "majestic and destructive grandeur."

Riley did not like what he saw. He proposed that they stay at sea another night and search for a landing place farther south in the morning. The crew disagreed. Their patience had been stretched to its limit. They demanded an attempt on the shore. They would land or go down that evening. Seeing that his mates agreed with the men, Riley reluctantly assented.

Had they sailed on, they would doubtlessly have reached a gentler coast, or with real luck, and another sixty miles of southing, they could have made it to territory under treaty with the British occupying Saint-Louis at the mouth of the Senegal River. In that area, the tribes knew there was a bounty for shipwrecked sailors, and it was their practice to take them into Saint-Louis to be redeemed.

Destitute as they were, the men had few preparations to make for the surf. Whether it was imprudent or not, Riley would not risk losing the last bottle of wine to the waves. He ordered it uncorked. Without prejudice to the offenders of the night before, they all took turns swigging it down.

Now Riley steered for the ironbound coast. "We could discover no aperture through which we might pass for some time," Robbins recalled. "At length we saw something that had the appearance of a sand bank. We made for it with all our little strength." The vertical wall of the continent raced at them like an opaque gale. In a dizzying frenzy of percussive waves, their bruised backsides slammed against thwarts. Suddenly, the longboat rose, rose, and fell. The wave swept out from under them. The boat crashed down. Its weary timbers exploded at their feet. Sand.

PART TWO

Ships of the Sand

Purgatory

◠◠ The sailors' destiny now manifested itself in a barren strip of beach not much larger than their destroyed boat. Towering over them was a cliff. The little that had survived with them included some articles of spare clothing, several hunks of salt pork, a number of bottles containing water or urine, and the bag of silver. The urine was more precious to them than the silver.

Even while at sea, the crew of the *Commerce* had opted for drinking urine over seawater. Riley reported that by the time they reached the desert, they were drinking their own shared urine "distilled" — having passed through their bodies — twelve times.[1] He called the drinking of urine a "wretched and disgusting relief."

Both anecdote and modern science indicate that drinking urine can be beneficial in small quantities for short periods of time. But in larger doses, when not diluted, its poisons and waste will overwhelm the kidneys and cause them to fail, a state known as uremia, which can ultimately result in brain damage and death.

According to a young Swiss surgeon named Savigny who was a survivor and chronicler of the raft voyage that followed the wreck of the French frigate *Méduse* on the Arguin Banks of Mauritania in 1816, the urine of some of those on the raft was "more agreeable than that of others." One passenger could not bring himself to swallow any at all. "In reality, it had not a disagreeable taste," Savigny conceded, "but in some of us it became thick and extraordinarily acrid." Its most peculiar quality, he noted, was that after drinking it, one immediately had the urge to "urine anew."

In 1877, a U.S. cavalry company lost in the desert drank their own urine sweetened with sugar, which, they claimed, improved it considerably. But an experiment by American World War I ace Eddie Rickenbacker, who after an emergency landing in 1942 was stranded on a raft in the Pacific for twenty-three days, was not so successful. He and his raftmates collected their urine in empty cartridge shells and left it exposed to the air and sun for days, hoping this might purify it. "That was my idea," Rickenbacker confessed. "It was a bad one." The smell became absolutely intolerable and the taste unimproved.

A very small number of known cases seem to belie science. In his narrative of the 1785 wreck of the *Ste. Catherine,* Pierre Raymond de Brisson reported that the ship's baker survived on nothing but snails and his own urine for ten days. In 1905, W. J. McGee, who was camped on the desert near Yuma, Arizona, studying the effects of light on desert life, rescued a Mexican who had been lost on the desert for eight days, existing for five of them solely on a burning desire to knife the partner who had abandoned him there — and his own urine. After examining the "shrunken and scrawny" man, whose skin had "turned a ghastly purplish yet ashen gray" and whose gums, nostrils, and eyelids had blackened, McGee recorded the facts of the case in minute detail and went on to conduct his groundbreaking research into thirst. Yet he could only struggle with the evidence when it came to *uriposia.* Ordinarily, drinking urine is "hardly helpful if not wholly harmful," he stated, but in this man's case it seems to have saved his life.[2]

The same is true for the Commerces, who now found themselves trapped in a terrifying place. "Over our heads," wrote Riley, "pended huge masses of broken and shattered rock." More of this could tumble down and turn the eye-blink of a beach into a craggy grave. He examined the dreary cliffs above, running from east-northeast to west-southwest as far as he could see, and figured they were somewhere near Cape Blanco. They had actually landed ninety miles to the north, near Cape Barbas, but with no map or navigational tools it was a reasonable guess.

Cape Barbas forms the southwestern point of the crescent-shaped St. Cyprian Bay. Ten miles to the east-northeast at the north end of the bay lies Morro Falcon, a flat-topped cliff that resembles a fort and reaches about a hundred feet above the sea. The St. Cyprian "river," really a wadi — a dry gully that flows only in the rare event of rain — lies just to the north of that. At both ends of the bay, the cliffs are made of white- to sand-colored strata turning maroon at the bottom. In between lies a sandy beach backed by dunes with steep rugged sides. The wind and surf shape all.

Riley did not know what exactly lay above their bit of sand beach, only that they had to find a way up while they still had the strength. He instructed the men to prepare a site for sleeping. He and Savage would explore along the shore to the west, where he hoped the cliffs sloped toward the water at the cape's point. They climbed over wet, jagged rocks until they reached a dead end — no way up and no way around. They returned after dark and broke the news that they had not found a route to the top.

The sailors wet their mouths with urine and ate shreds of salt pork. Before going to sleep in a huddled mass on a patch of sand partly sheltered from the wind by rocks, they prayed together.

At daybreak on September 8, the twelfth day since the wreck at Bojador, the rising tide was still half out, and one of the men found mussels on the rocks.[3] They all ate some, but the salt burned their sore mouths so much that they gave up. They began making preparations to head east along the rocky outcroppings of the cape. According to Robbins, they still held on to the scant hope of seeing a ship at sea and somehow waving it down. Not knowing exactly where they were, they also believed they might be able to return to the wreck on foot. In fact, they were more than two hundred miles south of the wrecked brig.

The men divided the little bit of water that remained, each having his own bottle and thus, within a narrow framework, control of his own destiny. Using penknives and rope yarn, they cut and sewed portions of the boat's sail and extra shirts into small satchels. Each man stashed his ration of salt pork and his bottle of water inside and slung the sack over a shoulder. They could not afford to waste any fluid. In an ever-diminishing cycle, they would now drink from and urinate into their bottles.

To reduce the weight and bulk they would have to carry, the men left everything else, including spare clothes, except for their jackets. They discarded the worst of the salt pork. Convinced that the silver had inflamed the Sahrawis' greed and cruelty, Riley also asked the men to leave behind any coins they had kept for themselves. It stood to reason that if a Sahrawi found one of them rich in coin, he might take the silver as his good fortune and murder or leave for dead the bearer; whereas if he found just a man, he would keep his new slave as his good fortune. The Americans buried the sack of dollars and flung away the rest as worse than useless. With reluctance, they also now abandoned the ship's colors; they could no longer afford the privilege to bear and the duty to protect their nation's flag.

Before setting off, they made a solemn pact to stick together and to help one another out. "It was not merely common danger that made us friends," Robbins later reflected. "We had become attached to each other by previous sufferings and mutual favors."

Porter and Robbins took the lead. The terrain to the east was even less promising than that to the west. The rise of the continent appeared either vertical or, worse, undercut by wind and surf and looming cavernously overhead at a dizzying height. Glacier-size hunks of the continent had ruptured and crashed to the sea, creating their path of boulders, rocks, gravel, and sand. They picked their way through tunnels formed by subsequent collapses and skirted impassable jumbles by traversing narrow strips of temporary beach or by wading. When there was no choice, they scaled ridges of scree, sometimes piled halfway to the summit. Hand over hand they climbed on slick, precarious ridges, knowing that one wrong move could send them tumbling into the breakers below.

At each summit they then dropped down toehold by toehold to the water's edge again. Where there was neither a strip to walk on nor a climbable outcropping, they waited for the surf to recede and then waded chest-deep along the wall to the next outcropping or

pile of scree, which they mounted between waves, each man helping the next up.

"Surmounting one obstacle seemed only to open to our view
another, and a more dangerous one," Riley later recalled. Two places
were nearly impassable. The first was a harrowing sight. A crest of
rocks deposited the men at a sheer face about fifty feet high. The
wall plunged to a deep churning sea, but a narrow ledge crossed it,
which Robbins estimated was about thirty rods, or 165 yards, long.
On the ledge and suspended over it in improbable crags, rocks, some
as big as cannonballs, rested, only temporarily halted on their journey to the sea. Riley and his crew paused to take in the situation.
Their shoes were shredded, their feet cut and bleeding. The sun
now beat down on their overheated bodies. The only thing worse
than pushing on — and risk falling into the sea — was not to push
on, only to die of exposure on the rocks. Below was death in the sea.
They had no choice but to cross the face.

Turning their satchels around to hang on their chests and stuffing things in front pockets, they placed their backs against the cliff
and eased out along the ledge. Robbins, who was still in the lead
with Porter, described it as "not much wider than a stone step."
Riley put the width at eight inches. In places, they had to creep
along on their heels with their toes hanging over the precipice. The
backs of their heads felt each tiny projection of the cliff. A horizon
of sea and milky space swam before them while below, the waves
crashed and washed away. But it was the heat that Riley would particularly remember. In strange juxtaposition to the heaving, foaming, spitting sea, the air was absolutely still, as if it had been
smothered. "Not a breath . . . ," Riley wrote, "to fan our almost boiling blood."

Partway across the narrow ledge, Robbins and Porter found a
recess in the wall. The crew filed into a space big enough for all of
them to rest in. A depression in the rock in the shape of a cooking
kettle contained a pool of warm water. Though it was too brackish
to drink, the men bathed their heads in it and found it greatly
refreshing.

As they crawled out of the crevice, Riley made a dire mistake. The passage was slim, and the men were forced to rub against the cliff. As he moved forward, he suddenly felt liquid wet his side. He knew without looking that he had broken his water bottle.

Riley was already exhibiting symptoms of McGee's fourth and penultimate stage of dehydration, in which saliva stops flowing altogether, the pulse slows, and breathing becomes labored. As mucous membranes dry out, the lips and gums tighten and the tongue "hardens into a senseless weight." Eyelids and nostrils retract. Deprived of moisture, the eyes and nose burn with grit. Riley was not yet suffering from every symptom of the stage. He did not have pounding headaches and hallucinations. Though his tongue had become as "useless as a dry stick," he managed to speak and be understood. But there could be no doubt: without his water, he was in deep trouble.

In the late afternoon, they waded around another precipitous rock. The sight of dead locusts on some rocks gave them hope that if they made it to the top, they would find vegetation to eat.[4] In reality, the surface above was so barren that the Sahrawis considered the arrival of a cloud of locusts — one of the biblical plagues — a gift from Allah: they harvested the bugs for food. But even if the sailors had been inclined to do the same, they would not have been able to — these bugs, Riley observed, "crumbled to dust on the slightest touch."

By nightfall, they had covered only about four miles and saw no break in the bluffs. "A harder day's travel was never made by man," Robbins wrote, though the next day's would rival it, producing an impediment that would stop them in their tracks.

With great relief, according to Riley, they found a stretch of beach to spend the night on. In the shelter of the cliffs about a hundred feet from the surf, they greased their mouths with salt pork fat and ate small pieces of it. Everyone but Riley washed this down with drops from their bottles. With the end approaching for all, he had no right to ask anyone to share, nor could he rightfully expect them to. Nonetheless, two of the men offered him their bottles. Riley gratefully wet his mouth.

They prayed together and then lay down in their wet clothes and slept. As the cold, moist sea air settled over them, Riley meditated on Horace's suffering. He had assured the boy's mother that he would take care of him, and he now vowed to himself to adopt him if they made it back home, to "watch over his ripening years" and share with him any fortune he and his family might be favored with. His mind wandered to his own children, to whom Horace would be a fine brother. Before dozing off, Riley wrapped his arms around the boy in a reassuring embrace.

On September 9, the sailors woke up stiff and numb, trembling from the cold in their sweaty clothes, which had not dried in the damp ocean air. They had no way to make a fire and only salt pork to eat, but the second night of sleep on land had helped them recover from the lack of it at sea. The wounds on their feet had healed enough so that they could walk again. Continuing along the coast would at least encourage blood flow.

They had not gone far when they caught a distant glimpse of a wide beach beneath a sloping bluff. As the crow flies, it was not far, but they had to stick to the contours of the coast, and here it was very rough, the cliff top having collapsed into the surf. As they picked their way forward, Riley studied the beach, searching for a spot near the bluffs where they might be able to dig a well, and recollecting one he had once dug successfully on a Bahaman key. It had produced drinkable water that he mistakenly believed was seawater filtered fresh by the sand.

The broken rocks reopened the wounds in the sailors' feet, and they moved slowly. Before long, they encountered a massive promontory undercut by the sea and looming over a half mile of surf thundering on boulders fallen from above. To reach the beach, they would have to somehow cross this chasm without being washed into the turbulence beneath the cliff. It was a deflating sight. Riley sized up their situation: "To advance by what appeared to be the only possible way seemed like seeking instant death; to remain in our present situation was merely to die a lingering one; and to return was still worse."

The sailors searched desperately for a solution. Then one of them spotted a large boulder about midway across the chasm, a boulder that revealed itself only momentarily as the surf washed out. It gave them a chance, anyway.

It was about nine in the morning, and Riley figured it was the depth of low tide. He told the men he would try to reach the boulder. A wave broke. The sea inhaled a giant's breath, and Riley plunged through the water. He reached the slick rock and grabbed onto its rilled surface. The next wave buried him and churned in the teeth of the cave, but the captain hung on. As soon as he could, Riley rose up again and dived in on the other side. He reached the far embankment just as the next breaker caught him. He desperately clung onto the steep rock face. When the wave receded, he scrambled up the face, exhausted but safe.

The rest of the crew followed. Riley had thought the tide was all the way out, but it continued to recede for another half hour, making each successive wave a little less violent. As the men reached the far side, they helped hoist up their soaked and battered shipmates.

Once recovered, they explored the beach. The continental wall looked more irregular here and the slope less severe, but first they would search for water. With their bare hands, they dug a well, eventually filling their hats and tossing the sand up. They found water, but it was salty. They moved back toward the cliff but had the same result. This disheartening process was repeated at several spots until near the cliff they dug down to solid stone.

Riley chose one more site for digging and set the men to work, but he had no hope for water now. "I will go and see if I can get up the bank," he told them. He promised to return soon with news.

Searching the bluff, Riley found a fault line. Though it was a long way up, the wall sloped enough to give him a chance. He used all his strength and clawed his way up. Though he had seen the tabletop horizon from the boat and feared that they were headed back to the desert, he was not prepared for what he discovered at the top. Then he had only had time to worry about getting the boat to shore. Now he gazed out on "a barren plain, extending as far as the eye could reach each way, without a tree, shrub, or spear of grass that might give the smallest relief to expiring nature." The tableau of emptiness rocked his soul: it was the earth before Eden; it was bones without flesh; it was nature that had gone mad and devoured itself. Riley dropped to the ground in shock and grief.

After a while — he did not know how long — he rose again, confused and nearly delirious. He cupped his hands, caught his urine, and soothed his burning throat with it. He felt an impulse to jump to his death in the sea, but it vanished as the faces of his men and of his wife and children flashed in his mind. He recalled what he had already survived and tried to find strength in it. He wandered east along the ledge, on a tightwire between the flashing waves and the sand. When a descent to the sea offered itself, he took it. At the bottom between two rocks he found a clear pool. He stripped off his salty clothes and bathed in the sun-heated seawater for half an hour, scrubbing at his defiled skin, but the desert ghost that had slipped inside could not be washed away.

When Riley finally returned to his men, he sat down on the sand. "We can go another two miles on the beach before we come to a wall," he told them. "On the way, you will find a pool for bathing and an easier route to the top than this one." He quickly changed the subject to avoid talking about what lay above: "Did you find any fresh water where you were digging?" he asked. But he already knew the answer.

The crew gathered up their bottles and satchels and headed down the beach, arriving around noon at the rise Riley intended to ascend. He now warned the men of the desolation at the top. Tired, hot, and discouraged, they decided to rest on a patch of sand in the shade under a ledge. The tide was out, and the air so still and humid that they had trouble catching their breath. They sank into a coma-like sleep for two hours.

Robbins opened his eyes to deep despondency. "I had become so inured to misery that she had adopted me as her child," he later reflected, "and I felt no dispositions to avoid her embrace." He felt they had run out of options, and he sensed this to be the general belief among the rest. Nevertheless, they crawled up the craggy slope, pulling themselves up with anything they could grab. Robbins described the climb as "next to dragging ourselves to the scaffold — it was becoming our own executioner."

When they reached the top, they gazed out slack-jawed on the dead landscape that Riley had warned them of. The ghost too slipped inside them, as tenacious as nausea. Like their captain, they experienced panic, confusion, and visceral, uncontrollable grief. Some collapsed on the hardpan, crying for the loss of hope, for their families, for the indignity of death so far from home. They always knew that something like this might occur. Now they wondered why they had not prepared for it better. They caught their tears with their fingers and guided them to their leathery tongues. " 'Tis enough," one man muttered in disgust. "Here we must breathe our last." Another groaned, "We have no hope of finding either water or provisions, or human beings, or even wild beasts. Nothing can live here."

What they looked out on, in 1815, had never been scientifically explored and was almost too mind-boggling to imagine. They faced the western edge of the world's largest desert. Occupying a third of Africa, it stretches more than three thousand miles east to the Red Sea and twelve hundred miles from the Sahel — the fringe of savanna in the south — to the Atlas Mountains in the north, mountains that snare almost all the moisture traveling down on the northeast winds. Relative-humidity levels, rarely above an abrasive 30 percent, are often as low as a lethal 5 percent, dry enough to kill bacteria and mummify corpses. On the coast, the heat of the Sahara clashes with the cold waters of the Atlantic, often creating heavy fogbanks that envelop the shore, and on many days the *irifi*, a powerful, searing wind, shrouds the region in a melancholy ocher veil of dust.

The Sahara was not always like this. From 5500 to 2500 B.C., it was relatively fertile, wet and inviting. Up until Roman times, antelope, elephants, rhinoceroses, and giraffes roamed a savanna densely studded with acacia, while crocodiles and hippopotamuses wallowed in lush rivers. Ostriches, gazelles, and antelope still persisted in 1815, but by then the Saharan climate was arguably the most extreme on earth. Its temperature could sizzle at more than 120 degrees Fahrenheit in the shade, the ground temperature soaring 50 degrees higher in the sun; at night, the thermometer could plunge as much as 85 degrees. These conditions, combined with frequent windstorms and less than five inches of average annual rainfall, made sustained life virtually impossible in many parts. As flora and fauna died off or adapted, the land itself deteriorated. While only about a tenth of the Sahara is covered in barren sand dunes, or *erg*, almost equally formidable are its stepped plains of wind-stripped rock covered in boulders, stones, and dust — the lower elevations generally known as *reg* and higher ones as *hammada*.

To the sailors — to the outside world — it was all a vast unknown. Period maps show the Sahara, then often spelled "Zahara" or "Zahah-rah" but better known as the Great Desert, as only a large empty space with a few tribal names scrawled on it. The sailors of the *Commerce* had landed in what would become in 1884 the Spanish protectorate Rio de Oro. In 1958, the Spaniards would combine this district with the Saguia el-Hamra district to the north to form Spanish Sahara; this in turn would become the disputed region of Western Sahara after the Spaniards left under duress in 1976.

In 1789, Brisson of the *Ste. Catherine* described the western Sahara in stark terms:

> These regions afford no variety, the country being entirely flat, and not producing any plant whatever. The horizon is there obscured by a reddish vapour. It looks as if there were burning volcanoes on every side. . . . Neither bird, nor insect, is seen in the air: a profound silence, that has something dreadful in it, prevails. If now and then a small breeze arise, the traveller immediately feels extreme lassitude; his lips crack, his skin is parched up, and little pimples, that occasion a very painful smarting, cover his body (pp. 381–82).

According to Robbins, when the sailors reached the *hammada*, their minds played tricks on them. Training their professional eyes on the horizon, searching for a reprieve from the void, they thought they saw a lake to the south. They briefly discussed going to it, before realizing that it was nothing but "the striking of the rays of the sun upon the dried sand." Some of the men were for stopping. Riley, Williams, and Savage urged them to get up, but the officers' exhortations rang hollow. When asked what he thought they should do, Hogan, the ordinary seaman from Massachusetts, replied, "I don't know — but what's the use of lying down to die as long as we can stand up and walk?" It was not what he said so much as how he said it: "with perfect apathy," Robbins recalled.

Paradoxically, Hogan's utter absence of enthusiasm motivated the men. No tinseled hope would spur them now, only the dispassionate notion that they might as well walk on simply because they could. They picked themselves up and trudged over the flint-hard red earth, marine sediment dating back 60 million years, which spawned dunes in only its most recent 2 million years: some live dunes, granular and yellow, unstable; and some dead in hard brown swells thirty feet high, covered in travertine and undercut by the wind. The sailors stuck to the familiar coast, where the desert ended abruptly, its broken surface having been tossed to the sea below, the dissolution of dead land.

Though it looked devoid of life, the desert around them was home to more creatures than they could have imagined. While the larger mammals had long since fled south, the hyenas and jackals, the wildcats, the reptiles and scorpions had adapted, often with exquisite efficiency. The Saharan cheetah can prowl fifty miles and needs only the blood and urine of its prey to slake its thirst. The horned viper, the Sahara's most feared snake, hunts with its body buried in the cool sand and its wedge-shaped head resting on the surface like a stone. When hungry enough, the ferocious gray monitor will attack a camel, and the foot-long lizard sometimes wins.

The Sahara yielded the sailors a few cryptic signs of accommodation. At first they ignored them: brittle shells of dead locusts and low, dry stalks that resembled wild parsnip. But they soon learned to adjust their sights. Toward sunset, they noticed small holes on the hard surface, according to Robbins, and decided they had been dug by some animal to get to the root of a weedy plant.

They found more of the plants and clawed in the hardpan with sharp stones.[5] The effort produced finger-length pieces of a root that tasted like celery, but the plants were too scarce and too dry, and the digging too difficult, to give them much hope.

Robbins later recalled seeing "large heaps of muscle [*sic*] shells, and the appearance of a former fire where they probably had been roasted by the natives." They thought they saw human tracks. In a haze of starvation, exhaustion, and thirst, it was becoming increasingly difficult for the men's brains to focus and analyze.

They next spotted in the distance a break in the cliffs and a gradual descent to a swath of beach. It was more of the same, but different, enticing now that they were treading over the bed-of-nails surface, bruising and puncturing their feet. It gave them a reason to keep going, and as night fell upon them, they marched forward. They had been reduced to finding hope and incentive in sand, enough inspiration to carry them another three miles to a place where they could at least lie down in relative comfort and die.

As they walked and the evening wind cooled them, the desert turned black. In the darkness, James Clark, whose keen eyes had served Ketchum before Riley, saw it first. In a hoarse croak, he called out to the others, "I think I see a light!"

Captured

∽ The men agreed that the faint light they saw flickering in the distance was a campfire. A simultaneous rush of joy and fear brought them back to life. At last there was a possibility of relieving the thirst and hunger that burned in their guts like fever. The fear, Robbins said, was that the medicine would be worse — if possible — than the malady. Though miserable, they were still free, and it was known that captives generally did not fare well among the coastal Sahrawis. Caravan merchants from the north were robbed and murdered. Spaniards whose Canary-based fishing vessels ran aground here were routinely slaughtered, and other Westerners endured brutal captivity. The band of Sahrawis that had captured Pierre de Brisson had amused themselves by watching hungry ravens pick at one of his shipmates, who was unconscious but still alive. Later Brisson discovered his enslaved captain's emaciated corpse, teeth sunk into hand: his master had stopped feeding him when he became too ill to work.

Though Riley felt his hopes revive at the sight of the campfire, he remained cautious. He recommended that they rest that night, so as not to surprise the men camped around the fire and send them into a murderous frenzy. The crew agreed.

At the break in the cliffs, they slowly picked their way down a maze of tumbled, broken rocks to the sand they had seen, still well above the sea on an awkward slope. The hardpan they had crossed had cooled rapidly as the sun set, but the sand retained its heat.

According to Riley, it was still hot enough "to have roasted eggs" on, but they were too exhausted to go any farther. The Commerces dug down to the cool sand below the surface, making shallow pits for their bodies and shoving the hot sand down the bank. They shared a bit of their remaining water, prayed, and then wordlessly fell asleep, all except for Riley, whose mind whorled. Despite his weariness, he lay awake mulling over their future and suffering from thirst. He bore the responsibility for his men heavily, especially the young ones: Savage and Robbins, whose families had such close ties to his own, and Horace, whose dead father he had loved and whose mother would now in all likelihood lose a son. The next day the Sahrawis would either kill them or enslave them. The best they could hope for was to eventually be ransomed. It was almost too much for him to bear.

Riley craved any end to his thirst, even death. Remorse was vanishing in the agony of his thirst. He had few reflections on his life, on his children, made no silent farewells to his wife. All thoughts of his family, he later confessed, with the candor of a compulsively truthful man, were "driven almost entirely from my mind"; he would sell his life, he admitted, for a "gill of fresh water."

Though he prayed for sleep, even just an hour, it never came. Bitter thoughts tormented him. He begrudged his men their successful stupors. Finally, in his despair, he broke down. Instead of trading his life for a gill of water, he forfeited his honor for a few drops of stale urine. "[I] stole a sip of the cook's water, which he had made and saved in a bottle," Riley later confessed. The briny substance only increased his fiery thirst.[1]

At daybreak on September 10, Riley awakened the men. They were reduced almost as much as a group of men could be: they had no food or drink to speak of — a few still possessed bottled urine and knots of pork — no shelter, little clothing, no weapons, and they were in a hostile environment, to their eyes devoid of resources. The equation was now simple and the eventual result clear. An outside force was necessary for their salvation, and they knew of only one outside force.

To prepare the men, Riley dispensed practical information. "If it is ever in your power, you must write Mr. James Simpson, the American consul general at Tangier, and tell him of the fate of our vessel and crew. Or write to any Christian merchant in Mogadore, Gibraltar, or elsewhere," he said. "Address the consul at Algiers, Tunis, or Tripoli if you hear those places mentioned.

"Remember," he added, "Providence has worked in our favor. Submit to your fate like men, and should we be made slaves, be obedient, as policy requires, to your master. We must submit to save our lives. Resistance and stubbornness will only make us more miserable and probably prompt the natives to murder us out of resentment."

As they prepared to walk to the campfire they had seen the night before, the men bowed their heads and Aaron Savage led them in prayer: "Heavenly Father, we implore you to protect and support us in whatever situation we might be placed, in whatever scenes we might be called to act, and in whatever sufferings we might be compelled to endure."

"Amen," they said together.

The men descended to a beach and walked northeast along it in the direction of the campfire. After about two miles, they came to a massive dune. When they climbed it, they saw a valley separated from the sea by a ridge of sand and from the desert by the coastal bluffs. About half a mile from them, camels and Sahrawis thronged around a well.

The sailors recoiled at the sight of these strange people and their ungainly beasts. It was one thing to pursue a distant flicker of firelight, which, at the end of a desperate day, had seemed a beacon of hope. It was another to beg for mercy from men they viewed as savages. Now the crew's opinions differed. Some wanted to wait and watch. "They might assist us," others argued. "This might be a caravan heading north." Riley was convinced they had no choice. They moved forward.

An Arab man in a haik and two women in flowing robes, who with some children had wandered off in their direction, spotted them first. As soon as he understood what he was seeing, the man drew his scimitar and made for them with the women and children at his heels. Those around the well soon realized that fate had put them at a disadvantage and set out with the zeal of men wronged.

Riley advanced with mates Williams and Savage. They bowed to the ground and then slowly rose. Riley continued to try to indicate their submission, but it quickly became apparent that this was not the issue. Possession was.

The man, whose name they later learned was Mohammed, charged ferociously at Riley with his scimitar poised overhead. Riley believed the man was about to cut him down. He waited, knowing that any sign of resistance would only guarantee it. He bowed down again. The man dropped his weapon and began to pull Riley's clothes off.

The two frenzied women did the same to Williams and Savage. Then, with their children, they fearlessly assaulted the rest of the crew, stripping off their clothes. Only Robbins and a few others managed to keep their pants. Mohammed now advanced on the crew, jabbing his scimitar at their chests and swinging the curved blade over their heads until they cowered together beneath him. Clutching Dick Deslisle, he returned to the officers before the charging horde reached them. He tore off his own haik, leaving himself naked, and stuffed all the clothes lying on the ground into it. He put the bundle on Deslisle's shoulders, indicating to Riley that he and Deslisle belonged to him now and that if they lost the bundle he would kill them.

Spears, scimitars, war clubs, and muskets glinted in a swirling storm cloud of dust and confusion as ululating tribesmen, dressed in animal skins or flowing white haiks and turbans, bore down on them. Some were on foot, others lofted to absurd heights on their frothing camels. As the beasts lurched to a halt, the riders leaped off and attacked.

The naked man and the two women unleashed their own fury,

screaming with atavistic rage, crouching and defiantly tossing handfuls of sand into the air to ward off the attackers.

"All seemed anxious to be the first sharers in the plunder," remarked Robbins, in the calm of hindsight, "when alas, they could find no plunder but our miserable bodies." Riley was still standing out front with Williams and Savage when the newcomers surrounded them and, disregarding Mohammed's prior claim, began to fight over them. Half a dozen shouting men vied for control of Riley, grabbing at him and pulling him in different directions. The same happened to Deslisle.

Like a cyclone in a thunderstorm, Mohammed leaped about, fending off the aggressors with threats and thrusts of his scimitar. He barked at the others to divide the rest of the sailors as they pleased but to stay away from these two. Some heeded his emphatic gestures and left to seize other men, but there were too few sailors to go around. They continued to fight for Riley, their weapons flashing at his sides and inches from his head, until the whir of their metal sounded to him louder than their shouts. He was the helpless fulcrum of a pitched battle, in which he observed them "hacking each other's arms apparently to the bone, then laying their ribs bare with gashes, while their heads, hands, and thighs received a full share of cuts and wounds." Blood soaked white garments. It was bedlam, and all that the horrified Americans could do was pray that a blade did not strike them down.

Over the course of an hour, factions of Arabs took possession of various sailors, separated them from the pack, and headed back to the well, until the melee had dissipated into a number of isolated scuffles. By eight o'clock, the issue was settled, at least temporarily, and all were regathering around the well. Some nomads exulted in their prizes. Others nursed their wounds, brooded, and plotted. Some returned with lesser trophies, having looted the bundle of clothes entrusted to Deslisle and any other items they could wrench from their owners during the confusion. The cook had managed to retain only his new master's haik, an item no one dared take.

Capture of Riley and ten of his crew by a tribe of wandering Arabs, near Cape Barbas
(from *An Authentic Narrative of the Loss of the American Brig Commerce*, 1817)

Urging Riley and Deslisle on toward the well, Mohammed's sisters, hardy women wearing tunics open at the sides and blue veils, beat them with sticks. As they stumbled along, Riley pointed to his bleeding mouth, abraded by sea salt and coated white by dehydration. He cared for nothing but extinguishing his thirst.

One by one, the sailors entered the dizzying scene around the well. In whirling dust and animal stench, the Arabs drew water, filled camel-skin troughs, and drove their one-humped beasts back and forth with guttural shouts and hard raps of their goads to the animals' rumps and necks. The camels, growling and gnashing their stained teeth at one another and their masters, jostled for space around the troughs, which held about twenty gallons each and accommodated half a dozen animals at a time. Once a camel had won a spot, its long neck stiffened downward, its jutting head froze as if in the moment of rapture, its broad jaws worked rhythmically, slurping down obscenely noisy drafts.

Exhausted, starved, pumped with adrenaline, scared but no longer morbid, the sailors milled about nervously like corralled beasts themselves. After nearly two weeks of exposure to the elements night and day, they were bearded, bony, and naked. Laughing bronze-colored children, equally naked, taunted them. Bare-breasted women and semiclad men alike shouted at them, calling them the lowest thing they could think of: *kelb es-sahrawi,* "desert dogs," or *kelb en-Nasrani,* "Christian dogs."

Finally, Robbins could stand his thirst no longer. He shouldered between two of the camels and plunged his head into a trough. This startled the massive, nine-foot animals, which began to shift and snort, and attracted the attention of the Sahrawis, who drove Robbins away with curses and their goads. Impressed by Robbins's size, strength, and gumption, the tribesmen began to fight over him again, three or four tugging him in different directions as they had done before.

A woman carried over a wooden bowl filled with an inky and fetid liquid Riley compared to "stale bilge water." As she set the bowl on the ground in front of Riley and Deslisle, Mohammed's sisters shoved the pair to their knees. Riley had previously advised his men that if they should come to a well they must take care not to guzzle. Despite this admonition and the impurity of the water, he and Deslisle drank like animals, draining half a gallon each without rising.[2]

More water was brought, and the women added to it a stream of sour milk from a goatskin. Riley declared the concoction, which the Arabs called *zrig,* "delicious," and he and his shipmates filled their bellies. Almost immediately, diarrhea rumbled through their intestines and shot down their legs. In the squalid circle around the well, their mess made little difference. The earthy scent of camels combined with the stench of camel dung and urine overpowered everything. The sailors' beggar's banquet continued until, racked by violent stomach cramps, they could no longer stand.

The captors separated their sailors out and took them off to the sides to be guarded. A large, raw-boned tribesman took possession of Robbins and placed him under the sharp eyes of his two sisters. Nearby, Robbins found Savage, Williams, and Barrett drinking *zrig* and joined them. Their thirst was immense. While the Arabs continued to water the drove, some four hundred head of bellowing camels, the sailors drank copiously. By ten o'clock in the morning, they began to feel like they had at last slaked their thirst. Now, they noticed, their appetites began to rage.

Modern science affirms this sequence of events. Given plenty of fluids, a person who is seriously dehydrated can rehydrate as much as 80 percent within half an hour, but he cannot do so fully without eating. The sailors' bodies were telling them that now. They craved food; they begged for it, but the nomads indicated that they had nothing to give them. This was shocking news: even their would-be saviors were empty-handed. With food and more water or *zrig,* they would have been able to rehydrate nearly completely within twelve hours, provided their dysentery was not too severe. As it was, the Commerces began their captivity on the Sahara with severe deficiencies in both nourishment and fluids.[3]

The bald desert sun pierced the human and bestial din now, and sweat rose freely to the sailors' pores. "Our skins," Riley observed, "seemed actually to fry like meat before the fire." The nomads vied to finish their watering. The fastest separated their camels and assembled their captives: Williams and Barrett with one master, in company with Robbins and his master; Porter, Hogan, and Burns each set out with their masters, as Riley, Savage, Clark, Deslisle, and Horace watched helplessly.

The breakup of the crew created new distress. Although the *Commerce* had brought them bad luck, they had survived it together. Until now, the brig still existed, at least as an organizing principle; they were still shipmates, sailors and officers, with ranks and responsibilities. In a stroke, this structure was demolished. Suddenly, each man was on his own, without the crew to depend on or to support. They did not know where they were going or whether they would all see one another again.

"It is wholly impossible to describe the feelings of my bosom at this adieu," wrote Robbins, who was among the first to bid farewell to his companions and felt palpable despair at this rupture, as if he were suffering his own death. "It left me in a state of horror and anguish which I then thought I could not but for a short time survive."

Each master made a camel kneel and directed his captive to mount the beast behind the hump on the sloping back and tailbone. The rising camel threw its rear into the air first, so the sailor hung there, against gravity, staring over the animal's head straight at the ground. The beast then lurched backward, its bony front legs extending and locking into place as the sailor clutched desperately to its short summer hair. Once up, it was like being aloft on a choppy sea. With no stirrups or saddles, the bones of the sailors' thighs and rear ends sat directly against the hard shifting anatomy of the camels. One by one, man and beast climbed out of the valley of the well, through a narrow chasm in the bluff to the desert above.

Of the four men who remained at the well with Riley, only Savage had somehow managed to stay partially clothed, in an old guernsey — a seaman's close-fitting blue wool shirt — and some ragged trousers. Clark, Deslisle, and Horace all worked at the well naked, hauling up water and filling the troughs until each camel had drunk as much as it could and the goatskins were full.

The Arabs tied two of these skins together by the legs and slung them over the camels' backs, where they hung on either side like bloated corpses. These *guerba* had been used to transport water since at least Neolithic times, and the Sahrawis were expert at decapitating a goat, inserting an arm into the warm cavity, running it around to detach the skin, and then extracting the flesh and bones without marring the skin. The neck, used as a spout, was lashed with a rope to a foreleg to keep it upright during transport.

The nomads saddled the camels, putting Riley to work fastening on a camel-skin basket, which sat on top of the hump and carried up to four women, children, or old people. (Some of the elderly Arabs looked so fantastically aged from decades of exposure to sun and wind that Riley believed it when he later heard they lived as long as three hundred years.) Swollen and cramped, Riley hoped to ride with the passengers in the basket but was disappointed in this. His master mounted the beast on a small saddle made of wood and camel hide in front of the hump, in the tradition of West African riders.[4] Riley clung on behind the hump, where there was no saddle. He was higher than he had ever been on an animal; the camel's motion combined the worst of a buckboard and a swaying mast.

Under so much weight, the camels' splayed feet sank into the yielding sand as they climbed up through the steep chasm that led to the desert. The drove stumbled forward, growing more furious with each cumbersome stride, barking like sea lions and spewing foam as if their insides were boiling over. The Arabs dismounted and ordered the sailors down too. While the former moved nimbly, the latter blundered along, sinking to their knees in the blistering sand. Sweat poured down their backs.

The Arabs were genuinely surprised by the clumsiness of their captives. At first they laughed and hooted with scorn. Then they cudgeled their backs, bloodying their peeling skin. The seamen grew increasingly desperate, flinging out their arms in order to keep their feet. The reflected sun scorched their downturned eyes. Still, the Arabs beat them.

On the lethal grade between the sea and the sun, the benefits of the water and camel milk and the corresponding lift in their spirits flamed away. A wrenching knot formed in their bellies: they now knew that the fate they had tried to escape at Cape Bojador was as bad as they had feared.

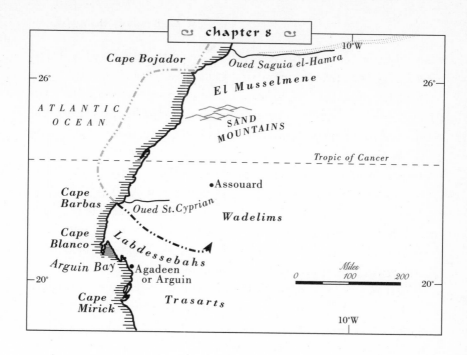

chapter 8

Thirst

As long as man has trod the western shores of the Sahara — at least seven thousand years — he has wandered and warred. In that time, no state or central authority has ever successfully controlled the remote desert plains. Even today, the smothering presence of Morocco's national police and military belies a tenuous grasp on the population of Western Sahara. And that is despite Morocco's having flooded the region with hundreds of thousands of settlers in the 1976 Green March and winning a two-decade war of attrition, not to mention possessing a historical claim to at least part of the territory.

"The Emperor, it is true, claims the sovereignty of the desert of Zahara, and the territory of Vled de Non [Oued Noun]," noted the British physician William Lempriere, who traveled in Morocco in

1789, "but his authority over that part of the country is almost nominal, as it entirely depends on the caprice & inclination of the Arabs who inhabit it." These Arabs, Lempriere wrote, "wander over the country in search of plunder, and are supposed, on some occasions, to extend their depredations as far as Nigritia, whence they carry off Negroes."[1]

By the time Riley reached the desert floor, he believed he was dying. He wished he would. Every step was a struggle.

Having noted the sailors' difficulty rising through the chasm, the Arabs now realized the extent of their exhaustion. They culled five camels from the drove, made them kneel, and again instructed the sailors to mount them behind the hump.

Gesturing and speaking Hassaniya Arabic, a dialect close to classical Arabic and Morocco's official language until the end of the nineteenth century, the Arabs demanded from the sailors the direction of the boat wreck. The sailors pointed and used their hands to indicate the distance. The Arabs hastily barked out instructions to the women, then lashed their camels and sped off to the southwest, leaving the sailors behind with the women.

As the women pushed the drove southeast into the desert, the Commerces discovered how painful it is to ride a camel over a long stretch. Unlike a horse, a camel swings both legs on each side in unison, making the rider sway heavily. It is no coincidence that a camel's gait is called a "rack."[2]

Bareback, slumped forward, clinging to the hair of the hump, the five seamen struggled to adjust. Sensing the inexperience of its rider, Riley's mount weaved in and out of the herd, bucking and bellowing, while the captain clung on for life. The camels' narrow hips and barrel-like stomachs, distended from the morning's water, gave the men nothing to grip with their legs, no way to support themselves. Mostly naked, their legs splayed wide, they flailed on the beasts' sharp spines. The insides of Riley's calves and thighs were chafed raw. Blood ran down his legs and dripped from his heels. The sun scorched the exposed parts of his legs and the rest of his body.

When the sailors begged to be allowed to walk, the women only drove the camels on harder than before. Inevitably, the seamen, pushed to the limit of pain, dropped off their mounts intentionally, sliding down the animals' steep rumps, balancing on the base of the tail before falling to the brutal *hammada,* then rising and running beside the drove. Although the stones were "nearly as sharp as gun flints," according to Riley, and cut their feet to the bone, for short intervals they seemed preferable to the camels.

As the sun started to sink and the women showed no intention of stopping, Riley's despair increased. The cold air, a relief in some ways, irritated the men's blistered skin. Delirious with exhaustion and pain, Riley could no longer stay on a camel or keep up on foot. He began to lag behind. He was losing not just the physical ability but also the will to survive.

"I cursed my fate aloud," Riley admitted, "and wished I had rushed into the sea before I gave myself up to these merciless beings." But that chance was gone. The captain began to search for a stone, "intending," he confessed, "if I could find a loose one sufficiently large, to knock out my own brains with it." But he did not find a good rock, and as this "paroxysm" passed, his reason returned. Realizing that it was now impossible to maintain the pretext of control, he reflected that his "life was in the hand of the power that gave it." This released a burden and lifted his spirits; he determined to "obey and please those whom fortune . . . had placed over me, and to persuade, both by precept and practice, my unhappy comrades to do the same."

Night descended. The sailors trudged silently in the gloom. At last, for fear of losing their captives, the women stopped the camels and made them kneel. The men climbed on. They rode again until around midnight, when they entered a shallow depression in the desert. The women halted the drove and made man and beast lie down. "Gliss, gliss!" they instructed the sailors, pressing them to the ground with the same unflinching hardness they showed the camels.

Riley estimated they had traveled forty miles. This was to be their bivouac. No shelter from the wind. No food.

Savage, who had started out with the group, had disappeared that day. Clark, Horace, Deslisle, and Riley all lay down together on the brittle earth, merging their scaly bodies into one mass to protect themselves from the wind. They rose again, however, when the women brought out a bowl of camel's milk and carefully doled out each man's share — about a pint. Still warm from the beast, the frothy liquid soothed their throats far better than the foul, gritty water in the goatskins and reminded them of all the comforts they lacked: their pipes and boots, their beds and their wives.

That night the Sahara showed the sailors just how distant those comforts were. A ceaseless wind buffeted their bare skin. Rigid stones poked into their backs and legs. Dust adhered to the moist surfaces of their wounds. Throughout the night, groans of pain and the wheezing, rattling, fretful sounds of dehydrated lungs emanated from them all. Despair counteracted their exhaustion, preventing sleep. They tossed and turned in a body, now to get relief from their spiky bed, now to expose a different face to gusts stinging with chill, grit, and sand.

It was, Riley said, "one of the longest and most dismal nights ever passed by any human beings."

Separated from his shipmates, Robbins's fortunes had seesawed repeatedly that day. He was paired initially with Williams and Barrett. Shortly after ascending through the broiling chasm and crossing an expanse of *hammada,* Robbins's owner, whom Robbins would come to know as Ganus, and the owner of Williams and Barrett ascertained where the boat was and, like Riley's owner, bolted to the west, leaving the women in charge of the sailors. With their combined droves, some forty camels, the women pressed on to the southeast, while the sailors suffered the rack of the camels and chose, like Riley, to trot on foot whenever possible. In both cases, the women seemed to be under strict orders to make all speed and ignored their captives' cries of pain.

Around two in the afternoon, a pair of menacing cameleers suddenly appeared from over a dune. The men had been at the well that morning and now swooped down on them. The angry women tried to fend them off but were unarmed, and the men easily brushed them aside. Fellow tribesmen would not steal one another's camels, which could be identified and reclaimed at a tribal council, but after the confusing melee at the well, ownership of the sailors could be disputed, and possession would count for much. In a flash, the men forced Williams and Barrett to mount behind them and rode off to the south.

Robbins was devastated by the sudden loss of his companions. Ganus's agitated sisters made it worse when they decided to take for themselves a scarce commodity on the desert: fine cloth in the form of his pants. Other men might come and take their last Christian slave, they evidently reasoned, but they would not get the valuable cloth in the bargain. The women filled up Robbins's hat with water and gave him a scrap of an old blanket. He fastened this around his waist with thorns.

In the evening, the reduced party reached two tents lying in a hollow on the desert floor. As soon as the travelers were spotted, half a mile from camp, family members rushed out of the tents to greet them. They held hands, embraced, and kissed. Robbins struggled to comprehend the strange people with whom it was his fate to wander on the desert. He considered them callous and barbaric, and this display of tenderness jolted him. Even he was welcomed. The gleeful children, all naked, held out their hands for him to kiss. A wrinkled old woman with breasts hanging almost to her waist clasped his hand in hers and then put her fingers to her lips in the Arab way of greeting, telling him to do the same. In her haggard face, he admitted, there was "something of humanity." But Robbins quickly resurrected his cynicism. They were only pleased to have a new slave "to serve them, and more probably because they hoped to make a sum of money by the sale of me," he concluded.[3]

The camels were driven up to the tent, which sat on a vein of sand in a basin of macadam-hard earth. Some of the camels bore two goatskins of water, others four, slung in pairs over their backs.

After they unloaded the beasts, Robbins was allowed a brief rest inside the family tent, a dozen sections of woven camel-hair cloth

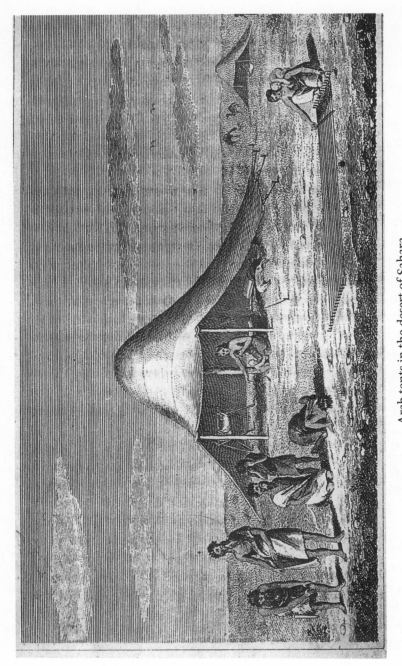

Arab tents in the desert of Sahara
(from *An Authentic Narrative of the Loss of the American Brig Commerce*, 1817)

sewn together and held up by poles and entered through a four-foot-high opening facing away from the prevailing wind. Ganus, his wife, and their three children — two girls and a boy, the oldest about twelve — all lived there, sleeping on a mat under a skin blanket. They had wooden bowls, *geddacks,* for cooking and eating and a few tools, including an ax and a knife. Otherwise, it was as empty as the desert itself. They could pack it up or unload it under half an hour.

Outside, around this tent and the other, where Ganus's mother, Annbube, and sisters lived, camels gnawed at the scattered knee-high bushes. The hulking beasts with their exaggerated chomping jaws looked particularly absurd next to these stalks already stripped of their scant foliage. The smell of dry camel feces and urine permeated everything.

The squalor of the camp staggered Robbins. He was no longer on his way somewhere, he had arrived — not just at a desolate place, but at a bygone era. One of the girls motioned him to follow her outside. She swung the ax into the sand at the base of a bush stalk until the stalk fell, then told him to cut more. Undertaking his first task as a domestic slave without significant reflection, he delivered three loads and was told to sit in front of the tent.

The wrinkled woman was Sarah, Ganus's wife, though she looked old enough to be his mother. The women, who did all the domestic work and were expected to take care of the children while keeping up with the men on the trail, seemed the more worn out. They did not even break to nurse the young. Their breasts "hang down to such a length," Robbins observed, "that they can furnish the child upon their backs with food . . . by thrusting them under their arms."

Sarah scooped out a hole in the sand and sparked a fire in some dried weeds, using a flint and steel. She rolled dry camel dung in her hands and placed it on the flame, blowing until it ignited too. She then laid the bush wood on top and dropped several fist-size stones onto the blaze. After slicing a morsel of Robbins's salt pork into a wooden bowl, she took the rocks from the fire and put them in the bowl, too. Robbins salivated as the meat sizzled on the scalding stones. The nomadic Arabs rarely cooked, and they ate little solid food. During lean times, they lived almost entirely on camel's milk. Because she was a Muslim, Sarah would not eat pork, but she fed the meat to her son, Elle, and her two daughters, and she placed a piece for Robbins in his hat. As a non-Muslim, Robbins would never be served from the same eating or drinking vessels the Arabs used. More than once, he would forfeit an opportunity to drink water for lack of a bowl.

Robbins spent that night on the sand under a corner of Ganus's family tent, the first night he or any of the sailors had had shelter since the shipwreck. Around eleven o'clock, after the camels had cooled enough to be milked, the Arabs woke him and gave him a bowl of *zrig*. Of his master's twenty camels, three were in milk, and each night they produced about six quarts, which was mixed with an equal amount of water and served among eight people. Robbins was given about two pints — the smallest share and only a fraction of the amount a man would require to sustain himself in the desert.[4] He could do nothing but take what was given. And Robbins was the best cared for of all the crew.

Later that night, Ganus returned. Robbins was stunned that his master had been able to reach the remote sliver of beach where they had abandoned the broken longboat and return so quickly. But he had plunder to prove it. Ganus and presumably the master of Williams and Barrett, with whom he had set out, were the first of the Arabs to reach the wreck, and the two had taken all they had found. According to Robbins, Ganus's share included a sack of rice the crew had ditched because it had been ruined by salt water.

Ganus had also retrieved a slab of pork that the sailors had not been able to carry with them, as well as a variety of salvage, including a scrap of sail, pieces of rope, and something that pierced Robbins with intense nostalgia: the brig's red, white, and blue colors.

The next morning, Riley and his three comrades received nothing but half a pint of camel's milk to share, barely a swallow for each man. After dawn, the Arab women hastily ordered them to drive the camels on. As they set out, their bare, mangled feet sent shocks of pain through their bodies. Soon they were trotting on bleeding soles to keep up with the drove.

After a while they reached a cluster of three or four tents in a depression where their masters were waiting for them. They were mingled in with other men, all heavily armed with double-barreled muskets, scimitars, and daggers. Despite the smiles and apparent decorum, all was not well here. Riley felt the strangers' eyes greedily examining him and his crew and sensed the tension roiling beneath the surface. Four rabbits had just entered a den of wolves.

It was not long before the wolves began to bite — one another. As the shouting and arguing grew more vehement, the Arabs drew and brandished their weapons. Each side grabbed onto the sailors, who found themselves the objects of another tug-of-war.

As the struggle ensued, Riley tried to comprehend the laws that governed these strange people. It was not quite a free-for-all. He could see that even as they pulled, they jockeyed verbally for the moral high ground. Possession was important, but just because one of the nomads took control of a sailor did not mean he would get to keep him. They continued arguing bitterly even as they all set out traveling in the same direction.

For the next several hours, the sailors found themselves shifted among different Arabs. In the end, Clark and Horace were hauled off separately by new owners. Riley, who had sworn to himself to protect Horace as a son, was powerless to prevent it. He and Deslisle remained with their original master.

They reached more tents around noon. The women in this camp examined the tattered Christians, whose skin had turned to chaff before the sun. Instead of arousing sympathy, the spectacle ignited a fit of disgust in women deeply encumbered with superstitious fears. In a culture where females were often denounced as conduits of evil, any contact with Christians was dangerous. They reviled the men with shrill curses and spat on them.

Such startling behavior had been related by Pierre de Brisson before Riley: "two of my fellows in misfortune were reduced to a most dreadful state; the women especially, far more ferocious than the men, took a pleasure in tormenting them." Charles Cochelet, a French survivor of a shipwreck off the west coast of Africa in 1819, also noted that if the women "by any accident happened to touch [us] . . . instantly spat in their hands, in order to wash them, testifying by that the horror and disgust which our presence inspired."

The Sahrawi women's potential for brutality was still being reported in 1934. During a battle outside the Spanish fort at Cape Juby, a mail plane arrived and scared away an attacking tribe. The Izarguien women — members of what some called the most civilized of the region's tribes — took advantage of the opportunity to dash onto the battlefield and gouge out the eyeballs of their enemy's dead.

Toward nightfall the sailors and their captors arrived at a large depression filled with dozens of tents. It now appeared to Riley that they had been heading here all along for the purpose of settling the tribesmen's conflicting claims to the sailors. That this quarrelsome group was united in any but the loosest sense was almost impossible to see. As far as Riley could tell, they had only one outward symbol of their kinship: four lean white mares, which seemed to be communal property and their greatest pride. To the nomads, the horses meant speed and maneuverability in battle and in hunting ostriches, much prized for their feathers, which were used as a currency on the Sahara. Having none of the camels' natural defenses against sand, heat, and drought, however, the mares had to be coddled. Indeed, they were treated far better than the sailors.

Riley's group was joined by Robbins, who arrived on foot, looking like a caveman, his unshaven face and hair now merged with a cape of skins hanging to his knees. Ganus had made his sisters return Robbins's pants, though now truncated at the knees, and he had given him shoes and a section of the ship's colors. Ganus's son had forced Robbins to trade the latter for the quilt of skins. In his pocket, Robbins nervously rubbed a string of knots: he had already begun to keep a calendar of his captivity. Others of the crew, weary, discouraged, and shedding skin, arrived throughout the day and were kept in the shelter of a tent while the Arabs prepared to debate their fate.[5]

Riley estimated that 150 nomad men of all ages, including some who were remarkably old, had convened here for the *yemma,* or tribal council. For the first time, he was able to listen carefully to their conversations and to clearly make out their words and names. His own master was Mohammed. Others were called Hamet, Abdallah, Seid, Sideullah. He had also heard Fatima, Ezimah, and Sarah for the women. By these names, he determined that they were "Mohamedans," and thus "Arabs or Moors."[6]

Arabs are often defined simply as Arabic-speaking people; thus, Riley was correct. They were also Muslims, further uniting them to the Arab world. Their ancestors had been converted by the waves of Islamic Arabs who had crossed northern Africa from the Middle East beginning in the seventh century; especially, in the west, by the Beni Hassan, a division of the camel-riding Maqil bedouins of Yemen, who had raided and rampaged across the northern Sahara, stopping only when they hit the Atlantic at Oued Draa in 1218. At first, the Sanhaja tribes that traveled between the Atlas Mountains and the Sahara had deemed the Maqil "locusts," pests that would devour and depart, but these Maqil warriors had come to stay.

Over time, the Maqil, fierce in nature but small in number, fused with and were subsumed by the Sanhaja tribes, a Berber people who were also the primary ancestors of the Sahrawis — including the Kabyles of Algeria and the Tuareg of the central desert. A strange thing happened, however: the culture of the smaller group came to dominate that of the larger. The Sanhaja of the western desert became largely Arab, adopting Islam and the Hassaniya dialect of Arabic. By 1800, these Arabized tribes had spread across the western Sahara and south into Mauritania, vassalizing the weak and creating a caste system.

At the bottom were slaves, mostly black Africans; craftsmen, mostly of Jewish descent; itinerant musicians; and the vassal tribes, known as *zenaga* or *lakhme,* "flesh without bones." These groups were dominated by the *chorfa* — religious tribes that adopted the lineage of the Maqil and supposedly traced their roots to the Prophet Muhammad — and by the warrior tribes, or "sons of the gun." In another twist of the Sahara, it was the warrior class that had the purest Maqil lineage and thus the strongest claim to descent from Muhammad, and the *chorfa,* whose lineal claims were largely trumped-up, who were among the most brutal and violent.

Animist traditions and the worship of holy men believed to possess supernatural powers remained strong on the desert, even among the *chorfa.* The Sahrawis did not look out on the same disheartening wasteland the sailors did but on a multifaceted realm of good and evil *yenun,* or spirits; of holy men with good magic, *baraka;* and enemies who could invoke the evil eye against them. Superstition pervaded everyday life. Good *yenun* in wells and trees deserved decorations and blood sacrifices of birds and small animals. Evil ones in the form of hyenas or sand tornadoes had to be vigilantly avoided. Shadows were to be dodged, and heed had to be paid to bad omens, such as being hailed at the beginning of a journey or seeing a crow on the path (seeing two crows was good). Newborn babies, especially attractive ones, were particularly vulnerable to the evil eye and so were hidden from strangers, kept dirty, and not addressed by their name.

When the *yemma* commenced, the tribesmen sat on the ground in circles of ten to twenty men, with their legs crossed under them, deliberating. Spoken in tranquillity, their elegant and fluid Arabic "thrills . . . like the breathings of soft wind-music," Riley reported. But spoken in anger, it sounded "as hoarse as the roarings of irritated lions." After intense discussion, one of the elders approached the tent where the sailors waited and spoke to them. Although neither Riley nor any of his men knew the language, Riley had an ear for foreign tongues, which he had honed in ports on both sides of the Atlantic and especially during his long stay on the Continent. The old man spoke distinctly, sounding to Riley like a Spaniard. With the help of signs, Riley was able to understand him. This was his first lesson in Arabic. As his and his men's lives were at stake, he would pick it up fast.

"What country do you come from?" the old man asked.

"Somos Ingleses," Riley responded, experimenting with Spanish. He claimed to be English because he knew that the Sahrawis had never heard of America and had no concept at all of land across the Atlantic Ocean. He might as well try to explain that he was from the North Pole, where the hills were made of ice.

"O Fransah, O Spaniah," the old man replied, indicating his familiarity with Europeans.

"Sí, Ingleses," Riley repeated, drawing a compass in the air and showing that they were from the north.

"We have seen your boat," he told Riley in a mixture of signs and Arabic, calling the boat *zooerga.* "Did you come all the way in that?"

Riley shook his head no. He elaborated by piling up sand to form a coastline and using sticks to indicate the size and shape of the brig. He showed that they had wrecked to the north at Cape Bojador by the force of a strong wind. Then he wiped out the image with his hand to signify that the ship was destroyed and a total loss.

A crowd of nomads had gathered around the two men. They listened intently to Riley and aided the old man in interpreting him. *Sfenah,* Riley noted, intent on grasping their vocabulary, was what they called the brig. At their prompting, he told them where the *Commerce* had been headed and what her cargo was. They gave him a bowl to show how many dollars he had had on board. Scooping up rocks, he filled and emptied the bowl three times.[7]

"They were much surprised at the quantity," Riley later observed, "and seemed to be dissatisfied that they had not got a share of them." When they asked whether others had seen it, he related how he and his crew had been treated by the inhabitants of that region, that their clothes, money, and provisions had been stolen and one of his men beaten and carried off.

The Arabs in turn informed Riley of the recent wreck of a Spanish ship up the coast. They asked him if he knew anything about "Marocksh," which he interpreted correctly as the city of Morocco. He said yes, he knew it. They asked if he knew the "Sooltaan." Riley clucked yes, in their manner.

"Soo mook," they demanded, trying to get him to name the sultan, but he did not understand. When they named Moulay Sulayman, he assured them that he knew him, that he had seen him with his own eyes, that Moulay Sulayman was a personal friend as well as a friend of England. They asked Riley where Morocco was, and he pointed correctly to the northeast, adding to his credibility. If they would take him and his men there, he pleaded, he would pay them very generously.

The nomads frowned and shook their heads. "It is too great a distance," they explained, "and at this time of year, there is no food or drink for the camels along the way."

The discussion ended. The Arabs returned to their council, and Riley to his men, who had not been able to follow the conversation. Despite the Arabs' refusal to go north, Riley took heart in the fact that they had consulted with him. He told the men he entertained the hope that they would be ransomed. "Yet they all seemed to think I was deluding them with false expectations," he acknowledged. He could not convince them otherwise.

Like his crewmates, Robbins could make little sense of the nomads. To him, the *yemma* was chaotic and confusing and appeared to be a forum for personal sparring rather than communal governing. He noted laconically that "Captain Riley seemed to feel some hopes that we might yet get released, and advised us all to keep up good spirits." But Robbins could not shake his depression. When he departed with Ganus at — according to his calendar, which varied somewhat from Riley's — around three in the afternoon on the third day, he took "a painful leave," of his shipmates, believing he would never see them again.

During the *yemma,* Riley had been awarded to a new master, a man called Bickri, who bade him lie down for the night in the dust outside his tent as if he were a camel. Alone, Riley lay shivering in the dark for several hours. At midnight, Bickri brought him a bowl of milk and water. After drinking it, Riley fell into a profound sleep.

He dreamed he was naked and a slave. Arabs with red-hot iron spears drove him through a firestorm raging up to his eyes and burning off his skin. Charred flesh hung from his bones, dropping to the ground in hunks. He looked up to heaven and prayed to God to take his spirit. He wanted nothing but to end his suffering. Yet the flames would not disappear. Then a bright spot opened in the

Moulay Sulayman: Son of the Emperor
(from *Sequel to Riley's Narrative*, 1851)

clouds above him. Rays of light beamed down from the sky. It was
an eye, and it directed him to go to the northeast. He turned, and
the fire vanished. The Arabs trotted beside him with their spear tips
poking him as they forced him over sand dunes and rocky wastes.
His dried skin continued to drop in hunks. He raced down into a
green valley. Trees appeared, flowering shrubs, grazing cows,
horses, sheep, and donkeys, and ahead a babbling brook. He threw
himself down on the stream's edge and drank in clear, cold water.
He drank until his belly felt like bursting. He drank until his throat
throbbed with cold. He drank for his mangled limbs, his scorched
lungs, his burned hair. Then he rolled over and into the brook and
extinguished his smoldering body.

He thanked God for his delivery.

But the Arabs were still there. They picked him up and forced
him on. The all-seeing eye was still above them, pointing out the
path. The path was no longer burning but crooked, thorny, and narrow. It rose over high mountains and plunged into deep valleys. He

was exhausted, but there was no stopping. Armed men on foot and horseback lined the way. Imposing fortified towns waited to absorb him should he stop. At another brook, a tall, youthful man dressed in Western clothes and mounted on a noble horse waited for him. Seeing him, the man dismounted, rushed forward, wildly joyful, embraced him, and addressed him in his own tongue: "brother."

Riley found himself in an opulent dining room, being pressed to partake of food and wine. "God has decreed that you shall again embrace your beloved wife and children," the man told him. Then Riley heard another voice, Bickri's, and opened his eyes on the frigid *hammada*.

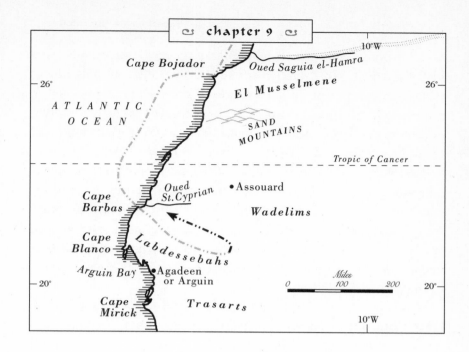

chapter 9

ATLANTIC
OCEAN

Cape Bojador

Oued Saguia el-Hamra

El Musselmene

26°   26°

SAND
MOUNTAINS

Tropic of Cancer

Oued
Cape   St.Cyprian   •Assouard
Barbas

Wadelims

Cape
Blanco   Labdessebahs

Arguin Bay   •Agadeen
or Arguin

Miles
0   100   200

20°   20°

Cape   Trasarts
Mirick

10°W

The Sons of
the Father of Lions

ᖃᔭ In June 1785, when the *Ste. Catherine* wrecked on the Saharan coast, envoy Pierre de Brisson prayed that she had reached the environs of the French settlement of Saint-Louis, Senegal. He was familiar with the tribes there and believed he could gain their help. Though he could not tell from the featureless shore, he suspected that they had not made it far enough and warned his shipmates, "I dread our meeting with some horde of the tribes of Ouadelims and Labdesseba, a savage race, whose only food is the milk of their camels, and who are for ever wandering up and down the desert."

When they did encounter the nomads, his shipmates, including the first and second mates, panicked and fled. Armed with scimitars and clubs, the Arabs "rushed on them with incredible ferocity,"

Brisson wrote, "and I soon beheld some of them wounded, and others stripped naked, and stretched out almost breathless on the sand."

Brisson calmly surrendered to a well-dressed, peaceful-looking man. He gave the man gifts of watches and gold that he had hidden in his pockets and asked him who he was. "Sidi Mahammet del Zouza," came the reply. "My tribe is that of Labdesseba."

"We were fallen into the hands of the most ferocious among the inhabitants of the Deserts of Arabia," lamented the Frenchman, who had been correct in foreseeing only "hardships and trouble." During his year-long captivity, he would be beaten, starved, and nearly killed in a tribal raid. He would witness the brutal deaths of two shipmates and see a third, caught sucking milk from a camel, strangled.

It was this same wide-ranging tribe, better known today by the French transliteration of its name, Oulad Bou Sbaa, that had captured the men of the *Commerce*.[1]

One of the *chorfa* tribes, the Oulad Bou Sbaa traced their roots to a fifteenth-century sharif of the Anti-Atlas Mountains named Ahmer Ould Hamel. One night when Ahmer, who was a descendant of Idris, founder of the Moroccan state, sensed that his flock was about to be stolen in a *ghazu*, or tribal raid, he prayed to Allah to turn his sheep into lions. His request was granted, and the lions scared away the raiders. From then on, Sidi Ahmer was known as "the Father of Lions," and was revered as a man awarded *baraka*, magic powers, for his piety. "Oulad Bou Sbaa" means "sons of the father of lions" and refers to Ahmer's three sons, Amar, Amran, and Numer, patrons of the tribe's many branches, based around the city of Morocco. Early in the eighteenth century, the tribe rebelled against the sultan, Ismail. Fearing retaliation at the hands of Ismail's formidable army of French-trained black Africans, the Oulad el-Hadj branch of the Oulad Bou Sbaa fled northeast to Oran. They were eventually pardoned and returned to the Morocco area.

The Oulad Brahim, the branch that now held Riley and his men, fled to the desert, where they grew in number and eventually sprawled from the Saguia el-Hamra wadi, near Cape Bojador, over

the vast expanse of desert to southern Mauritania. The various factions came to consider themselves independent tribes, though they
all used the name Oulad Bou Sbaa. Having never been pardoned by
the sultan, they roamed for a century. They shared a fierce, austere
nature, prospered and perished by the *ghazu*, and measured their
wealth in terms of camels and slaves.

To the men of the *Commerce,* the Bou Sbaa's desert transhumance
that they were now a part of was as inscrutable as a merchant fleet's
sailing maneuvers would have been to the nomads. The tribe was
broken down into *friqs,* groups of half a dozen or fewer families,
units large enough for mutual protection but small enough for effective grazing of the animals. Within the *friq,* families with no slaves
traveled with their camels, sometimes banding together with another
family and combining their droves, which they could separate again
with an ease the sailors found uncanny. Those families with many
camels and slaves to drive them sometimes roamed more freely away
from their beasts. The *friqs* moved together but apart in a sort of
chaotic harmony. To the Commerces, who were distributed among
these small groups, however, the arrangement felt harum-scarum.
They never knew which of their shipmates they might see that
night or ever again.

 They could discover little purpose in wandering from one thicket
of thornbushes to the next, stopping along the way at smaller
patches of thornbush to graze the camels. It seemed like the farther
they went, the worse off they were. In fact, as they moved east with
the nomads, they appeared to travel solely to find ever-diminishing
shrubs to feed the camels, which produced ever-diminishing milk,
the nomads' lifeblood. Instead of living off the land, the land seemed
to be living off them, consuming their bodies and minds.

 The nomads owed much to the Arabian camel. By the time their
Sanhaja ancestors had acquired the peculiar humped beasts from
the east — between the first and fourth centuries A.D. — desertification had long since intensified, clustering people around oases,

where they could grow food. As the land grew more arid and infertile, the black tribes migrated south, while the Sanhaja adapted to nomadic life with the camels, living like bedouins long before the first wave of bedouins arrived. Though not considered ruminants, camels, with their complex, three-compartmented stomachs, regurgitate and rechew their forage, turning poor vegetation into protein and energy even better than ruminants do. It was the camel, which could convert scrub brush into nutrient-rich milk, that allowed the Sanhaja to stay on the desert.

Oddly enough, camelids originated not in Africa but in North America. During the Pleistocene epoch, the ancestors of the llama, alpaca, vicuña, and guanaco migrated south to South America, while the ancestors of the camel crossed an erstwhile land bridge at what is now the Bering Strait to Asia. As the camelids were dying out in North America, camels migrated across Eastern Europe, the Middle East, and North Africa. By 3000 B.C., however, wild camels had become extinct in North Africa too. They were reintroduced on the Sahara as desertification increased their utility there, and they quickly became the most important thing a man could own. He who mastered the camel mastered the land.

At daylight on September 12, the Bou Sbaa moved on. Bickri ordered Riley to drive the camels forward. Separated from his crew and even missing Mohammed, his original captor, whose ways he was familiar with, Riley felt especially low. Bickri showed no signs of warmth, and Riley derived no hope from him. The captain shuffled forward in a wary crouch, ready to shift his weight whenever he felt another jab coming to the underside of his mutilated feet.

Riley never explained how Bickri gained possession of him, probably because he did not know. Something had happened at the meeting. Mohammed, who had retained Deslisle, had been forced to hand over the captain or had decided to sell him to Bickri. Now Mohammed saw Riley shuffling across the plain. He rode up on his camel and haggled with Bickri. After a while, he pulled the blanket off his back and handed it to Bickri, then drew up beside Riley, told him to stop walking, and made his camel kneel. Mohammed placed a skin on the camel's back behind the saddle and secured it under the girths, helped Riley mount it, and steadied him while the camel rose. Bickri rode on at a fast trot in the company of a handful of other heavily armed men. Riley had been bought for a blanket.

It was impossible for him to enjoy this bit of luck, however. The blood pulsed through his swollen legs in dull thuds, while the sun flogged his upper body and head until it was "racking and cracking with excruciating pain." To escape his anguish, Riley recalled his dream of the night before. Unlike most seamen, he had never put much stock in omens, visions, or dreams, but this one clung to him, or he to it. As he turned it over in his mind, he felt certain there was a message, that the "all-seeing eye" was guiding him north. If he could find his way to Morocco, someone would save them. The narrow escapes he and his crew had experienced, he assured himself, had happened for a reason. God was watching over them.

This belief kept him going over the many miles that ensued, until in the early afternoon they rode into the middle of a *friq,* six tents in a depression with scattered shrubs. Mohammed made the camel kneel and was mobbed by his joyful children. Riley needed shade and staggered toward a tent. The women and girls, their animosity sudden and stunningly palpable, threatened him with sticks and stones. Though Mohammed had directed Riley toward the tent, he did not come to his rescue, and the captain was prevented from entering. For Riley, there would be no refuge from the intense afternoon rays, and certainly no sympathy for his travails.

In the evening, Deslisle returned to Mohammed's camp with the camels he had taken out for grazing. Mohammed had put him straight to work as a camel driver. Deslisle had mastered the job quickly and was rewarded with a large serving of milk daily and a corner of the tent in which to sleep. Riley attributed the cook's good health to this and to the fact that, because he was also a domestic slave, he had managed to filch water and some sour milk.

Ultimately, Deslisle could expect more or less the same treatment as the Arabs' black African slaves as long as he performed his tasks willingly and converted to Islam. This could mean a substantial degree of freedom around the camp and nourishment on a par with the family. He might eventually, after long servitude or a signal service to his master, be liberated, admitted to the tribe, and allowed to marry and to own camels.

Adopting their faith, however, was not as simple as making a vow and participating in their prayer; a man had to be circumcised to be a Muslim, and this procedure marked one forever as a Christian apostate. Representatives of Western states shunned such men. Arabs fought to keep them.

Mohammed had also bought Hogan, who joined them that night and told Riley that Horace was in the camp as well. The captain went in search of the boy and soon found Horace's master, whom he described as an "ill-looking old villain." The Arab addressed Riley as *Rais,* or Captain. "What is the boy's name, Rais?" he asked.

"Horace," responded the captain.

"Hoh-*Rais,*" the Bou Sbaa mimicked, pleased with his pronunciation, which to him proved the boy's kinship to the white chief. He took to shouting the boy's name frequently. When Riley tried to speak to Horace, however, the foul-tempered nomad chased him away, threatening to beat them both with a stick.

Riley, who was not wholly above the racial prejudices typical of his era, had higher hopes for Mohammed, in part based on his light complexion. On the Sahara, many of Riley's preconceptions would be put to the test. Any illusions he had of Mohammed's benevolence were shattered that night. Even though a patch of sand lay not fifty yards from the tents, their captor forced Riley and Hogan to sleep on the *hammada.* Struggling to remove the stones beneath them, they scraped up their fingertips until they bled. Approaching his master, Riley pointed to the sores on his body and held out his bloody hands. He indicated that they would like to sleep on the sand, but Mohammed turned steely. "Stay here," he warned, "or no milk tonight."

Riley and Hogan tried to sleep on the hardpan, but the stones poked into their wounds, and the cold, damp night air — "as salt as the ocean," Riley said — made them burn. They shivered and shifted until midnight, when Mohammed brought them each a pint of milk and then retired to his tent. After drinking the milk, which Riley averred was "pure and warm from the camels," he and Hogan crept over to the sand and slept soundly.

From dawn to dark, Robbins had ridden on the back of his master's camel. Because he had chosen to ease the pounding by sitting on his animal skin rather than wearing it, the tropical sun had ravaged his torso. After traveling sixty miles to the east, even the nomads were too exhausted to bother pitching the tent. Instead, they loafed and visited other campfires nearby. When Ganus's sister Muckwoola returned to the tent and told Robbins that she knew where two of his shipmates were, he rose again. Babbling incomprehensibly to him all the way, she led him to a campsite by a patch of dry thornbushes.

There he found Williams and Barrett squatting by a low fire, cooking the remnants of a piece of salt pork that their master had retrieved from the beach where the longboat crashed. They rose and shook hands with Robbins, whose joy quickly turned to disgust as he got a close look at his comrades. "Did you see the long-legged deer they call gazelles today?" he asked, making conversation to cover his shock. "They came right up to us, as tame as sheep, but my master would not shoot any. He said it's not the season to take their skins." In the crimson firelight, Williams looked like a leprous demon, both gaunt and bloated. The sun, starvation, thirst, and the pounding of the camels had produced in him a look of dissipation. His dead skin hung in sheets, the new layer beneath already covered in red blisters. His face was pinched.

Focused on what he was doing, Williams did not speak at first. He knew he looked hideous, and he seemed resigned to his own death. At forty-eight, he had already lost his parents and several siblings. When he had signed on to the *Commerce,* he had left behind in Wethersfield not only his wife but two orphaned nieces, Almira, age twelve, and Elizabeth, six, the daughters of his younger brother Richard and his wife, Hannah, who had both died during the recent war. Williams spoke lovingly of the two girls and with great concern for their future. By the flickering campfire, he rambled on until grief stopped him.

At daybreak on September 13, Riley and Hogan gingerly brushed the sand from their wounds and set off in a southeasterly direction behind Deslisle and the camels. They were so stiff from dehydration and the hard night that they could barely keep from wailing with every step. As the morning advanced, the blistering Saharan sun lashed their backs.

Three hours after they set out, Riley spotted one of his men in the distance, mounted on a large camel so that he floated queerly above the drove and the dust. Riley veered in his direction. Something was not right, he realized as he hobbled nearer on his bruised feet. The rider moved without purpose, like the boom of a drifting boat. Head and arms flopped about in response to the camel. Riley limped faster, catching up when the camel stopped to chew on a bush. The rider sat propped on the beast like a swollen corpse. His skin had burned off, and the sun glistened bizarrely from his body as if he were lit from within. Aghast, Riley examined an unrecognizable face. The man, entirely naked, muttered in a barely audible voice about his woes. It was Williams. That morning his master's wife had greased his body with animal fat to try to save him, but now it cooked his skin. "I cannot live another day," he gasped to Riley, who gently held his trembling hand. "Should you ever get clear from this dreadful place and return to our country, tell my dear wife that with my last breath I prayed for her happiness." He began to sob.

Riley searched for words to console his first mate, but before he could produce any, inadequate though they necessarily would have been, Williams's master suddenly appeared, scolded them vehemently, and lashed the camel. As it wheeled around, Riley saw ruby streaks on its coat where the inside of Williams's leg "hung in strings of torn and chafed flesh."

"God Almighty bless you," he called to the dying man. In an instant, the first mate was gone. Riley was left alone to contemplate the gruesome sight and his inability to help.

His reflections were brought up short by his own trouble. The encounter had lasted no more than a quarter of an hour, but during that time the desert had swallowed his master's drove without a trace. In his sudden isolation, he hit a wall of hopelessness. "My God," he cried, looking around, "suffer us not to live longer in such tortures!"

Lurching forward, he ran, grimacing, in the direction in which his master's camels had been heading. With each strike of his feet on the stones, he shouted in anguish, but he did not slow down. Having witnessed the agony of the first mate, he was almost indifferent to his own physical pain. Mohammed saw him coming and stopped the drove. As Riley neared, staggering like a madman, the Arab raised his cane to strike him. Then, almost as if it were not worth the effort, he changed his mind. Instead, he lit into him for thinking he could do whatever he pleased. He ordered Riley and Hogan to drive the camels on as fast as they could, and he rode off in a huff.

When Mohammed returned about an hour later, he was accompanied by a tall, fearsome-looking old man, whom Riley described as being as "black as a negro." The old man was with his two sons and a number of heavily armed men on foot. The dark Arab, who was Clark's master and whose features Riley thought "showed every sign of the deepest rooted malignity," looked him over and made an offer to Mohammed. The two quickly came to terms. Riley never mentioned what he was traded for, but Mohammed probably recouped his investment — a blanket — and was satisfied at being rid of a nuisance. He still had Hogan and Deslisle.

Riley's new master, whose name was Sideullah, and his entourage walked even faster than the camels, and Riley could not keep up.[2] Sideullah snarled at him to move faster and struck his back with a cane. Riley staggered, but his animal instinct for survival kicked in, and he kept pace until one of Sideullah's sons saddled him with his musket and powder horn. Beneath the weight, exaggerated by his fatigue, he lagged again, hating the young man and waiting for Sideullah to come beat him once more. The old man, however, was preoccupied with other matters. He strode on, leaving the others to make their own way to camp.

Haunted by the lingering image of the dying Williams but compelled by it too, Riley kept his feet moving. How could he pity himself with the chief mate in such a state? He could see the far-off horizon in every direction, broken only by camels, which rose above the skyline like distant ships. All around him, they were hull up or hull down. To keep his bearings, he needed only to follow them. He had to keep his feet moving. He prayed for Williams, willing him on and himself too.

It was late afternoon when he reached Sideullah's camp. The nomads relieved him of his burden and told him to lie down in the shade in the tent. He begged for water, to no avail. Sideullah and his son prayed and then left to visit other tents. "I tried to soften the hearts of the women to get me a little water," he said, "but they only laughed and spit at me." Mercilessly, they drove him away from the tent. Riley sat on the smoldering hardpan, absorbing the last rays of the sun. He could think of nothing but his thirst.

At sunset, Riley's new master returned with his sons and two dozen men and led them in prayer. He seemed to be their spiritual leader. For all their piety — they prayed regularly and devoutly, as their religion required — Riley wondered how the Arabs could ignore the fact that under their care he and his men lacked the most basic necessities of life and suffered inhumanly.

Riley was distracted from his brooding when James Clark arrived with Sideullah's camels. These meetings had become what the men looked forward to and what kept them going, but here was another shipmate whose condition was not just deplorable but heartbreaking. Clark had two youngsters at home. "He was nearly without a skin," Riley later recalled. "Every part of his body exposed; his flesh excessively mangled, burnt and inflamed." He looked almost as bad as Williams. "I am glad to see you, sir," Clark told Riley, "for I am afraid I cannot live through this night. If you get to our country again, please tell my wife, my brothers and sisters how I perished."

"You're not going to die now," the captain assured him matter-of-factly. "The food we have, though meager, is enough to keep us alive, and the desert, while it is roasting us, is preserving us at the same time. Look at our wounds. To be sure, they hurt like the dickens, but even in the worst of them there are no signs of putrefaction. We are being saved for some other fate."

Clark looked scared. Riley searched for other encouraging words, words that he himself did not believe, anything to convince Clark to hang on for another day. He told him truthfully that one old man had said that when it rained, they would all go northeast to sell the sailors. "I assured him," Riley told Clark, "that a great ransom would reward them for delivering the entire crew to the land of the Moors."

Riley begged Sideullah to let them sleep in a corner of the tent, as his two black slaves, who attended the herd, did. The Bou Sbaa agreed, pointing to a place for them to lie down, but again the women objected and drove them off. Sideullah did not countermand the women, but in the night he and his sons brought Riley and Clark warm milk, a quart each, and after the women were asleep, Omar, the son who had foisted his gun on Riley, came to them and led them inside the tent to sleep on soft sand. He did so in such a manner that Riley decided he had misread Omar, that he had made him carry the gun not out of laziness or cruelty but to give Riley an excuse to lag behind so that he could walk in peace. Omar was, at least in part, kind.

The group stayed put the next day. In the morning, the women in the tent chided and jabbed at Riley and Clark, who played possum until the blows became too painful. Although Arab women hold authority inside the tent, Sideullah, who wanted the sailors to regain their strength, scolded them. Riley and Clark remained under the tent all day, sharing a pint of camel's milk in the morning and each having a pint of water at noon. By the afternoon, Riley could feel the swelling in his body subside, especially in his pulverized feet.

While the sailors lay in the tent, Sideullah's powerfully built black slave, Boireck, and two Arab boys had spent the day driving the camels off to find shrubs. In the evening, Boireck seated himself at the fire, stretching out his long, tired legs on either side of it. Seeing Riley and Clark inside the tent and resenting the fact that they had rested all day, he got up to run them out. When Sideullah stopped him, Boireck became even more riled.

That evening he amused the family and some visitors by taunting the Christians. He pointed at their slack genitals and laughingly compared them with his own. His sneering references to the gaunt Riley as "*el rais*" brought howls of laughter. He poked their wounds with a sharp stick and made fun of their skin, which died and turned foul beneath the very image of Allah, the sun. What further proof was needed that these miserable white heathens were worthy only of slavery and scorn?

Clark fumed. "It's bad enough to be stripped, skinned alive, and mangled," he whispered to Riley, "without being obliged to bear the scoffs of a damned negro slave."

"It's good to know you're still alive, Jim," Riley responded with a nod. The milk and water they had consumed that day, the rest, the shade had boosted his spirits. He would not let Boireck's buffoonery beat him down just now. "You feel the need to revenge an insult, but let the poor negro laugh if he can take pleasure in it," he told Clark. "God knows there's little enough here to provide that. He's only trying to gain favor with his masters and mistresses. I'm willing he should have it, even at our expense."

Over the next three days they pushed southeast, deeper into the desert, at a rate of about thirty miles a day. The terrain became flatter, with shallower depressions and fewer thornbushes, mostly dead and dried up. The camels' powerful molars ground the wooden stalks with the strength of mill wheels, but still they could not fill their stomachs. The plants the nomads used to supplement their own diet also became scarcer. "In every valley we came to," Riley wrote, "the natives would run about and search under every thorn bush, in hopes to find some herb, for they were nearly as hungry as ourselves." A small plant resembling shepherd's purse Riley found disappointingly bitter and salty. The pleasant-tasting, onion-shaped root of a plant the Bou Sbaa called *taloe* was scant. Underneath its single grasslike blade, about a hand high, hid a walnut-size root, which they dug up with a stick; a good day produced no more than half a dozen, their benefit negligible. Riley and Clark continued to lose strength. Indeed, Riley had eaten so little that nothing solid had passed through his bowels since their capture.

Lack of food was not the only problem. The stores of water were nearly finished, and the milk had begun to fail. The sailors, naturally, were the first to suffer. Their ration was reduced to a cup of milk a day, with no water. Even the nomads seemed enervated, stopping earlier, pitching their tents for the night in the midafternoon, and paying little heed to the sailors as long as they gathered sticks for the fire. Riley and Clark spent afternoons and nights in a corner of the tent.

Ironically, the lack of sustenance made walking easier in one way: they could endure the stones better as they became lighter. But as chronic dehydration intensified, their joints stiffened, and they found it exceedingly difficult to stand. Riley observed that he was literally shriveling up. Every day that he had been on the desert, he had relieved his thirst in part by continuing to catch and drink his own urine. "But that resource," he wrote, "now failed me for the want of moisture."

Robbins's situation was no better. Ganus's water supply was also running out, and his slave's begging now elicited only harsh rebukes. Each step, Robbins was convinced, was another away from civilization. He had encountered none of his shipmates for days, and he had decided he never would again.

When Savage suddenly appeared behind him in the company of two Arabs, Robbins was incredulous. He had not seen the second mate since the well; he lagged behind his master's drove to speak to him. Savage was skeletal. He said that he had eaten nothing solid since being captured. Robbins regretted that he had no means of helping him. "I'd share the small remains of my pork with you," Robbins said, "but my master never lets me carry it myself." They could talk no more. Robbins had to catch up to Ganus again.

Two days later, Ganus scouted ahead, leaving Robbins waiting near a bush. For the previous four nights, the nomads had not bothered to pitch a tent, and exposure had taken its toll. Each morning, Robbins had woken up wet from dew and stiff in his joints. The cold, moisture, and sand irritated his blistered body. He now collapsed in unconsciousness.

Midway through the afternoon, he was awakened — not by the threatening command of an Arab but by Savage. Robbins was glad to see the second mate again and to have the opportunity to spend some time together and talk. Savage was in a better frame of mind now, but he told Robbins bluntly that he was nearing "absolute starvation" and bitterly cursed his cruel master. The two wandered off in search of the snails that nestled their round, trumpet-mouthed shells in the dome-shaped euphorbia plants and thornbushes. These shells — about an inch in diameter, thick to keep the elements out, and bleached white by the sun — each yielded a chewy, coiled morsel that tasted like dirt. Savage gobbled down a few, but neither of the sailors had the stamina to continue the hunt. They were quickly exhausted, and the heat drove them in search of shade, where they sat with little to do but disparage the nomads. Before returning to their tents, they offered up a terse prayer to God.

Neither group moved the following day. Robbins visited Savage's tent, where the two stole some water from a goatskin. Savage told Robbins that his master had removed a wen from a camel that morning, and he knew where it was. They went and found it lying on the sand, already in two pieces, looking, according to Robbins, "not unlike a shad-spawn." They started to cook it furtively in the sand under coals from the fire, but when they saw Savage's mistress approaching, they dug it up and gobbled it down.

On the night of September 18, the Bou Sbaa assembled for another *yemma*. As a full moon illuminated the sand around them, they decided to return full circle to the well by the sea. Riley was devastated by this news, which confirmed that the nomads could not find water where they were. By his estimation, it was three hundred miles back, seven and a half days' hard traveling. "As the camels were almost dry," he reasoned, "I much feared that myself and my companions must perish before we could reach it."

In the morning before they turned back, Sideullah watered the four mares. Every other day, a family in the tribe, each in its turn, gave them as much water as they could drink. Sideullah emptied his last goatskin into a bowl. When they finished, Riley, who had not drunk water for days, begged his master to allow him to lap up what was left, but Sideullah refused. Instead, he sprinkled this dross on the ground as a sacrifice to Allah while the Arabs prayed for rain.

Over the next few days, they walked and foraged. Riley could not understand how the Arabs kept up such a pace on what little the desert yielded for them to consume. He and Clark had even less. In one sandy depression overlooked by the camels, they found snails on squat thornbushes. Most came off with a crisp snap, indicating they were long dead, dry, inedible, but then came a clinger and another. They hid the live snails in their clothing until dark, when they discreetly roasted them in the fire, but they found they could barely eat them. The body needs fluid to digest food, and they had drunk no more than a gill of milk that day. Burning with thirst, Riley and Clark sought out a staling camel, caught its amber stream in their hands, and drank. "Its taste was bitter, but not salt," Riley said, "and it relieved our fainting spirits."

Hunger began to derange the seamen and threatened to prove true, with ultimate irony, the myth that cannibals occupied the Sahara. At their lowest, some of the men ate the skin off their peeling arms, gnawing into their own flesh. Horrified, Riley tied one man's arms behind his back. Two others lured an Arab child away from the tents. Riley discovered them and rushed up as they were about to kill him with a stone. "I convinced them that it would be more manly to die with hunger than to become cannibals and eat their own or other human flesh," he later wrote, and he assured them that their masters would feed them at least enough to keep them alive until they could be sold. For the moment, Riley had succeeded.

September 21 brought about a change even more inexplicable than the sudden about-face to a well Riley believed they could never reach. The Wandering Arabs, desperate for water, did not wander. Sideullah and some of his tribesmen pitched their seven tents, rested in them or tended their camels, and prayed at the usual times, cleansing themselves with sand. Riley wondered if they had taken the wrong path. He could think of no reasonable explanation for simply stopping. Had the Bou Sbaa lost hope too? Were they simply surrendering to the desert?

Sidi Hamet's Feast

⮂ At midday, after the nomads had taken refuge from the sun in their closed tents, two strangers on heavily loaded camels entered the valley. By desert custom, they should have stopped well short of the tents, dismounted, and waited for the head of the family to come out and greet them. These men, who peered out from slits in their swaddling and kept a hand near the double-barreled muskets on their saddles, rode directly into the *friq*.

From the corner of a tent, Riley, stupefied by the heat, eyed them warily. No matter how bad things were, he had learned that on the Sahara, they could always get worse. Beside him, deeper in the shade, Clark lay barely lucid, dying. He was "a perfect wreck of almost naked bones," in Riley's words, "his belly and back nearly collapsed, and breathing like a person in [his] last agonies."

It would have been customary for the tent owners to offer the travelers water, but there was none.

No one left their tents. The two fierce-looking men, whose haiks concealed the scars of wounds sustained on two failed caravans to Tombuctoo — both having cost the lives of many men and many camels — made their beasts sit in front of Sideullah's. They dismounted and sat on the ground, each propping his musket on a knee to keep it out of the sand. Riley wished that his master were there, but he and his sons had taken up their arms and ridden off with the other men before dawn. Or perhaps they had reached the end of the line and had abandoned them along with their own wives and children. If so, it would only be a matter of a day or two before they died.

Riley felt the palpitations of his frail body and listened to Clark's grating breaths. Sometimes they sounded to Riley like distant wood chops in the forest, confusing him as to where he was and sending his mind reeling. Clark's tattooed cross seemed to levitate on fresh crimson skin. The two sailors had descended into the zone where death inexplicably claims some men and spares others. Water makes up between 60 and 70 percent of the human body. Men have been known to die from losing as little as 20 percent of their water (or 12 percent of body weight); others have survived losses of up to 40 percent (or 28 percent of body weight). Riley's and Clark's relatively long, steady slide into severe dehydration had perhaps allowed them to endure to the extreme end of the spectrum.

Clark teetered on the edge, and Riley had also entered the later stages of dehydration, in which the body milks secondary systems to channel fluid to the blood so that it can perform high-priority tasks such as delivering oxygen and nutrients to the cells and carrying away heat to the skin to be released. Both men's circulatory systems siphoned their joint oil, causing them to move in a stiff, jerky way. Their mouths produced no saliva, their eyes no tears.

"One feels as if one were in the focus of a burning-glass," a sufferer of severe thirst once wrote. "The eye-balls burn as though facing a scorching fire. The tongue and lips grow thick, crack, and blacken." In the agonizing final moments of thirst, the blood becomes viscous and loses its ability to transport heat to the skin. The victim is consumed by his own body heat, suffering a sort of internal meltdown.

The nomad women maintained their sphinxlike indifference to the sailors' suffering. Sideullah's wife and a daughter emerged from their tent, carrying a large skin and a roll of camel-hair tent cloth toward the strangers. The men rose. "Labez, Labez-salem," they greeted the women. "Labez-alikom." Peace, peace be with you.

The women retrieved tent poles and constructed a shelter. They unloaded the strangers' camels and arranged their goods and saddles in the shade. Then they brought a rack to hold the visitors' most precious cargo: two bloated goatskins. Riley strained to hear as the women sat and talked with the men, who, it was now clear, were traders, asking them the usual questions of the desert: "Where did you come from? How long have you been traveling? What goods do you have?"

The elder of the two, a large, gray-bearded man with pointed ears sticking out from beneath a fat turban that shaded his eyes, motioned to the other, who rummaged through the packs. He brought over blankets, ostrich feathers, and blue linen for them to examine. The blue linen, which Sahrawi women use to cover their heads and take great pride in, had its intended effect: they could not help smiling as they fingered it approvingly.

Afterward Sideullah's wife poked her head into the tent where Riley and Clark slouched in the stagnant air. "Sidi Hamet has come from the sultan's dominions," she said suggestively. "He can *buy* you." She left, and Riley pondered her words. He trusted no one. A wrong move could send him into a deeper circle of this living — albeit barely — hell.

For the next few hours, he laid low, turning the question over: Should he approach the traders? His head was too muddled for reason. At last, thirst drove him, bowl in hand, to the tent. Standing filthy, tattered, and speechless before them, he pointed to his sore-ridden mouth. He knew that in their eyes he was a repulsive infidel. With his peeling skin and his scarred body, he had all the charm of a rat trying to join them for lunch. Sidi Hamet's younger brother, Seid, wanted to strike him for his impudence and run him off, but Hamet stared at Riley. "El Rais?" he asked. Are you the captain?

Riley nodded. After a moment, Hamet motioned for his brother to take the bowl. Seid refused. Hamet got up and filled it himself. Riley held the bowl in his bony hands and examined its contents in awe: nearly a quart of clean water.

"Sherub, Rais," Hamet ordered, raising his cupped hands. Drink, Captain.

Riley gulped down half the water. It was the best he had had since leaving the brig. It stung his chapped lips and awakened deadened nerves in his mouth. "Besmillah, Sidi Hamet, and God bless you," he croaked in broken Arabic, lowering the bowl.[1] He intended to take the rest to Clark. As he turned to go, Hamet stopped him and motioned for him to finish it.

Riley pointed to his tent and explained as best he could that he wished to give it to a dying shipmate. He feared the usual rebuke, but Hamet's expression did not register anger. He nodded consent. Riley was surprised. He had seen Arabs — even the most brutish — dole out water to other men's slaves, as Hamet had just done, but he had not seen one tolerate any sort of effrontery from a Christian slave.

Clark lay facedown on his mat. Riley turned him over and held his shoulders up. "Here is water," he said. He held the bowl to Clark's lips, and he drank, his sunken eyes brightening.

"This must have come from a better country," Clark wheezed to his captain. "If we were there, and I could get one good drink of such water, I could die with pleasure."

Sideullah returned in the late afternoon. Riley was not surprised that he brought back nothing from the day's outing. It was typical of what Riley had seen so far. No matter what show of industry they made, the tribesmen seemed to produce nothing, to gather nothing, except when they milked the camels or decided to fill their goatskins, the latter a duty bewilderingly now abandoned. None of the men had been to a well in more than a week.

News of the arrival of the northern traders spread, and Bou Sbaa began to materialize as if by magic from the empty desert. By dusk, Riley estimated, two hundred men, more than he had seen at any gathering, milled about his master's camp, conversing with the northerners and one another and gesticulating in their fervent manner.

At sunset, Sideullah led them in their prayer. First they stripped off their haiks and washed themselves with handfuls of sand.[2] Then, bowing repeatedly to the east, they chanted: "Allah Houak- ibar" — God is great. This was followed by the Shahadah, their dec- laration of faith and call to prayer: "Hi el Allah Sheda Mohammed Rahsool Allah" — I testify that Muhammad is the Prophet of God.[3]

Then Sideullah delivered a long prayer. They ended by reciting a chapter of the Quran together. Once again, Riley wondered about the inherent contradiction between their piety and their indifference to the suffering of their fellow men, especially Clark, whose light was fading with the day's.

By ten o'clock the *friq* was quiet again. Riley and Clark were banished from the tent. Riley helped his comrade move to a spot not far away, where they collapsed on the bare sand and dozed, fitfully, shivering, short on the fuel necessary to maintain their body heat. They had eaten only snails and roots for three days. At midnight, Sideullah woke them up and gave them each a pint of sweet fresh camel's milk. Riley later asserted that this saved Clark's life.

In the morning, Hamet took the captain aside and questioned him. Again, Riley did not attempt to explain that he was from across the Atlantic but said that he and his men came from England. Hamet nodded understanding. Using his hands, his expressive face, and the rudimentary Arabic he had picked up, along with a smattering of French and Spanish, Riley related the events that had brought him there, pointing out the direction of the wreck. He described his wife and his children, eliciting an unexpected heave from his own chest. He claimed that Horace was his oldest son.

To the Arabs, hardened by life on the desert, tears from a man were shameful. When the Frenchman Brisson was reduced to weeping in front of the Bou Sbaa, he wrote, "some women perceiving it, instead of being moved to compassion threw sand in my eyes, as they said, to wipe away my tears" (p. 369). Riley expected no sympathy, but Hamet, having recently returned from a disastrous caravan of two miserable years, had seen his family — his wife, two sons, and a daughter — only briefly before taking to the desert to try to clear his debts. Moved by Riley's suffering, so similar to his own, the trader teared up too.

"Men who have beards, like me, ought not to shed tears," Hamet said, brushing his face with his arm before walking away.

Riley was encouraged. Here was a man who might be willing to help. He began to formulate a plan.

A short time later, he found Hamet alone.

"I have a friend in the north," he told him. "If you will buy me and my shipmates and deliver us to the realm of the Sultan of Morocco, my friend will pay you a large sum of money."

As Hamet peered into Riley's eyes, the Arab showed no hint of a reaction. He and his brother were in debt to his father-in-law, Ali, a ruthless sheik who lived near Wednoon, and he had been weighing what opportunity the Christian sailors presented, if any. A Marrakech Bou Sbaa of the Oulad el-Hadj Ben Demouiss branch, Hamet was growing convinced that Allah had led him to this lowly band of Oulad Brahim, his Bou Sbaa cousins, to right his misfortunes. His instincts told him to trust the bold captain.

"No," Hamet responded. "Impossible. I might be able to take just el rais to Swearah." This walled town, called Mogadore in the West, was the emperor's international trading post on the Atlantic.

"I have seen the sultan," Riley told Hamet. "He is a friend to my nation."

Hamet listened and then ratcheted up the stakes. "Mohammed Rassool?" he asked. Muhammad the Prophet? Riley bowed. He pointed to the east and then to heaven, indicating that he knew the Prophet came from the east and that he believed he had ascended into heaven. This pleased Hamet. "How much money?" Hamet asked.

Riley scooped up a handful of small stones and counted out fifty. "This many Spanish dollars for myself and the same for each of my men."

"I will not buy the others," Hamet said. "How much more for you?" Riley added another fifty stones to the pile.

"Is the money in Swearah?" he asked, using his hands and words. "Or must it be sent from your country?"

"My friend in Swearah will pay," Riley replied, though he knew no one there.

"You are lying," Hamet scoffed.

"No," Riley said, placing a fist over his heart and shaking his head. "El rais does not lie."

Hamet held him in his piercing gaze. "If you deceive me," he said, making a slashing motion with his hand, "I will cut your throat."

Unflinching, Riley nodded his consent. He pleaded again for Hamet to buy his "son," Horace, but the trader said he could not get any others off the desert. "Say nothing about this to your master," he concluded, "nor to my brother or anyone else."

Despite Hamet's reluctance, Riley was encouraged by his manner. He was direct and clever and spoke with understated force. Riley felt sure that whatever he decided would come to pass.

The captain went to hunt for snails and found Savage, whom he had not seen in many days, and Hogan doing the same. They stumbled around in vain, for they had already exhausted the supply at this site. The camels had mauled the scattered thornbushes, devouring all the branches less than an inch thick.

Returning to camp, Riley fetched Clark, who had recovered to a remarkable degree, though he still moved feebly, like an old man. The four Commerces sat down outside Hamet's tent. "I have great hopes," Riley told them, despite the trader's naysaying, "that we should be bought by this man and carried to the cultivated country." Sidi Hamet came out and sat down, silently though unabashedly examining the men. Even he, who had seen horrific suffering on the Sahara, grimaced at their deplorable state. "He will not take us," they whispered. But as Riley had hoped, Hamet was interested. He began openly sizing them up for durability and worth. He asked Riley if any of their group had died, if they had wives and children, what they had been fed. Riley answered in their favor, assuring Hamet honestly that even Clark, who was so emaciated, was the husband of a beautiful woman named Ruth, the father of two children, and a soldier who had won glory in battle.

As Riley was about to discover, a Christian's value as a ransomable commodity depended on his rank, wealth, health, and location. On the desert, where a tent with a life of four years was worth a camel, and a camel was worth a dozen goats or half a dozen sheep, a Christian's worth fell somewhere between a tattered blanket and an adult camel, except in rare circumstances. Officers were worth more than seamen, though the Arabs, desperate for practical skills, would hold indefinitely a gunpowder maker, a surgeon, or a smith who naively admitted it. Married men brought more than single men for their perceived added wealth. The Arabs quickly noticed a man's fine accoutrements. Brisson, who had lavished watches, silver buckles, and money on his first captor to ingratiate himself, was sold from one owner to another for five camels, while the ship's baker went for one. Ultimately, Brisson regretted the gifts, which served only to inflate his ransom price.

To ransom a Christian, a Sahrawi had to deliver him to the imperial port of Swearah, where foreign merchants or consuls could make the payment. To get there, they had to cross the desert, past hostile bedouin tribes, past the fortified Berber towns of the Souss region, and finally past the operatives of the Sultan of Morocco, where Christian slavery was technically illegal and the sultan was fond of the "gifts" Western nations paid for their citizens' freedom. All the while, the captor had no guarantee he would actually receive the agreed-upon sum. Instead of making the long, risky journey, a Sahrawi often sold his slave locally at a small but sure profit to a buyer who would sell at a small profit to another buyer.

In this way, in an agonizing peristalsis, the Sahara slowly yielded Christians north one territory at a time, the nearer to Swearah the higher the price, with the medium of exchange switching from bartered goods to cash at Wednoon, on the edge of the desert. On the Sahara, the French merchant Saugnier was traded once for a barrel of meal and a nine-foot bar of iron, and later for two young camels. He was sold twice at Wednoon, first for $150, then for $180. Seamen with him brought $50 to $95. Robert Adams of the *Charles* went in the latter range, once for $50 worth of blankets and dates and a second time for $70 worth of blankets, dates, and gunpowder.

In 1810, the English merchant and author James Grey Jackson proposed paying a fixed rate for Westerners delivered to Mogadore. "A trifling sum would be sufficient," he maintained, if it was always on hand and the policy well known. This would eliminate the uncertainty that led to the repeated reselling of Christians and extortionate ransom prices. Jackson estimated that $150 per man would be enough, "a sum rather above the price of a black slave." The British adopted the practice to the south at Saint-Louis, on the Senegal River, where in 1816 the speedy recovery of some of the passengers of the *Méduse* proved its soundness, but no such standards existed for Christians being transported north.

On the morning of September 24, the Bou Sbaa broke camp and moved northwest all day. When they stopped at dusk, Sideullah's women pitched tents for the family and for Hamet and Seid, who had ridden with them. The next day, the group stayed put, and Hamet and Sideullah discussed business. They haggled over the items Sideullah wanted from the traders, and over Riley. For him, Sideullah demanded two coarse haiks, a bundle of ostrich feathers, and the blue linen his wife coveted. On the desert, where such goods were rare, it was a hefty price and one that reflected Riley's rank as captain. At length, Hamet agreed. On the coast, these goods were worth less than half a British pound, or two Spanish dollars. Riley had promised to pay *fifty* times that for his freedom.

Later that day, Horace and his master and Savage came to Hamet's tent. With tears in his eyes, Riley embraced Horace and gave him and Savage some snails he had found that morning, further impressing upon Hamet his bond with the boy. After the visitors left, Hamet told Riley that they would depart in two days and that Horace's master, whose cruelty and possessive nature Riley had already witnessed, would not sell the boy at any price. This news shook the captain, whose determination to look after Horace had earlier saved him from despair. "Let me stay in his place," he pleaded. "I will be a faithful slave to his master as long as I live — carry *him* up to Swearah. My friend will pay you and send him home to his mother. I could never face her without him."

Hamet was moved by Riley's anguish. "You shall have your son, by Allah," he swore. He took the matter to the tribe's elders, who called a council. Hamet and Horace's master each ardently stated his case, and then they began to shout and hit each other with their fists. They drew their scimitars, but before blood was shed, the men were pulled apart. In the end, as Riley had foreseen, Hamet prevailed. "But," Hamet told Riley, "the price the council set was steep. You must pay as much for the boy as for yourself."

Undeterred, Riley now urged Hamet to buy Savage and Clark. "It is impossible," Hamet told him again, "for two men to transport four Christians to Swearah. It would be easier to lead gazelles through a lion's den." To get to Swearah, they would have to run an eight-hundred-mile gauntlet of bandits and warlords, who would think nothing of killing him and Seid to steal their slaves. It was not simply a matter of greed, it was also a question of power and control of lands. No sheik would let them pass carrying such a valuable cargo without paying a tribute. It would belittle him. Hamet and Seid had only a small amount of money and no power base from which to forge alliances and promise goodwill in kind. They were anybody's prey. The more Christians they had, the slower they would travel and the more attention they would attract.

Riley turned a deaf ear to this reasoning. He fell to his knees and begged Hamet to buy Savage and Clark, but this time he had gone too far. "Skute. Ferknâ ferknêe!" Hamet roared. Shut up. Leave me alone! He swatted Riley with the flat of his scimitar blade as a warning.

The following morning, however, Riley, like a bulldog, pursued Hamet again. He recited the names of all his crew, even those whose whereabouts were unknown, urging the trader to inquire about them. This time, Hamet insisted only that he would not buy Clark, who, he said, would die within three days. Riley swore he would pay the same amount for Clark even if he died along the way.

That seemed likely. Though he had rebounded slightly from dehydration, Clark's sun-scalded scalp had cracked open in raw, oozing sores. Hamet and Seid pushed his matted hair apart with sticks and prodded his patchy flesh. This led to a closer inspection of Riley as well and muttered conversation between the brothers. Seid was not convinced that they should buy any of the sailors. They were emaciated, and their skin was as riddled as a tent in its fifth year.

Realizing that the starving sailors had to be fed before the journey, Hamet bought a worn-out *jmel*, or male camel, from Sideullah for just a blanket. In the desert there was no such thing as a bargain. Both men knew that the old beast, which could no longer keep up with the drove, was fit only for slaughter, and since by Islamic custom meals were communal among desert dwellers, anyone who could get there had a right to join in. In reality, Hamet had traded not for a whole camel but for the right to play host: to control the time and place of the slaughter, to feed his slaves, and to keep anything left over, which he would dry for the journey ahead. Even the withered *jmel,* with its flaccid hump, would produce several hundred pounds of rich blood, marrow, flesh, and organs, an abundance of food to the nomads, who were accustomed to living off camel's milk, water, and roots for weeks or months on end. That is not to say that Hamet would not try to keep the slaughter preparations as quiet as possible.

At midnight, he roused Riley and Clark by clucking. He had bought Clark for a pittance and had also bought but not yet taken possession of Savage. Hamet directed the two men to bring the brush and camel dung they had collected. In the light of the moon and stars, he, Seid, and Sideullah led them and the camel wordlessly to a secluded gully, where they forced the beast to its knees. Seid tied a noose, looped it under the *jmel's* fat jaw, and pulled its head around until its snout reached its rump. He lashed the free end of the rope to the firm base of its tail. Hamet placed a copper kettle under the camel's neck about a foot from its chest. The aged bull strained briefly as Hamet drew his scimitar through its flesh, opening a vein on the right side of its neck near its shoulders. A dark stream thrummed inside the kettle, the melancholy sound echoing on the silent dunes, as Riley watched a flame of sticks and dung sputter to life and grow, crackling and sending sparks into the night, like fireflies.

When the kettle held about a gallon and a half, Hamet and Sideullah set it on the fire. Riley squatted in the orange glow of the blaze, warming his shins, which were raw to the bone, as the traders stirred the simmering blood.

The smell drifted over the hill to the tents, waking the hungry nomads, who poured across the dune. At first they made a show of helping with the butchery, but by the time Hamet set the pot in front of the captain, saying "Kul, Riley," — Eat, Riley — they had crowded around like hyenas. Riley and Clark dug into the steaming blood with their bare hands. The mob surged forward. Hamet and Seid attempted to fend them off, but there were too many. The two sailors devoured the congealed blood, now as thick as calf's liver, as fast as they could, while the nomads battered them, snatching hand-fuls of the rich food. When the blood was gone, the frenzy abated as quickly as it had started. The nomads turned their attention to strip-ping the hide and dressing the camel. They placed the small intes-tines, with their contents still inside, in the kettle, along with the liver and lungs. One man slit open the camel's rumen — its first and largest stomach, where it partly digests its food before regurgitating it as cud — reached inside with a bowl, and scooped out some of the chunky green liquid. Soon the concoction bubbled on the fire.

At no time were fewer than half a dozen Bou Sbaa working on the carcass. The ones who arrived first warded off those who came up afterward. Then they disappeared with their loot and were replaced. In the dark of the early morning, they managed to carry off more than half the camel's hide, bones, and flesh. Hamet and Seid worked and kept watch. While their presence limited the thievery, they avoided confrontations that might start an out-and-out battle, which they could not win.

Riley had never seen anything like it and later expressed his dis-may: "Though our masters saw the natives in the very act of steal-ing and carrying off their meat, they could not prevent them, fearing worse consequences than losing it: it being a standing maxim among the Arabs to feed the hungry if in their power, and give them drink, even if the owner of the provisions be obliged to rob himself and his own family to do it."

Wilfred Thesiger, the famed British explorer of Arabia's Empty Quarter in the 1940s, was equally perturbed by this practice. "I . . . knew from bitter experience that while we were in inhabited coun-try every Bedu for miles around would come to feed at our expense," he wrote. "It would be impossible to refuse them food: in the desert one may never turn a guest away, however unwanted he may be" (p. 79). T. E. Lawrence observed that "the desert was held in a crazed communism by which Nature and the elements were for the free use of every known friendly person for his own purposes and no more" (p. 84).

While Riley found the custom barbaric, Hamet understood the realities of the desert and was not aggrieved. Fair or not, the Sahrawis shared in one another's fate, the strong providing for the weak, including children, the elderly, and slaves. This social pact allowed them to exist on the harshest terrain on earth. In accordance with the teachings of the Quran, Hamet expected nothing in return and received nothing. When the entrails were cooked, he and Seid fought for their own share.

Outside the circle of light, Riley and Clark dozed fitfully. As their dehydrated bodies struggled to digest the congealed blood, they became overheated, and a craving for water vexed them. In the buff morning light, Riley saw a teenage boy plunge his head into the camel's gaping rumen and drink. Hamet, seeing Riley's interest, told him to remove the boy and take his place.

Riley scooped the nauseating cavity with a bowl and poured the ropy green fluid down his throat. What he swallowed could not have been more refreshing had it been the springwater he once dreamed of turning into a spa. "Though its taste was exceedingly strong," he later wrote with his usual equanimity, "yet it was not salt, and it allayed my thirst."[4] Clark followed suit.

As Hamet, Seid, and their tenacious helpers continued to butcher the camel and spread the meat out to dry in the sun, the other nomads and their children hovered around, wheedling, begging, and pilfering. The result was as inevitable as the *irifi*. By nightfall, Hamet had less than fifteen pounds of meat left. Any hope of having a full stomach for the duration of the journey was shot.

The notoriety of Hamet's feast did have a positive result for the sailors, however. As word spread through the tribe that the traders were preparing to depart and that they were buying the sailors, other owners of *Commerce* crewmen scrambled to reach them.

Around noon, Horace was delivered by his former master, who had stopped feeding him after being forced to sell him. In three days, he had drunk little and eaten nothing but a few snails, miserable provisions even by Saharan standards. Hamet had saved him some boiled camel meat and entrails, and Riley brought him a bowl of rumen water to wash it down.

While the boy had been expected, Burns had not. Shortly after Horace arrived, an Arab showed up with the worn-out seaman, dressed in rags. Hamet asked Riley if he was one of his men. Riley nodded yes. "He is old and good for nothing, but I can buy him for just this blanket," Hamet told Riley, holding up one inferior to that swapped for the old *jmel*. Riley assured him that he would pay as much for Burns as for any of the men. Despite his appearance, Burns still had spirit. His joy at exchanging his miserable isolation for the company of his shipmates, plus a meal of offal and the hope of freedom, was infectious and boosted their morale.

The next Oulad Brahim to arrive was Mohammed, Riley's former master, the first to claim them at Cape Barbas. He had Hogan with him. Hamet negotiated for the Portlander and bought him for a fine blanket. But as Riley congratulated Hogan and Hamet fed him, another Arab showed up and began to argue with Mohammed, claiming to be a half owner of Hogan. After a heated discussion, he and Mohammed turned to Hamet and demanded another blanket. Hamet was outraged. Their dispute was none of his business. But the two Oulad Brahim pressed their case. "He is a stout fellow," they claimed. Soon all three were shouting. Their hands felt for the hilts of their weapons, but with Seid nearby, neither side had a decisive advantage. No one drew. In the pregnant moment, Riley intervened, pleading for Hogan, but the Brahim and the trader had dug in their heels. It was now a matter of pride, and neither side would back down.

Finally, Mohammed flung Hamet's blanket back at him and seized Hogan. Grabbing the sailor's long hair, he thumped him across the back with his camel goad, a thin two-foot club, and drove him out of the camp.[5] "My heart bled for him when I saw the blows fall on his emaciated and mangled frame, but I could not assist him," Riley lamented. "All I could do was to turn round and hide my face, so as not to witness his further tortures."

The next morning, the captain made another mark on his leg with the thorn he kept for that purpose. According to this crude calendar, it was September 27. After eighteen days away from a water source, the Oulad Brahim planned to set off the following dawn for a well two days to the northwest — the same well where Riley and his men had tasted their first life-saving drink on the desert. Hamet, wishing to avoid this gathering place, would head east instead, to another well he knew, and then turn northwest from there.

Riley both longed for and dreaded the departure. The five of them — Riley, Burns, Clark, Horace, and Savage — would be leaving behind six shipmates. He had not seen Williams, Barrett, or Deslisle in days and doubted Williams was alive. Riley had not come across Porter since the well, nor Robbins since the council the next day. And, of course, now Hogan was gone too.

That morning, Hamet took Riley aside and told him that he was now in charge of their possessions, the camels, and the sailors. As a sign of his trust, he gave him a small knife, hanging it in a case around his neck. The captain soon felt the burden of his new responsibilities. Hamet expected him to delegate chores, but his men were mostly incapable of strenuous work. The previous day's optimism at their new chances had withered in the noontime heat. Facing what seemed an impossible journey, they were nearly as moribund as before. Riley coped with his troubles the way he did at sea. He worked tirelessly, tending to their chores and even to minor details, none of which alone seemed overly important, though in sum they might mean the difference between life and death. He repaired his and Clark's meager clothing with camel-hair threads filched from the tent; he cleaned their drinking bowls with sand; he drained the blisters on their feet; and he prayed.

Among the preparations Hamet and Seid made that day for the journey was to drain about two gallons of liquid from the camel's paunch into a goatskin. Using their fingers as sieves, they strained out the thickest filth from what would be, for a week, their only source of fluid other than camel urine. They made sandals for the barefoot sailors out of the camel's hide, giving Riley and Horace the best, with two layers of skin, while those for Burns and Clark contained a single layer.

That evening Hamet called Riley over and informed him that Savage would soon arrive and that he had now risked everything he owned for the captain and his men. He could buy no one else, he said. Hamet confided in him his hope that the ransom money would allow him to repay his father-in-law for his losses in a Tombuctoo caravan that had gone awry. Lowering his voice, he said he needed Riley's help not just for external threats: "Seid is a bad man," he warned. Then he called over his brother, who remained contemptuous of the sailors and wary of the scheme. "Riley, repeat your vow," Hamet demanded.

Riley said that his friend in Swearah would pay the ransom. "If I am lying," he assured them, "you may cut my throat."

Savage's arrival late that night should have lifted their spirits, especially Riley's. As the son of one of the brig's co-owners and the second mate, Savage was the captain's nearest equal and most likely confidant in the crew, but while the others had exulted, at least briefly, in rejoining their shipmates, Savage sulked. He had divined the presence of the traders over the past week from rumor, but his young master, Abdallah, had remained silent about them; Savage had tormented himself with the belief that his shipmates had left him behind. The prospect of freedom and the camel's intestines that Hamet had saved for him to eat did little to cheer him up. Angry and fearful, possibly on the verge of insanity, Savage had turned surly. The humiliation of captivity was magnified for him by his strict Baptist upbringing. His mother's brand of religion brooked no compromise and, as she once wrote in a sermonizing letter to his father at sea, tolerated no one "friendly of Babilon [sic] or AntiChristians." Nodding at Hamet and Seid, he snarled, "I do not believe a word these wretches say." He as much as accused Riley of fabricating their prospects of liberation. "I can understand nothing they say," he grumbled, "and I do not believe the captain can either."

Savage also questioned the plot Riley had hatched and even carped about the ransom he had agreed to. "He will find nobody willing to advance that sum of money to him, because he is poor," scoffed Savage — a galling snipe, for Savage was the only one in a position to know the gravity of Riley's financial woes.

Riley was furious. Not only was Savage's talk impertinent, it undermined the captain's authority. On board the brig, it would have amounted to mutiny. Even in his diminished state, he could have snapped Savage like a dry twig. But that, he realized, would have been worse than pointless. What really mattered was the effect dissension within the ranks might have on Hamet and Seid. Their confidence in Riley was the linchpin of the deal. If that collapsed, their escape would be in jeopardy. Riley held his tongue.

That same night, Robbins was still out on the desert at ten o'clock. The temperature had plunged thirty degrees since sunset, and the moon would not rise for another two hours. Dressed in nothing but his cutoff trousers and wide-brimmed leather hat, Robbins shivered as he rode behind Ganus on his camel. The only part of his body that stayed warm was his legs where they pressed against the camel. As he rode north over uneven terrain, a northeasterly wind gusted in his face. Robbins's mind swam with fatigue. The stars stretched from one flat horizon to the other, giving him the strange and ironic sensation of riding through the heavens.

He did not know where they were headed, only that Ganus had asked him if he wanted to go see "Aarone," which he took to mean Aaron Savage. He had replied that he did but then began to suspect that Ganus had other intentions. For seventeen days, his master had paid little enough attention to him and had never asked him to accompany him away from camp. Now Robbins worried that he meant to sell him, a possibility he feared, for Ganus, unlike some masters, was at least diligent in providing food and water.

Over the next three hours they traveled rapidly, covering about twenty miles. At last they stopped at a patch of low thorny shrubs so that the camel could feed. Robbins lay down on the sand to rest.

An hour or so before dawn, he felt a nudge in the side. He awoke with sand pressed through his beard onto his jaw and Ganus standing over him, ready to move on. Though Robbins was in better shape than most of his mates, his body throbbed from the effects of long-term dehydration aggravated by the hard riding and the cold night. He rose stiffly.

They mounted the camel and rode until near sunrise, when they entered a *friq* where men were roasting a camel. Robbins's mouth ached for the charred meat, but all Ganus could get for him was a helping of boiled blood. Robbins placed it in the crown of his hat. "Kul, Robbins," urged Ganus. But his mouth was so dry he was afraid he would not be able to swallow it.

They took off again as the sun approached the rim of the earth and oblique morning light crept over the rippling crests of sand waves, leaving the troughs in darkness. Fatigue and the numbing cold lulled Robbins into a trance. His mind wandered. Had he been on board the *Commerce* out at sea, this would have been the sunrise watch, the bow rising and falling on choppy waves, the pangs of hunger in his gut soon to be appeased by Dick's breakfast and hot coffee.

When the camel topped a hill, Robbins was jarred from his reverie. To the east, the sun, a vivid orange-pink ball, rose above the horizon, a glowing ogre head approaching from the far side of the world. In front of it, a silhouette of camels stretched across a valley and over a dune. In a place of few landmarks and fewer maps, the nomad's standard unit of measure for distance was the span over which a camel could be seen clearly, a little over a mile. Robbins, accustomed to discerning an object and judging its direction and distance from a rocking masthead, quickly pegged them at about one camel away.

There was a brief pause to take in the sight, and then Ganus goaded his animal's neck, directing it toward the camel train's place of origin. Less than an hour later, they loped into a narrow valley dotted with tents, where Robbins listened intently when Ganus asked an old woman, "Where are the kelb en-Nasrani?" — the Christian dogs.[6]

She pointed toward a hill to the east. As they approached it, Robbins saw smoke rising from a fire. Their camel, having covered more than forty miles that night, stumbled over the brink of the dune, sinking in deep sand as it instinctively lurched toward the camp at the bottom of another narrow valley. For the second time that morning, Robbins smelled roasting meat, and it nearly crazed him with hunger.

Dismounting after Ganus, he blindly approached the fire, only half in his senses, intending to beg or steal. What he saw brought him up short: Scattered around the campsite, tending to the duties of packing, were Clark, Burns, Horace, Savage, and Riley.[7] Immediately Robbins forgot his hunger, his thirst, his misery and sank to his knees. "Something whispered to me that my deliverance was near," he later recalled, "that the day of my redemption had come."

Ganus, a short man, approached Hamet and Seid, who towered over him, and the three fell into conversation. Ganus intended to sell Robbins. As they discussed his fate, Robbins, still marveling at seeing his friends, traded some of the boiled blood in his hat to Horace for a piece of gristle. The gristle was inedible, so he swallowed it whole.

Riley edged toward his new masters and Ganus. When it became clear to him that Hamet was refusing to buy Robbins, he got down on his knees and begged him to. Hamet told him to rise, insisting he had nothing left to trade. Although the deal for Hogan had failed the day before, he had since bought a young camel. His claim was not a ploy. He became irritated, kicked sand at Riley, and ordered his group, including Savage's master, Abdallah, who had joined as a partner, to begin moving up the dune.

Robbins was stunned. His shipmates began to look away, as if he were a condemned man whom they could not face in his worst moment. He had come tantalizingly close to the hope of being saved. Instead, he was about to be left behind.

Riley could not interfere any more with Hamet. He knew it was dangerous to linger. He embraced Robbins. "Keep heart," he said in an anguished whisper. "Do your best to stay healthy, and to encourage the others. You will find a means of liberation. If I make it, I will do everything I can to retrieve you."

As his five shipmates trudged up the dune to begin a grueling march across the desert, Robbins broke down in tears. "While I rejoiced at their good fortune," he later wrote, "I grieved, in the very depths of sorrow, at my own calamities." His best chance to escape the desert had just passed before his eyes, and once again Robbins was alone.

PART THREE

Journeys and Sandstorms

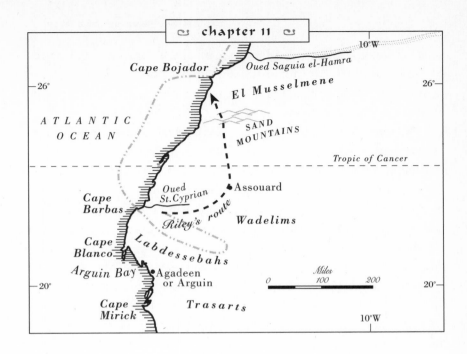

chapter 11

Is It Sweet?

Phoebe Riley had seen nothing like it before. An oppressive heat, as if a mysterious visitation from faraway equatorial regions, had permeated Middletown for several days. Then on Friday, September 22, the Gale of 1815 hit the coast of New England like a blast of grapeshot. Waves six feet high broke on the streets of New London. At Potapaug, a falling tree crushed a stretch of the ropewalk, the roof of the Episcopal church blew off, and two ships sank. As the furious wind whipped up the sea, brackish rain salted fields a mile inland and coated apples on trees with a briny frost. Winds funneled up the Connecticut River, lifting roofs, knocking down barns, and scattering hay in the meadows. All along the coast, merchant seamen, having already fastened down or stowed everything that could move, cursed and prayed for their vessels.

Left alone with five children, one a baby, Phoebe had her hands full on a normal day; to watch the Valley flood and blow down around them and to have to try to calm her brood's fears at the same time was almost too much.

The wind had started to blow on Wednesday. Soggy and sullen, it dropped down chimneys and suffocated fires in fireplaces. On Thursday, Phoebe and young James had closed the shutters, put the animals in the barn, and brought in everything that might blow away. By Friday, the wind was howling at fifty miles an hour. Still young and supple, her husband's poplars, the ones he had planted on Prospect Hill and then had to abandon, bowed to the ground, but they were no longer hers to trouble with. How they had dreamed: a grand spa with a four-story brick mansion, pools of bubbling mineral water for bathing, broad esplanades for strolling, and formal gardens. But that chimerical vision was as far away as her husband now seemed.

On the river, the men battled the rising tide. They secured wharves and warped down vessels to keep them from being driven ashore. The houses nearby stood on foundations of brownstone, but if the banks flooded, they would soon be under and, like the vessels, pummeled by fallen trees and other large objects caught in the sweep of the floodtide.

But Phoebe had even darker thoughts in the back of her mind. Some said the storm and its torrid air had blown all the way across the Atlantic from Africa. Her husband would be in constant danger from such weather. Everyone was talking about the disappearance of the *Épervier,* which had set out from Gibraltar in early July. Decatur had dispatched the brig with a copy of the new U.S. treaty with Algiers, ten captives he had freed, and Captain Lewis and Lieutenant Neale, who had married sisters just before embarking for the Mediterranean. Word had it that the British West India fleet had caught a glimpse of the brig in a vicious gale that sank a number of the fleet's merchant ships. The *Épervier* had not been heard from again.

The *Commerce* had been crossing the Atlantic at exactly the same time. Phoebe had not received a letter from James since New

Orleans. This in itself was not a cause for concern, but now she could not help wondering what might have happened. Had this gale hit the *Commerce* at sea? And if it was this fierce after blowing all the way from Africa, what must it have been like for her husband and his men?

As the citizens of Middletown set about repairing their water-logged village, part of the crew of the *Commerce*, with visions of Connecticut's pristine fields in their hearts, set off across the Sahara. Riley, of course, knew nothing of the storm or of Phoebe's recent worries, but he ached to see her and the children, all the more so now that he saw a glimmer of hope of one day returning to them.

A band of Oulad Brahim rode along briefly with Hamet, Seid, Abdallah, and the five sailors, bidding them a raucous farewell and getting a head start on disputes over future transactions that might never be. The clamor gave Sideullah a chance to commit a last bit of malice against Riley, whom he and his family had "shunned as they would a pestilence" ever since selling him. While Riley was watching the drove, his former master sneaked up to one of the camels and slashed a rope holding a large slab of meat from the recent slaughter. Riley tried to stop him from taking it, but his shouts went unheard. Sideullah merely glared at him with disdain and rode off with his prize, leaving Riley dumbfounded that his former master, a leader of worship and a respected member of his tribe, would brazenly steal another man's food, and troubled over what his own punishment might be when the loss was discovered.

While Riley was thus distracted, Hamet's big camel strayed off, following a drove heading northwest. The old *jmel* stood out like a ship of the line among frigates. Riley tore off in pursuit, finally catching him after an exhausting run. Hamet put Horace, Burns, and Savage on this towering animal. They clung to its packsaddle and one another in a shifting stew of flesh and sweat, of matted hair and woolly beards. Burns, wearing an old jacket, and Horace and Savage, draped in ratty goatskins, looked like desperadoes. Riley, shirtless, and Clark, clad in a fragment of sail, rode on Seid's camel while

Seid shared Abdallah's. Hamet straddled the new, young camel, which he was breaking in, bareback, behind the hump.

They rode eastward at a purposeful, long-striding rack, a beating for the feeble sailors, made worse by the constant sun on their backs. At midday they stopped in a shallow depression to adjust the saddles. Hamet pulled a checked shirt out of a saddlebag and gave it to Riley, declaring that he had stolen it for him and that he had tried to find another for Horace but failed. "Put it on, Rais," he said, looking at Riley's raw skin. "Your poor back needs a covering." Riley kissed Hamet's hand and put it on. Although he was surprised that even Hamet, on whose trustworthiness he had staked his future, would steal from a fellow tribesman, he could not deny that he was grateful that he had.

The rest of that afternoon and the following day, Hamet pushed them east across the *hammada,* stopping only to feed the camels on thornbush and at night to camp by thornbush. The second night, they shared out the last of the rank rumen water, about four quarts, equally among the eight men. Swearah lay north by northeast, but Hamet continued to head east, deeper into the desert.

Riley would at first figure, based on his observations of the sun's height at noon, that they traveled as far south as 20° N latitude, into the deepest, driest section of the western Sahara. This would have placed them in what is today the region of Adrar, Mauritania. But this is a hilly region, and Riley did not encounter hills on this leg of the journey; nor did he mention crossing a long wadi that bisects the route.

It is probable that Hamet's course was more northerly than Riley originally thought (in fact, a map that accompanies later editions of his memoir shows a northeasterly route). Hamet might have been making for a water source in the granite of Zug, or even more likely, for Assouard, a remote wadi, where the Oulad Bou Sbaa were known to congregate.

It is certain that Hamet's path through the stubby sand hills and shallow valleys took them at times toward all easterly points of the compass. The route would have been impossible to accurately track without scientific devices and the means for keeping notes. Because the region was uncharted, Riley did not even have a template on which to transfer his memories.

It seems likely that they did not travel as fast or as far as Riley believed either. He recorded that the camels reached speeds of up to seven miles an hour and, on consecutive days, covered 63, 105, and 50 miles. Though camels are rightly prized for their stamina, the speed and distance they can travel has long been a matter of lore. In 1791, William Lempriere reported that they ran so fast "their riders are obliged to tie a sash round their waists to preserve the power of respiration" (p. 708). But Lempriere, who said it was normal for camels to cover five hundred miles in four days, had been fooled to a substantial degree. In his 1959 classic, *Arabian Sands,* desert explorer Wilfred Thesiger told of once dashing 115 miles on camelback in twenty-three hours and covering 450 miles in nine days, but that was on the "finest riding camels in the Sudan."

With only four camels for eight men, five of whom were frail, ailing, and inexperienced riders, the pace of Hamet's company could not have approached Thesiger's, nor even that of the French adventurer Michel Vieuchange, who journeyed to Smara, the forbidden city of the warrior-sheik Ma el Anin on the Saguia el-Hamra, in 1930. "I know now that I can cover 110 to 120 miles in forty-eight hours, going day and night, by camel and on foot," he scrawled in his diary, but his camels could not keep up the pace. As he fled back to civilization, Vieuchange had to abandon two of his three mounts, which were too exhausted to continue. In 1817, Robert Adams, of the *Charles,* gave the most unvarnished assessment of a camel's pace and a more applicable benchmark for Riley's rate of travel: A fresh, lightly burdened camel, he said, will travel from eighteen to twenty-five miles a day, but when loaded down and poorly fed, as is usual, only about ten to fifteen miles.

On the second day, September 29, Hamet led the party across another stretch of gnarled tamarisks, saltwort, and stones.[1] After the Arabs prayed at noon, they all caught camel urine in their hands and drank it. Hamet assured Riley that the Arabs considered camel urine good for the stomach. Indeed, as is recorded in the *Sunnah,* the book of traditions relating to the Prophet Muhammad, the Prophet himself had directed its use for medicinal purposes. Riley noted that the sailors preferred the beasts' urine to their own.

That evening, Hamet searched futilely for a sheltered place with forage for the camels. Fifteen hours after setting out, they stopped in a shallow depression that offered neither. "The remaining flesh on our posteriors, and inside of our thighs and legs, was so beat, and literally pounded to pieces, that scarcely any remained," Riley wrote. Their bones "felt as if they had been thrown out of their sockets" by the constant jarring. Crying out in grunts and slurred oaths, the sailors fell from the kneeling camels to their hands and knees. They rose like drunken men and reeled about, joints cracking, trying to regain the use of their legs.

The Bou Sbaa, using flint to make sparks, started a blaze despite the gusting wind. They roasted about a pound of the dried camel meat and shared it out among the eight men. Living on so little nutrition, with no cushion of fat or fluid in their bodies, the sailors experienced food and drink with biological profundity. Hunger and thirst played a seesaw battle, each tip in the balance sending an acute signal. Even these small portions of charred meat required more liquid for digestion than their bodies had to spare. They ate voraciously; then, inflamed by thirst, they surrounded a staling camel, drank, and were soon famished again. They lay down on the ground, huddling together against a gale. Their bruised muscles ached so badly that Riley compared the agony to the tortures of the medieval rack. Despite their exhaustion, they could not sleep. They were too exposed. A century later, Michel Vieuchange would affirm Riley's experience in simple but compelling words: "The cold nights of the Sahara," he scribbled in his diary. "I suffer from the cold a great deal more than from the sun" (p. 223).

On the morning of September 30, Riley showed Hamet his bleeding sores and other evidence of the men's deteriorating condition. The Bou Sbaa was genuinely chagrined and a bit mystified at the sailors' infirmity, but he could see with his own eyes that they were not merely grousing. Clark and Burns were flopped on the ground like empty panniers, drained of all energy. Still, they had to move on, Hamet told them. "We should come to good water soon. After that we will not travel so fast."

As they rode, Riley brooded over the shipmates he had left behind. Robbins's anguish at their separation was indelibly stamped on his heart. Williams he believed would die soon if he had not already. Porter was strong and clever and might survive, and the two Portlanders, Hogan and Barrett, had a fighting chance. Still, for all but Deslisle, the margin between gaining or losing the opportunity to leave the desert had been wafer thin. As for Deslisle, who Robbins said was "esteemed by the crew as a faithful, active cook," he never had a fair chance. Being black in a place where most blacks were slaves, coming from a country where the same was true, and having neither wealth nor a devoted benefactor, he had virtually no hope of escaping slavery on the Sahara or its purlieus.

After four hours of riding farther to the east, they descended into a vast boxy canyon, a "dreary abyss," according to Riley. After they had driven the camels down the steepest pitch, Hamet sent Seid and Abdallah to search for a spring in the far wall. By the time the others reached the bottom, the two Bou Sbaa had disappeared on a boulder-strewn and pathless floor, which Riley determined, as they picked their way across it, had once been a river or possibly an "arm of the sea." Though the water that had flowed in it was now long gone, the hooves of the camels crunched through a crust of salt, all that remained, he imagined, of an evaporated sea and cruelly reminiscent of a crisp fresh snow.

Riley was awed by the otherworldliness of the Precambrian bedrock, more than 2.5 billion years old, and the vastness of the chasm, which was eight miles wide in places and ran, by his reckoning, three hundred miles southwest to the coast. As Riley had guessed, the sea had washed over it, and the sea had receded, only to return again in another age, many times over. Each washing had left its layer of marine sediment to become another stratum of rock, some less porous than others and able to trap water. It is said that when rain falls in the western Sahara, a third of it evaporates, a third of it goes to the sea, and a third of it remains underground. Scattered beneath the western Sahara were pockets of trapped water — some vast, many ancient, some extremely deep, others shallow enough to wend through tortuous rifts and bubble to the surface. Occasionally, where the surface floor had sunk to form a canyon, water from one of these pockets seeped through a fault in the vertical wall.

Following Hamet, the seamen kept the camels in a line. They passed through a smaller, more recent riverbed etched into the larger one but now, like its predecessor, eerily still. The fact that they were heading east, not north, the direction Mogadore lay in, made the sailors anxious. Savage grumbled, and his insinuations lingered like the bitter taste of cotton-mouth.

As they walked, Hamet motioned for Riley to join him in front. Since leaving the Oulad Brahim, the trader had had time to consider their venture and wished to impress upon *el rais* the importance of his promise. Hamet and Seid had traded everything they owned for him and his men, he reminded Riley, fixing him with his dark eyes. "Be candid with me, Rais," he said. "Have you been to Swearah?"

The clever Arab had timed his inquisition well. Hollow eyes in the horned skull of a sun-bleached ram watched them pass. Nearby, the neck of a curled camel skeleton that could not make it up a slope arched back in enduring agony. Riley was as tired, thirsty, hot, and oppressed by the canyon as the others. It was clear that Hamet held their lives in his hands. If he rode off and left them, they would never find the spring. Should Riley come clean to the Arab who had shown that he was a friend? And if he did not, what were the odds that erratic, petulant Savage might give him away at any time?

Riley was aware that the expression on his face was as crucial as the words he spoke. "I have been to Swearah," he said.

Hamet, who made his living by reading other men, studied Riley for the merest twitch of guilt. "Are you telling the truth about having a friend who will pay money for you?" he asked.

"I am, Sidi Hamet."

"Do you own property in your country? Tell me," Hamet asked, more forcefully. "I am your friend. Allah will deal with you as you deal with me!"

Riley allowed a reflective instant to pass, a hardly discernible pause, to give these words their due and to allow their power to dissipate. "I have a friend in Swearah," he said calmly, looking Hamet squarely in the eye, "who will advance me any sum of money I need."

Hamet persisted. So, too, did Riley, although to avoid some specific questions he pretended not to understand. Hamet found one thing in particular hard to believe. "Will you really buy Clark and Burns?" he said. "They are good for nothing."

"They are my countrymen and my brothers," Riley replied. "I will if you carry us to the Empire of Morocco and to the sultan."

"No," Hamet answered. "The sultan will not pay for you, but I will carry you to Swearah to your friend. What is his name?"

"Consul," responded Riley.

The Arab nodded to indicate that the answer satisfied him. Using his hands, he showed Riley how to count to twenty (*ashreen*) in Arabic. He produced from his djellaba the seven dollar coins that he and Seid still owned. "Riley, you must pay ten times twenty dollars for yourself and the same for Horace. For the others, ten times ten dollars each. In addition to that, you must pay for all the provisions on the road." The sum was growing, but at this juncture it mattered little to the captain, who agreed without protest. Hamet asked him to point in the direction of Swearah. Riley, who was getting more and more accustomed to communicating with the Arabs, used his knowledge of the coast, the position of the sun, and the direction of the prevailing wind, and pointed correctly just east of north.

"Now, if you will agree before God the most High to pay what I have stated, in money, and give me a double-barreled gun, I will take you up to Swearah," Hamet concluded, tacking on another reward. "If not, I will carry you off that way," he said, pointing to the southeast, "and sell you for as much as I can get, rather than carry you all the way across this long desert, where we must risk our lives every day for your sakes.

"And know," he added with chilling candor, "that if we get there safely and you cannot comply with your agreement, we must cut your throat and sell your comrades for what they will bring."

Riley nodded his head in assent, and Hamet took his hand. "You shall go to Swearah," he said, "inshallah."

It was midafternoon when they finally reached the far side of the canyon, about five miles from where they had entered it. Hamet called, "Hoh, Seid! Hoh, Abdallah!" Their names echoed off the overhanging north wall, which long ago had been undermined by running water. Talus had massed beneath the bluff to three hundred feet, shelving just a hundred feet shy of the canyon rim. Hamet called again as they walked along the base of the scree.

Finally, they heard the reply: "Hamet, amet, amet!" and Seid appeared from behind some large upright rocks. He and Hamet called back and forth. "Stay," Hamet told Riley. "They have not found it." And he proceeded up the slope on foot to search for the spring while the camels foraged and the sailors rested their heads on stones.

An hour later, Hamet called down and told Riley to come up, and the captain fumbled his way up the tumult of debris. Worried that his legs would give way, he hoisted himself up between the bigger rocks with his arms. His sores cracked open as he stretched and bent. His hands and wrists quivered under the strain.

When he finally reached the spot where Hamet stood, he saw nothing but rock and dust. The spring was dry. From the open sea, to the coast, to the desert, and now to the dusty canyon, it had been a steady, mind-boggling descent. At each phase he had thought it could not get worse. But this was the worst place. It appeared their luck had run its course. He began to sob.

"Look there," said Hamet, pointing through a narrow fissure in the rocks. Riley stared into a dark crevasse. As his eyes adjusted to the shadows, he made out a reflection. There *was* water below. But how would they get to it?

Hamet indicated a place among some boulders lower down but

not far away, where the spring surfaced in a more accessible groove. "Sherub, Riley. Drink," he said. "It is sweet."

Riley followed a crooked path under and behind boulders fifteen and twenty feet high, then squeezed through a narrow passage along the face of the canyon. He tasted the water — "cool, clear, fresh" — and gave a shout. Soon Burns, Clark, Savage, and Horace were scrambling up the slope. "Where is the water?" they called eagerly. "For God's sake, where is it? Oh, is it sweet?" Yes, it was sweet beyond imagination.

Not far from where Riley had left him, Robbins surveyed the place where Ganus and three dozen other Arabs had pitched their tents and reckoned it the Valley of the Shadow of Death — only without the benefit of an actual shadow. Its merits consisted of a few feed bushes for the camels and hills to break the wind. Lying in the corner of a sweltering tent, he surrendered to despair, slipped in and out of waking dreams. His subconscious interwove threads of past and present, wefting him to his parents' hearth, to the smell of baking bread and the feel of blackberry jam in his mouth, and warping him back to the unctuous odor of the remaining boiled camel blood in the crown of his hat and the knot in his gut from being left behind.

He and Ganus had found the family's relocated tents late two nights before. The shock of seeing his shipmates depart had left that long day a grotesque blur. The next morning after dawn prayer, he had learned from Sarah through signs and words that they would not go north until the rainy season, probably January — another blow to his sinking spirits. Under a scorching sun, nearly vertical at noontime, they moved fifteen miles to the east, crossing hills and descending into the southwest end of a broad canyon. They crawled along a dusty rubble floor until, in the late afternoon, they saw three tents in a gully in the canyon's south wall.

They drove the camels into the gully, where Robbins felt an immediate drop in temperature but not much relief. The Arabs in the tents had invited Ganus and his family to drink and eat with them. Alone, Robbins watched the camels and felt deeply dejected. This and his burning throat drove him, as he watched the Arabs lift the bowl to their mouths and then pass it, to ponder the unthinkable: If he became a Mohammedan, as they were constantly urging him to do, they would always share whatever food and drink they had. Could anything be worse than what he was already experiencing? This thought was interrupted when Ganus waved to him to drive the camels in closer. As he did, a boy pointed to a tent and indicated that one of his shipmates was in it.

Inside, wearing the remnants of an old coat and trousers hacked off at the knees, was Porter, who greeted Robbins like a lost brother, elated to learn that he was not alone and that another had survived. Robust by nature, Porter was less beaten down than the others. But they had barely exchanged more than a greeting when Ganus had called "Robbinis!" and they had moved on.

The next day, frustration and hopelessness consumed Robbins again. Porter, his closest mate among the crew, was just a valley back, but he might never see him again. Porter had told him that Hogan and Deslisle were in the valley where Robbins now lay, but he could not make himself get up to look for them. The sounds of camp, of the women's careless voices as they combed and braided one another's hair — to "divest it of the vermin that generally colonize it" — taunted him. He could not understand their complacence. On occasion they spun wool or wove, but usually, he complained, they were "listless, inactive, and stupid." In his rage over their cruelty and his desperation, it did not occur to Robbins that the Sahrawis might have chosen this way of life for a love of the desert, despite its hardships, or that they were amazingly well adapted to it. He cursed their world. He cursed their God, and his God. He rued the day he was born.

Near midday, from where he lay muttering to himself, Robbins caught a glimpse of a shuffling, stooped figure wearing a small animal skin and a piece of sail. "Hogan?" he called out. John Hogan looked up and walked over. "Robbins, how are you?" he croaked.

Staring at Hogan's gaunt face, Robbins could not produce words. The Portlander's mouth had contorted into a lopsided scowl that made him look demented. Burned and cracked, his eyelids were merely retractable scabs, his eyes the fresh part of a wound. Robbins felt his empty stomach convulse. He embraced his shipmate, the strong and audacious youth who on a stormy night — ages ago, it now seemed — had led the way down the hawser from the wrecked brig to shore.

Robbins took Hogan back to his tent and begged his mistress to allow them to enter. At first she refused. Then, taking a look at Hogan, she relented. Inside, the sailors exchanged news. Hogan told Robbins how on that recent fateful day the traders had bought him from Mohammed and then returned him when a dispute broke out with Porter's master. The feud had raged on afterward until the two came to blows. Ever since, Mohammed had treated him worse, feeding him even less and forbidding him to sleep inside the tent. Mohammed also owned Deslisle, who tended his camels from dawn to dusk. The cook ate better than Hogan did but was often beaten by their master.

Robbins related his own near miss with the traders and his news of Porter and shared the rest of the three-day-old camel blood with him. Hogan gratefully swallowed the rich morsel down. Sarah gave them *zrig,* and Hogan remarked that compared with his mistress, she was an "angel of mercy." The two sailors remained together mending each other's spirits into the evening. They made plans to hunt for food together the next day, and Robbins urged Hogan to bring Deslisle with him. Hogan replied that Mohammed would never allow it.

In the morning, Robbins rose with the family at dawn. They went outside to the sand in front of the tent, and the few who had them slipped off their camel-skin slippers. Facing east, they dropped to their knees, with what Robbins deemed "peculiar solemnity," for the first of their five daily prayers.[2] Robbins knew that after their morning worship, the women would remove the reed baskets that covered the camels' udders so that the young animals could nurse.

The women would milk what was left over and share it with the others who had prayed. All he had to do was join them.

"My master Ganus bade me follow his motions," Robbins recounted. Ganus and the others knelt and rubbed sand on their hands, arms, and faces, their ablutions in the absence of water. "I did the same," confessed Robbins. Always facing east, Ganus rose up and loudly exclaimed the call to prayer, which Robbins recorded as "Sheda el la lah, Hi Allah — Sheda Mahommed — Rah sool Allah." Robbins repeated the words, not knowing what they meant, and continued to follow his master's example. Ganus was delighted.

In the desolate canyon far to the east, Riley and his men reveled in water as pure as a Connecticut creek. They drank and drank, so much so that they grew giddy and water-drunk. Even as Riley admonished them not to consume too much too fast, he continued to guzzle himself. Their stomachs twisted like Turk's heads, they bent double, and still they heedlessly drank more. Just as they had at the well the first day, they fouled themselves like infants while the Bou Sbaa, who were fastidious in such matters, looked on in disgust.

Seid and Abdallah drove the camels up switchbacks to within fifty yards of the spring. At the top, Riley filled a four-gallon goatskin and handed it down to his men, who were stationed in a line and carried it down to the *selaï,* the large bowl used for watering the camels. Even the intense griping of their stomachs and the cramps in their sides barely diminished their feeling of satisfaction as they went about the work.

The camels had not drunk for twenty days. Their dung had become so dry that as soon as the pellets dropped, they could be used as fuel for the fire. The sailors filled the goatskin fifteen times for Hamet's big one alone and grew more amazed with each delivery. "Is he not done yet?" they cried. "He alone will drink the spring dry!" Unlike the men, the big camel would retain with great efficiency the sixty gallons it absorbed.

The unusual ability of the camel to endure thirst would not be accurately explained by scientists until the twentieth century. When dehydrating, camels sustain their plasma volume, losing tissue fluid first and maintaining good circulation. Even as a camel's blood thickens, its small red blood cells circulate efficiently. When water becomes available, camels can drink great volumes because the liquid is absorbed very gradually from their stomachs and intestines, preventing osmotic distress, and, whereas the red blood cells of other species can swell with water to only 150 percent of their normal size, a camel's can grow to 240 percent.

When all the camels had finished, the men filled two skins with the chalky water that remained in the pool.[3]

Riley thanked God for Sidi Hamet's profound knowledge of the desert and for taking them out of the hands of the aimless nomads. How had Hamet discovered the hidden pools pinned to the side of the remote canyon? Riley had seen "not the smallest sign of their ever having overflowed their basons," nor any other clue to their existence. He could not help but look at Hamet with greater respect.

On the desert again, dire reality soon prevailed. They were alive, and they had water, but they could feel their hunger the more severely, and the landscape was no more promising where they emerged from the canyon than where they had entered it. As far as they could see, the desert was empty, "no rising of the ground, nor any rock, tree, or shrub," Riley wrote. "All was a dreary, solitary waste." One crucial factor did change, however. They altered course, heading northwest.

They rode several hours as the sun dropped toward the horizon, momentarily a pleasant, glowing ghost of itself casting shadows behind them before leaving them in empty desolation. Finding no shelter, they finally stopped in the middle of the plain. Before lying down to sleep, they ate the last of the dried camel meat, about an ounce for each man. Since Hamet's camels produced no milk, they had no more nourishment. They would now have to forage. That night, the frigid north wind pummeled them like buntlines on a billowing canvas, and the next day the wind continued, gusting in their faces. The rejuvenated camels walked so briskly that those on foot had to trot to keep up. The sailors struggled with hunger and monotony until, in the afternoon, Hamet called out, "Riley, shift jmel" — I see a camel.

Riley searched the horizon. He saw nothing. The other sailors could not make out any sign of a rider either, but Hamet looked delighted as he altered their course to due east. Two hours later the sailors glimpsed the small outline of a camel on the horizon. By sunset, they had reached a large drove of camels and herders, who invited them to their camp. It was after dark when they reached four tents on the plain. They stopped at a distance and collected brush for the fire.

After traveling forty miles in fourteen hours without food or water, the sailors were in bad shape. Their wounds had reopened from the jolting, and their "various and complicated sufferings," wrote Riley, caused them great discomfort. They were certainly feeling the effects of scurvy or some other form of malnutrition. They had no shelter to protect them from the wind and no sand to lie on, only the spiky hardpan. They had been promised food, but on the desert such promises, they knew, were fleeting. As the hours passed, they lost hope for anything but milk, which would be served around midnight, if at all.

An hour shy of that, Hamet called Riley over to the circle of light and handed him a bowl. Riley returned to his men and gleefully displayed its contents: boiled meat. They tore it into five portions, cast lots for them, and ate voraciously. The meat was tender and aromatic, not ashy or burned, just enough to fill their stomachs. As the sailors lay down again to sleep, the Arabs brought them a large bowl of zrig. "This was indeed," Riley glowed, "sumptuous living."

In the morning, one of these generous nomads proudly produced an acquisition he had made on the coast. It was shiny and new and, assuming from its appearance that it would fetch a vast sum, the Arab presented this novel and mysterious object to el rais to ask its value. It was the spyglass that Riley had bought in Gibraltar. He told the man it was worth about ten Spanish dollars, a not inconsiderable sum. Hamet wanted to buy it, but having only seven dollars, he was not able to.

Hamet's party left this company of nomads and continued traveling northwest on the *hammada* until late afternoon, when they met up with another party of Arabs whose camels wore *selaïs* on their sides like armor and lugged full waterskins. Another invitation was issued and accepted. They followed these men two hours to the southwest to reach their camp of fifty tents and the first sheep the sailors had seen on the Sahara. When they went out searching for firewood, a crowd gathered to see the pale blond-bearded men who had come from across the northern sea. They identified Riley as *el rais* and asked him questions about his ship, about the country they had come from and their families.

Hamet's group stayed with these nomads two more days, traveling fifteen miles north with them. The tribe treated both the Bou Sbaa and their captives as honored guests, erecting tents even for the Christians. Although their sheep were perishing, barely able to stand and graze on the brown moss, the Arabs lavished milk on their guests at night. Unsure when they would eat again, the sailors gorged until they vomited.

On October 5, they left this band of Arabs, who had impressed Riley and his crew with a generosity that was as liberal to the lowly slave as it was to the master. Hamet bought a sheep and traded his young camel for an old one and a calf. The old camel soon proved to be lame in the right forefoot. They called it Coho, "Lame," and the calf Goyette, "Little Child," though it was big enough to carry an emaciated sailor on its back.

Riley led the sheep with a rope tied around its neck until noon, when they reached a small valley with a *bir* sunk amid bushes with thick roots. This was no small find. Until recent times, Western Sahara, a region the size of Colorado, possessed only about a hundred known sources of potable water. Wells tapping them — categorized by their depth, a *hassi* being as deep as forty feet and a *bir* anything deeper — are so essential and the land otherwise so devoid of landmarks that even modern maps show their locations.

They pulled up bucket after bucket from the deep well, each man drinking as much as he wanted. After watering the camels and filling two goatskins, they slaughtered the sheep, which could not keep up. When Riley started to clean the entrails, the Bou Sbaa stopped him, put them, still intact, back inside the carcass, and slung it across a camel. They mounted again and continued northwest, driving riderless Coho on in front.

That night, the Bou Sbaa roasted and ate two of the mutton quarters while the sailors devoured the offal nomad-style — with its partially digested grain still inside. On the morning of October 6, they set off on foot, driving the camels on in front of them. Since leaving the chasm, Riley had noticed that Hamet, Seid, and Abdallah had more trouble navigating. Before, they had steered by the desert's landmarks. Now they seemed more concerned about their location, frequently checking the sun and the wind and dismounting at sandy patches on the *hammada* to smell the sand. By the middle of the morning, even the sailors began to notice signs of change. The sand that lay in small, loose heaps began to mount. The distant terrain took on an ominous, choppy look, like the sea under an approaching storm. By early afternoon, wind-borne grit stung their skin.

For another week, Ganus's family remained in Robbins's so-called Valley of the Shadow of Death, where, empty-handed, they searched farther and farther afield for sustenance and pushed the limits of tribal obligation, borrowing, cajoling, and filching from those who still had milk or a cache of food or water. One of Ganus's camels had gone dry, reducing their milk supply to four quarts a day.

Robbins and Hogan crossed the hill to the east into another valley, where they found snails. Robbins stashed his in his sailcloth satchel until they could take fire from a camp and roast them. So reduced were the Arabs that when the pair returned to Ganus's tent for *zrig* and Ganus discovered what they had found and eaten, he scolded them for not sharing. It was a fair rebuke, Robbins had to allow, since Ganus was always as generous as his circumstances permitted.

What Robbins could not abide was the Sahrawis' resignation in the face of starvation. As he put it, "to waste away and go down to the grave for the want of food was too much for the small portion of philosophy imparted to me to endure with fortitude." How maddening it was to persist on the barren Sahara and not make an effort to leave it while they still had strength. What sailor becalmed in the horse latitudes would not make every effort to set his vessel in motion again? Unable to fill their stomachs on snails, Robbins and Hogan now investigated the refuse around the camps. A pile of decaying camel bones had already been gnawed by dogs, but the sun had softened them. Robbins dug into a crevice with his teeth for a bit of gristle and nearly dislocated his jaw.

The next day, Robbins saw Deslisle for the first time since leaving the well near Cape Barbas. The cook was returning from the hilltop where he had been keeping the animals. He appeared relatively hearty and had better clothes than Hogan. Robbins and Hogan greeted Deslisle eagerly, but his mistress saw him at the same time and ordered him to keep moving. Anxious to speak to Robbins, Deslisle lingered, which infuriated the woman. She attacked him, cuffing and clawing his head. Deslisle did not dare strike back. She dragged him up the hill, scolding him loudly, and at the top, Mohammed knocked him down and clubbed him repeatedly. Deslisle could do nothing to defend himself. As he cried out in pain, Robbins fumed. "Never did I more ardently pant to revenge the injury of a shipmate," he recalled later. "I was desperate but knew I must be humble and see my shipmate mauled to pumice."

Near dusk, Robbins went to check on Hogan and Deslisle. He wore a new article of clothing that he had made to protect his skin from the sun. He had folded a yard-and-a-half square of the brig's colors, cut a hole in the center, and sewn up the sides, leaving holes for his arms, to approximate a shirt. His mistress had sewn a dress out of a larger section of the flag and was vainly sashaying about camp in the latest fashion of "striped bunting." Relishing the irony,

Robbins mused that this was probably the first U.S. flag to fly over the Sahara. Arriving at Hogan's master's tent, Robbins found that Deslisle was still out with the camels. Hogan was moribund. Robbins strutted around in his absurd new attire to cheer him up. "If you like this," he jested, "you should see my mistress. She has also *covered herself in glory.*" He chuckled at his own joke, but Hogan could not shake his dark cloud. His effort at laughter ended in a sorry hiccup of despair.

"Yesterday," he muttered to Robbins, "good Dick brought me some cooked snails. But our confounded master would not suffer me to eat them. I will starve soon." Robbins tried to reassure Hogan, but nothing seemed to work. He wished Deslisle would come in, but the cook still had not arrived by the time Robbins had to return to his master's tents. He never saw Deslisle again.

A blast of heat hit Riley like campfire smoke in a sudden gust, and he broke out in a clammy sweat. It had been just three days since he, Savage, Horace, Clark, and Burns had saturated themselves with water, laughing like children. Now as they labored through burning sand, chronic diarrhea plagued them. Clark and Burns and the rebellious second mate appeared wan even in their desert color. As thin as scarecrows, they looked like they might combust and vanish in a puff. Horace was already little more than a vapor.

Before the group had trudged long, Hamet assigned the men to camels. As the beasts rose, the sailors looked out on an awe-inspiring sight. Stretching to the north and south as far as they could see, dunes towered hundreds of feet high. Wind-ripped crests gave them the appearance of storm-churned sea rollers, Poseidon's anger writ in grit.

The trade winds, which had cooled their bodies under the broiling sun, "now blew like a tempest" and became their "formidable enemy," Riley wrote. "The loose sand flew before its blasts, cutting our flesh like hail stones, and very often covering us from each other's sight, while the gusts (which followed each other in quick succession) were rushing by."

On the sliding hills, the camels faltered and sank into the sand. An anxious Hamet ordered everyone to dismount. He, Seid, and Abdallah went ahead to find a route. On foot, the sailors struggled to keep up with the camels, especially on the downhill slopes. At the same time, they had to make sure that old Coho, walking with no load at all, did not lag behind, or they would be beaten.

Wind and sand. Sand, wind. They saw nothing else for two days, as the *irifi*, the region's legendary desert wind, unleashed its fury on them. The two elements sucked and scoured all the moisture out of their bodies and tore at their skin to get more. The first day, they struggled on for five hours until around dark, when they discovered a flat trough, like a "lake surrounded by mountains," where some shrubs grew. While the camels chewed the leaves and limbs of the bushes, the men pushed sand up against the saddles to form a barrier against the wind. They cooked the remainder of the mutton, pulverizing the bones with rocks so that they could eat them too. "It was sweet to our taste, though but a morsel," Riley wrote.

At dawn the next day, Hamet ordered Riley to gather the camels. He, Savage, and Clark quickly found the two strongest, which were fettered, their forelegs tied together about a foot apart, so that they could hobble around to feed but not run far. Riley went for Seid's, the spunkiest, leaving Savage the big one. The captain, who was fast learning how to handle the beasts, which were never bridled or haltered, made the camel kneel, took off its fetter, and climbed on, using a goad and soothing words to guide it.

While he was doing this, Savage made the mistake of unfettering the big camel before making it kneel. Just then, lame and recalcitrant Coho, who had given the men so much trouble by lagging, bolted to the south. Goyette, the calf, followed. Bellowing, Hamet's big camel wrenched free of Savage's grasp and dashed off at a full gallop. Abdallah's camel followed.

Riley struck his swift camel with the goad. He soon caught up with the runaways and maneuvered in front of them. He tried to head them off, but they bumped him and dodged by, at a full gallop, weaving around the dunes. The impulse to flee was contagious.

All at once, Seid's camel went berserk trying to free itself of Riley. It bolted, bucking its suddenly flexible body, bellowing and growling like a wild animal. Rafts of stinking froth flew from its mouth into Riley's face. He hung on desperately. In response, the fiendish camel lay down and rolled over, dumping him, then reared its head and gnashed its teeth against his thighs. Riley leaped back on the animal before it could rise to its feet again.

The camel's fury was spent. He had beaten it. He guided it near the others, now a good distance from camp, but he could not make the stubborn brutes turn. Fearing that he was lost in the tortuous sand hills, he stopped his camel and turned back.

The three angry Bou Sbaa came running over the dunes. Hamet shouted for Riley to make his camel lie down and to get off. Catching up, Hamet leaped on, wheeled the rising animal, and sped off with Seid and Abdallah tailing him on foot. Riley followed their tracks back to camp, where he ruefully collected some skins that Goyette had dumped. The Arabs did not return for three hours. As the time passed, Riley grew increasingly frightened for Savage, who would certainly be severely beaten for causing this trouble and might not survive it in his current state.

As the Bou Sbaa rode back into camp, Riley encouraged Savage to apologize or plead for mercy, but he refused, enraging the Arabs even more. Riley begged for forgiveness on Savage's behalf, but the Arabs, fuming and hungry for vengeance, ignored him, grabbed Savage, and beat him with their camel goads. They accused him of driving off the camels on purpose, spat at him, and pronounced him *foonta,* or bad. Savage survived, but he would suffer further from this reputation.

It was nine o'clock before they set out again, as close to north-northwest as the sand hills would allow. For two hours, they wound through passes between slopes at a trot. Then the hills became so thick and treacherous that Hamet feared for the camels and bade the men all to dismount. The Bou Sbaa went ahead to scout a route, spreading themselves out so that they could relay directions. The sailors followed with the camels, taking the utmost care to keep the beasts in line.

They walked at a miserable pace through sand heated until it felt like "wading through glowing embers." Wind-borne grit coated their bodies. For twelve chafing hours they marched with nothing to consume, finally stopping aloft on the sea of dunes, where there was no forage at all for the camels. Exhausted and frustrated, the men each had a drink of water before collapsing in comalike slumber. In the dead of night, Riley awakened with a start. He heard and felt in his shivering body a low, distant rumbling to the north that was not just the wind. The noise reverberated with the force of a hurricane. It must be a hurricane of sand, he reasoned, which will bury us alive.

He rose in a panic and woke his men, who listened in shocked silence, convinced that the distant thunder was the sound of their impending death. At first they were certain it was a noise unlike any they had ever heard before. But soon someone noticed that the rumbling, though persistent, grew no closer and the wind no stronger. Suddenly acutely aware of his mistake, Riley announced, "It's the sea!"

On October 3, Archie Robbins hiked seven miles over the hilltop to see William Porter and amuse him with his sartorial use of the Stars and Stripes. His timing was fortuitous. Porter's master and another Arab were heading up the valley to a tent where a camel had been slaughtered. Porter and Robbins carried the Arabs' muskets — "good double-barrelled pieces," Robbins noted — as they walked.

Robbins's nostrils twitched with hunger as the aroma of thornbush smoke and roasting camel filled the camp. Porter's master and his friend devoured the meat they were given and tossed the warm bones to the sailors, who tore at them with their teeth and fingernails, scraping away every shred of gristle and cracking them open for the marrow. While the Arabs drank milk afterward, the Americans went thirsty.

The following day, however, Robbins and Porter were provided for in the most unimaginable way. Among the more primitive of the Sahrawis' animist beliefs were those regarding that rare event, rain.

When dark clouds appeared, the nomads took great pains not to upset them; in fact, they were forbidden even to look at them, except through eyes darkened with kohl. Nor were they allowed to talk about them. Children's games were halted out of respect.

In this instance, the Bou Sbaa behaved to the clouds' satisfaction. In a land where rain falls as rarely as once every six years, they received their small miracle: a brief but violent shower. As soon as it began, the women took up their *geddacks* and sponges and rushed over to the rock slabs on the hills, according to Robbins. They did not set their bowls out to catch the rain, because — however perverse — this too was forbidden by Sahrawi custom. Only after the shower had passed were they free to sponge up the standing water and squeeze it into their *geddacks*. Heedless, Robbins lay on his stomach on the rocks and slurped up little rivulets. After a few minutes, the sun returned as strong as ever. He "licked and sucked" the rocks until they were dry.

The excitement did not wear off right away, and the nomads celebrated with gleeful chatter. The shower had brought something more valuable than water to Robbins too: hope. Perhaps his life did not depend entirely on the nomads. Perhaps Providence would play a role. He could hear laughter coming from the tent where the women had returned after filling a goatskin, and for once he did not resent it.

Two days later, Ganus and his sisters, Ishir and Muckwoola, set off with the camels to find water. Those who stayed behind had only snails and the dregs of the goatskins to live on. Robbins begged at neighboring tents, invoking his mistress's name to elicit generosity, but the valley was used up and the nomads were beginning to leave. As the number of tents dwindled, Robbins cast a wider circle. Five miles from the tents, looking up from the hardpan, he saw a large turbaned Arab racing toward him on a straining camel. Above his head, the man waved a gleaming scimitar ready to slice him in two. A nauseating fear overwhelmed him, yet it was tinged with relief. The end, it seemed, had finally come.

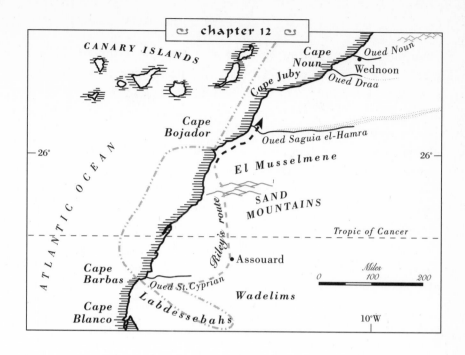

chapter 12

Honor Among Thieves

⌒◯ Captain Riley and his men had come full circle. The Sahara
had taken the *Commerce* from them, reduced them, and sent them
away, but now they were back. They could hear the waves crashing
at Cape Bojador — a fact that Sidi Hamet confirmed — over the
bones of the *Commerce*. They had regained lost ground and reached
a milestone. The news boosted the morale of the sailors, especially
those who had remained skeptical of Hamet's intentions. They quietly rejoiced at the proof that they were in fact heading toward the
Empire of Morocco. At the same time, Hamet added an ominous
fact: "You will get no more zrig," he told Riley regretfully, shaking
the collapsed goatskin.

Late in the morning of October 8, they began to see hard flat surfaces blown clean between the dunes, as if the mountains of sand

were merely piles sitting on a giant tabletop. Around noon they reached a clearing to the northeast, where they gazed out on open *hammada,* something the sailors had never thought they would be grateful to see. They were now within a day's ride of Cape Bojador and entering a more populous region of the desert, occupied by two dozen tribes. Most, including the Oulad Bou Sbaa and their rivals the Oulad Delim, were deemed "ferocious" or "savage" by Moroccans as well as by Westerners. Brisson called the Oulad Delim "so . . . rapacious, that friends, or enemies, they are almost equally to be feared."

As they neared the northern limits of the desert, they would have to penetrate the regions of the Reguibat tribe, near the Saguia el-Hamra wadi, and of the Tekna, who lived between the Saguia and Oued (wadi) Draa. North of the Draa, where the desert gave way to arid hills and then fertile valleys, lay Souss, the land unsubdued by the Sultan of Morocco and dominated by warlords with troops of mercenaries who roamed the countryside. They controlled the caravan traffic to Tombuctoo and the ransoming of shipwrecked Westerners whenever they could, both for profit and for the prestige it brought them. Hamet would have to elude them, as well as his own greedy father-in-law, who lived near Wednoon.

The sailors had hoped to bathe in, or at least gaze upon, the sea, preferably at Bojador, where they could find out whether the brig remained, but the dunes to the west did not diminish. When the breakthrough came, they headed nearly due east over deep but not piled sand. As they rode along the southern side of a ridge of dunes, the Bou Sbaa spotted two distant camels heading in a northeasterly direction. In urgent need of food and water, they lit out for them, with the sailors trailing behind.

As they approached the camels, they saw that they were loaded with goods in large tent-cloth sacks. Lashed to their sides were an earthenware pot and a few small skin bags, but there was no sign of any owner. The Bou Sbaa smelled a trap. Scanning the terrain for hidden enemies, they unsheathed their guns and primed them. They dismounted by the indolently grazing camels and motioned silently for the sailors to do the same. Only Savage, who had lagged behind on Goyette in the dash, had yet to reach the scene.

With his loaded gun ready, Hamet milled around, scanning the convoluted terrain for hidden enemies or the owner of the pack camels, who was obviously a trader. At the same time, he worked his way toward Savage, still struggling forward and vulnerable.

Stepping over a rise, Hamet nearly stumbled on a swaddled Arab fast asleep on the sand. Without making a sound, Hamet stooped and studied him, searching first for a weapon, then for an injury or a wound. He saw nothing, only a small bag of valuables by the man's head. The trader must have traveled all night; he slept as soundly as a snake that has swallowed an egg and settled in the sun. Hamet approached him and silently eased a hand toward the bag. He snatched it and backed away just as furtively. The trader did not move.

When Savage caught up, Hamet directed him behind the dune where Seid and Abdallah were rifling the trader's packs. They untied a sack and found what they were looking for: barley. Quickly they poured out about fifty pounds of the grain and stuffed it into one of their leather bags. They preserved the remaining grain as if it were their own, tying up the neck of the sack and carefully repacking it.

To the sailors, it was a curious act of thievery. Although the disappearance of fifty pounds of grain would be obvious to its owner even if the robbers vanished without a trace, they had taken the time to make everything appear in order. They could have just as easily made off with the man's camels and all his possessions and never seen him again, the sailors thought, and so they would have preferred. They were starving and did not care about the stranger. If they were going to be accomplices to a crime, they might as well take what they wanted and run.

But their masters seemed in no great hurry to depart. They rummaged through a number of smaller bags of personal effects. The bag Hamet had discovered on the slumbering trader contained the best find: barley meal, barley ground into an edible state. The Arabs dumped the meal into a bowl and stirred in some water. They wolfed down the gruel with their hands and then fixed a bowl for the sailors, who dispatched it with equal enthusiasm.

Finally, the Bou Sbaa mounted their camels and hustled the group off to the southeast, leaving the trader's camels behind.

Less than half an hour later, a man came running across the dunes, waving his arms and calling for them to stop. Hamet, Seid, and Abdallah calmly ignored him and goaded on the camels. Still, the stranger gained on them. It was the trader. "Poor devil!" Hamet said to Riley as he approached. "He does not even have a musket, and he let me take his bag while he was asleep."

Riley later admitted that he, like the others, had only one concern at the time: that they not give the barley back. "If I had a loaded musket," one of the sailors bluntly muttered, "I'd soon stop him and save the barley."

The persistent man made to head them off. Seeing that they could not escape a confrontation, the Bou Sbaa prepared their muskets as they rode. Hamet warned the stranger to keep his distance, but he approached them fearlessly. Armed with only a scimitar, he cut them off and brought them to a standstill. What the man did next shocked the sailors more than if he had pulled out a hidden gun and aimed it at them. He threw up his hands and appealed to Allah. As they looked on, mesmerized, he bowed to the ground and began to pray loudly. Then he declared that he had lost part of his property and that he knew it was they who must have taken it. "I am your brother and would rather die than commit a bad action or to suffer others to do it with impunity," he announced. "You have guns and believe you can kill me in an instant, but the God of justice is my shield and will protect the innocent. I do not fear you."

"Leave your scimitar on the ground," Hamet replied. "You have nothing to fear." He made his camel kneel, and he dismounted.

The aggrieved man, still suspicious, came forward. "Is it peace, then?" he asked.

"It is," replied Hamet, offering his hand. "Peace be with you. Peace be to your house, and to all your friends."

As the sailors stood with the camels, the Arabs sat down on the ground in a circle. Hamet did not deny that they had taken the barley. "But," he countered, "our slaves were starving to death," a fact clearly exhibited in the gaunt faces around him. "You would not have denied us a morsel, if you had been awake."

After more discussion, Hamet ordered the sailors to dust off an area on the hardpan, and he poured out the barley they had taken, showing the trader the inside of the leather bag to satisfy him. The trader loaded the barley into his own sack. They handed over what was left of the barley meal, along with a small bag of opium. Hamet assured the stranger that, other than what they had eaten, this was all they had taken. They prayed together and the man left on foot as he had arrived, seemingly bringing the affair to an end. It had cost them a little more than an hour, but they had gotten a good meal out of it — as well as the bag of valuables that Hamet had denied taking.

Hamet and his company mounted their camels and rode off to the east as fast as they could go, but Savage, who was now relegated to the lame Coho, and Horace, on Goyette, slowed them to little more than a man's walking pace. Disregarding their inferior mounts, the Bou Sbaa harangued the two laggards and beat them with their goads. They rode on all afternoon and into the night, covering fifty-six miles, according to Riley's calculations, before they heard voices ghosting on the wind from the north. The Bou Sbaa immediately stopped and listened in silence.

Fettering the exhausted Goyette, they led the other camels into a wadi, unsaddled them, and fettered them too. The Bou Sbaa checked the priming in their flintlocks and scrambled across the sand and up the bank, motioning for the sailors to follow. Unsure whether they were the hunters or the hunted, the five Commerces crept along on hands and knees, up to the dark place where earth and space seemed to meet, where the moon seemed far closer than Connecticut. At the brink, the nomads waited for the sailors to catch up and then suddenly broke out in a chorus of animal bellows, including what Riley took to be the sounds of a lion, a tiger, and "the sharp frightful yell of a famished wolf." The Bou Sbaa, more likely, were imitating the Saharan wildcat, hyena, and cheetah.

At dawn, they returned to the wadi where they had left the camels. Riley was still mystified by the Arabs' actions the night before. After half a night of hide-and-seek with an unseen enemy or potential victim, they had circled up and collapsed in exhaustion, the Bou Sbaa clutching their guns, "as if afraid they should lose their slaves." In the light of day, Riley noticed that the willowy bushes growing in the old riverbed seemed to be of a different species than they had seen before. They were thornless, taller than the big camel, and their trunks were as thick as a man's leg.

Other camels grazed here, and an old woman and a boy wandered into their makeshift camp. After conversing with the Bou Sbaa, the woman sent the boy off. He returned with goatskins and the remnants of a boiled sheep or goat. The Americans did not know what had transpired, nor did they much care. The Bou Sbaa tore the carcass apart, devoured the meat and entrails, and tossed the bones to the sailors, who crushed and ate them. They washed down the splinters with *zrig*.

Leaving the riverbed, Hamet's party resumed its journey along a ridge of high dunes. The camels, too, had been weakened by the fast pace and the lack of water. Since Burns and Clark were too frail to do anything but ride, Riley and Savage walked. The Bou Sbaa goaded any stragglers more often and more brutally now, ignoring Riley's pleas for mercy. Under this constant strain, some of the sailors showed signs of cracking.

Despite Riley's constant agitation on their behalf, one man in particular had taken to cursing him to his face. Any act of kindness only enraged the man further. "In the ravings of his distempered imagination," Riley recalled later, "he declared that he hated the sight of me, and that my very smiles were more cutting to him than daggers." The captain refused to name the belligerent shipmate but allowed that he had "transformed into a perfect savage," perhaps suggesting by double entendre that Aaron Savage, already aloof and antagonistic, had slipped another notch toward insanity, or at least blind hostility.[1]

In their ill humor, the Bou Sbaa were not pleased to see a lone cameleer approaching them from the direction of the hills. While he was still far away, they dug holes in the sand and buried two small bags. As he neared, Riley could see what his masters had known immediately. The trader had tracked them down again.

The lone Arab, more aggressive this time, accused Hamet of deceiving him. Hamet had not, as he had vowed, returned all that he had taken. Hamet earnestly denied the charge, insisting that the man satisfy himself by searching their bags. "Allah as my witness," he said, "we have nothing of yours in our possession." The trader searched in vain. As the defeated man rode off, Riley was once again impressed by the ease with which his master deceived.

When they were sure the trader was gone, the Bou Sbaa dug up the bags. Hamet told Riley, with a laugh, "The trader wanted his bags and things, but he has not got them yet." He opened a small box and showed Riley a reddish-brown substance, which was opium, and several hollow sticks as wide as a man's finger containing gold dust. The other bag held tobacco and some herb roots, which the Sahrawis smoked in a goat-bone pipe to ward off the evil eye.[2] Under its influence they fancied themselves invincible, which made the herb more valuable to them than the opium or the gold dust.

As they rode on and Riley reflected on the robbery, he grew less and less sure about the deal he had struck. He did not question his own lie, which he knew was born of necessity and uttered in good faith, but he struggled with Hamet's deceit, which seemed to have crossed the line from necessity to profit. Before Riley, the French traveler Saugnier had wrestled with the Sahrawi ethic regarding property. According to him, on the desert things stolen unperceived became rightfully the property of the thief, and things unwatched, it followed, deserved to be stolen. "In vain would the owner recognize his own property in his neighbour's tent," he observed. "He cannot reclaim it; it ceases to be his from the moment he has been negligent in its care. Hence arises this people's inclination for rapine; they do not think they commit a crime, and only follow, in this regard, a custom allowed by their laws." Riley deduced only that, on the desert at least, the Arabs "regard no law but that of superior force."

They rode hard into the night and camped late. Hungry and —
lashed by the northeast wind — bitterly cold, the men hugged the
unyielding ground and one another through the wee hours. They
rose early and, having nothing to eat or drink, rode on with no comforts. In the afternoon, they discovered tracks. Desperate for food
and water, the Bou Sbaa followed them until they found a drove of
camels grazing in a depression alongside sheep and goats rooting
among the rocks for patches of short brown moss. They approached
the herders of these animals, who invited them to their nearby camp.

In a valley half an hour away, twenty tents sat beside a thicket of
thornbushes. After introductions were made, Hamet attended to
their immediate needs, trading for a kid. Seid and Abdallah slaughtered it and gave the entrails to the sailors. Adopting nomad custom, the hungry sailors did not clean them out before roasting
them. The sailors were well aware by now that Arab manners
demanded the sharing of meals and that no one would be bashful in
claiming his portion, so when the camp's curious began to surround
them, they grew nervous of their intentions. Reaching a quick con-
sensus by whispers and nods, the sailors extracted the smoking
food from the fire and divided it with their hands. Before anyone
could insist on a share, they devoured the entrails, warm but still
raw. Their hurry was unnecessary. None of the Arabs disturbed
them. Nor would their hosts accept any of the meat Hamet offered
them. Riley took this as a good sign, indicating that the tribe had
plenty and that his party was nearing more fertile territory. These
Arabs gave them water and returned at midnight. The bowl they
offered up contained five pounds of what Riley called "stirabout or
hasty pudding" and the nomads called *lhasa,* boiled semolina with
a hole pressed in it and filled with fresh sweet milk.[3]

The sailors scooped it up with their bare hands. The hot mush
scalded their mouths and throats, but they could not control their
craving to feed. Riley commented that it was the first "kind of
bread" they had eaten since leaving the wreck. It warmed their
stomachs and had the salutary effect of soothing their dysentery-
plagued bowels. The best meal of their journey was the gift of men

they did not know and would never see again. Like so much on the Sahara, it opened their minds to the unexpected, and to small graces in the midst of adversity.

The next day, they reluctantly left these friendly Arabs and traveled ten hours northeast to reach a brackish well surrounded by a horde of men and camels. There, beasts sucked down long throaty drafts and then fed on nearby thornbushes to fill their rumens. The sharp smells of freshly belched cud and wet dung contrasted markedly with the dry whiffs of ancient dust on the *hammada*. As Riley prepared to water the camels, Hamet, having studied the crowd of cameleers, stopped him. He ushered the sailors aside. In the south, he had worried primarily about surviving the harsh environment. With just 150 miles of desert to go before they reached cultivated lands, he began to focus on negotiating the Sahrawi clans. Although his party had been greeted amiably, they were in a region dominated by the powerful and quarrelsome Tekna, a fusion of Lamta Berbers of the Oued Noun region and Maqil Arabs, part nomadic and part sedentary, living in walled villages from the fringes of the desert to the foothills of the Anti-Atlas, and the ascendant Reguibat, a tribe almost purely of Sanhaja Berber blood, though they had adopted Islam, spoke Arabic, and claimed *chorfa* status, as descendants of Muhammad. Hamet did not want to excite anyone's envy, so he ordered the sailors to sit down and keep to themselves. After a long day riding and walking, this came as a relief to Riley. "We were so extremely reduced and weak," he wrote, "that we could not without difficulty stand steady on our feet."

As Hamet had feared, trouble was not long in coming. Seid and Abdallah drew water from the well and filled a *selaï*. One of the other cameleers led his beast to it. Seid told the stranger to take his camel away. The man glared at him brazenly and declared that his camel would drink from their bowl. "Keep filling it," he added.

Seid dropped the bucket, leaped at the stranger, and punched him squarely in the face. The man staggered but did not go down. He drew his scimitar and slashed at Seid. Seid dodged, but the thrust grazed his chest, throwing him off balance. The man lunged forward, with the scimitar ready to strike again, but found himself looking down the twin barrels of Hamet's musket. Others quickly moved in, pulled the man away, and ushered him to the other side of the well. There they watered his camel and sent him on his way, muttering curses.

Hamet decided to push on. An hour's ride to the east, they reached two more wells. Recently dug and even saltier than the one they had just left, these wells had also attracted a mass of camels, but they belonged to a single owner. Hamet talked to this man and then told Riley to help with the watering of his drove. "Their owner is a good man," he said. "He will give us food." They worked until dusk and then followed the drove east three miles through the valley. The wealthy man, however, spurned them, and for once Hamet's persuasiveness failed him. They had nothing to eat.

A strong gale blew that night. The men rose early, cold and stiff and hungry, and continued on unnourished. They pushed the well-fed and watered camels harder now, keeping them at a brisk walk across fifty miles of *hammada*. They rode on until well after dark, finding little inducement to stop. When they did break, they did not stay long, rising before dawn to move on.

Around noon the next day, they encountered an abrupt rift in the plain, which they entered on a natural ramp to a deep, sand-covered riverbed and floodplain. They had reached the famed Saguia el-Hamra, a wadi stretching 210 miles across the desert like a neatly sewn scar from the slopes of the Anti-Atlas Mountains to the coast. There its mouth is dammed by a profusion of fused crescent dunes, sculpted by the trade winds, the Sahara's proof that sand trumps water. Widening to two and a half miles in places, the Saguia el-Hamra, or "red channel" — named for its clay walls, or for the blood they have absorbed during centuries of turf wars — was the area's cradle of civilization, a blooming oasis when water filled its riverbanks or, as when Hamet's party arrived there, the last stronghold of desert plants for grazing after years of drought.

The men rode due east on a firm shelf above the bed for two more hours before the Bou Sbaa announced that they saw camels. The sailors could not see them for some time; indeed, it took another four hours riding at a fast trot and kicking up dust like *ghazu* raiders before they reached the unattended drove. They searched for the owners, but whoever they were, they had seen the Bou Sbaa and sailors coming and had either hidden or gone for help. Hamet decided to avoid any sort of confrontation and ride on. At the end of the tongue of land they were on, they dropped into the powdery riverbed, kicking up the pale dust of sandstone, marl, and lime-stone laid down by the sea more than 50 million years earlier. In the distance, in the fading light, Riley saw what looked like an island in a lake. They reached it around ten o'clock, having traveled, Riley estimated, seventy miles that long day. But the desert had fooled him and his shipmates again. The lake turned out to be an oasis of bushes and stunted trees, argans and white-spine acacias with trunks twisted by the winds. The water was all underground. The Bou Sbaa cautioned the sailors not to make a noise as they entered the oasis.

They encountered no one as they silently made their way to a clearing in the center of the copse. Still, they did not risk lighting a fire. The sailors, like the Arabs, had nothing to eat that night, but at least they were protected from the wind. They slept soundly in the shelter of the oasis and in the morning had to be roused from their dreams.

At daylight on October 14, the group watered the camels and filled a goatskin at a brackish well near the bushes. Riley and his men tried eating some of the leaves but found them too salty. The Bou Sbaa brusquely urged them onto the trail again.

Before long, they dropped down a steep bank into the lowest part of the wadi, where each step of the camels broke through a crust of salt. Riley gazed in awe at the view in front of him. They had entered what appeared to be a vast, ancient bay, with embankments rising hundreds of feet in places and signs that it had once been filled nearly to the top with water.

Riley and his men now stood in what the Scottish trader Donald Mackenzie would describe in 1875 as a channel connecting the "Great Mouth," on the coast near Cape Juby, to the "great depression called El Juf" (now called the Tindouf Depression), which he claimed was five hundred miles long and reached nearly to Tombuctoo.

Mackenzie proposed clearing the sandbar that blocked the mouth, thus allowing the Atlantic Ocean to flood El Juf and create a shipping lane into the heart of Africa. In this way, Britain could advance trade with the interior, generating hundreds of thousands of pounds of profits while eliminating the dangerous and costly trans-Saharan caravan. Mackenzie's grandiose scheme was embraced by London's newspapers, which relished the vision of steamships running from Liverpool to Tombuctoo, "sending civilized influence into the interior of this vast continent" and returning with ivory, gold, and gum. However, it never came to pass.

Victorian England's fantasy for this place could hardly have contrasted more with reality. After traveling several hours through the wasteland, Hamet and his group spotted two men driving camels down the sand slopes. It was quickly grasped by every man in the party that whatever food those riders possessed, the group had to partake of. Hamet, Seid, and Abdallah rode off to intercept them while the sailors waited behind. From a distance, they watched the meeting. The two riders then continued on their way with Abdallah while Hamet and Seid returned.

"There are goats there," Hamet announced, pointing to the east-southeast. "We shall have meat soon." With threats and harsh words, Hamet and Seid drove the sailors up the most direct route, a hot, two-mile climb over steep sand hills. Coho stumbled on his lame leg, rising slowly. A little later, he toppled again. The brothers cursed the poor beast, summarily pronounced it *foonta,* and, without hesitating, left it behind. Driven to extremes by heat, hunger, and trail weariness, they seemed dangerous now, Riley thought, like "madmen."

Hamet, frustrated by the pace, pushed ahead alone. The sailors continued up the incline under the watch of Seid. At a peculiar cavity in the sand, Seid sniffed the ground like a dog and announced that the entrails of a camel had been cooked. As they emerged from the Saguia onto the desert plain again, they heard a gun fire, then saw Hamet driving a frightened shepherd and his flock of goats toward them.

Seid waded into the flock, culled out four stout goats, and drove them to Riley, who later wryly noted that the two Bou Sbaa "considered possession as a very important preliminary" to making a deal. What they did not realize was that the frightened shepherd was not alone. Like the great Bou Sbaa patriarch summoning the lions to defend his flock, the shepherd produced, out of nowhere, a wife. She was as defiant as her husband was cowed, scolding the bully brothers with contempt: "I will not part with any of the goats, even if my husband will. What is your name?"

Taken aback, Hamet told her.

"Sidi Hamet," she crowed, "how can you be such a coward as to rob an unarmed man? The whole country will ring with your infamous name and actions, Sidi Hamet!"

Seeing the ugly looks on Hamet's and Seid's starving faces, the shepherd begged her to be quiet, but to no avail. Eyes bulging, she continued to rant: "I will find a man who will avenge this injustice, Sidi Hamet!"

What the shepherd could not accomplish, Seid's musket raised to his eye and trained on her chest did. He warned her that if she said another word he would fire.

Hamet took advantage of the sudden hush to tell her that not far back they had left a good camel that had tired and that they would trade for the goats. Although she plainly did not believe him, and her mistrust would be borne out if she managed to find Coho, she had little choice but to accept. She insisted on swapping a different goat for one of the ones that Seid had selected, and the deal was done. Hamet and Seid roped the four goats together by their necks, turned them over to Riley, and then rode ahead to find the best passage back to their trail.

As hunger, thirst, the oppressive midday heat, and the yielding sand all conspired to sap their wills, Riley pressed his men to keep up the pace. Spiky euphorbias, bulbous gray plants hoarding their moisture in poisonous latex that not even the thirstiest animal would attempt to drink, studded their path. Savage, unable to resist temptation any longer, picked the leaves of a short green weed that grew among the euphorbias. "It's delicious," he announced, in a demented voice, "as sweet as honey."

"Savage, do not swallow it," Riley urged. "It might be poisonous. Wait and let me ask Sidi Hamet if it's safe."

Savage ignored him. He found more of the weed and ate it. Riley examined some and warned him that he thought it looked like Indian tobacco, better known as gagroot. Over the next two hours as Riley, Horace, and Savage, all on foot, tried to keep up with the goats and with Burns and Clark on the camels, Savage's stomach convulsed in spells until he was heaving blood. His pace slowed to a crawl. Soon the camels had disappeared over the horizon. Riley now made a calculated decision, which he later stated unapologetically: "I could not wait for him."

Faced with being left behind, Savage found reserves he did not know he still had. Over and over he stopped to retch and then ran to catch up. Riley, focused on tending to the goats and not losing sight of the camels, encouraged him but did not slow down. As he and Horace crested the summit of a hill, they stopped and scanned the terrain to find the camels, but they were nowhere to be seen. They searched further on the horizon, but all they saw was a narrow dark stripe shimmering between dune and sky. At first they did not know what it was. Riley took it to be an "extensive ridge of high woodland." Horace disagreed. "It's too dark and too smooth for land," he said.

Riley stared hard. The boy was right. It was the ocean. Riley clapped him joyfully on the back. For a moment they forgot hunger and thirst as they breathed deeply. They could smell the sea. They could taste it in their mouths. They laughed. It tasted, they thought, like freedom.

Riley found camel tracks near a breach in the face of the bluffs. He and Horace herded the goats over the edge and picked their way down the steep dunes, followed at a distance by Savage. They reached what he deemed a "tolerably inclined plane" of sand covered with lustrous egg-shaped stones in hues of ocher, charcoal, and maroon.

The stones had been buffed as smooth as bone china by ancient seas, whose violent surf had once crashed there before receding to its present reach. Riley scanned the coast for the others but could neither see nor hear any sign of them. The flush rays of the sun setting across the sea gave horizontal surfaces a rosy brilliance, etched with deep shadows. To the north, cliff faces receded in what seemed to Riley like infinite regression, imbued with futility and loneliness. If the sight had not been so magnificent, it would have crushed him.

Suddenly, Hamet emerged from behind a knoll and called him. They were much closer than Riley would have thought possible. Behind the dune and under a tarp of skins, Hamet, Seid, and Abdallah sat with several families, while camels foraged around the hidden camp. The Arabs instructed the seamen, who had just walked thirty miles, to collect brush on the steep bank and to place it around the camp as a windscreen and for use in the fire.

Savage was still retching. Riley made him a bed and left him to rest. When he returned with an armful of brush, however, he found Seid beating him for not helping. Riley pleaded with him to leave Savage alone. He tried to convince him that he was too sick to work and that he himself would do Savage's chores. Seid grudgingly relented.

Hamet slaughtered a goat, severing its head and holding its neck over a bowl to catch the blood. He slashed its hide free of its legs and extracted the carcass from the skin through the neck cavity, preserving the skin in one piece. He butchered the meat and gave the intestines to the seamen to boil. They drank the resulting broth and shared a small piece of meat as well. Riley called the meal "a seasonable relief."

In the night, the Arabs fed the men a barley pudding and camel's milk, but they refused to serve Savage, who was still ill. Riley kept a piece of meat for him and gave him some of his pudding. Hamet saved Savage's portion of pudding to give to him later, but in the morning, while they were preparing to break camp, Abdallah devoured it.

They now proceeded between the bluffs and the shore, along a plain of sandstone and lime-cemented sands, the seafloor of another age, filled with the fossils of fish and mollusks and littered with centuries' worth of bleached snail shells. Although there were now five goats to tend to, Hamet having bought two more from the nomads, Riley did not have to worry about losing his way if he lagged behind; he only needed to follow the coast. Savage had a long day ahead, but Riley was in a better position to help him now that everyone had eaten and the Bou Sbaa were less edgy.

At dusk they came upon an Arab encampment. Hamet and Seid ingratiated themselves with the leader, a man named Hassar. His band was also traveling north, and in the course of the evening Hamet and Hassar agreed that they should proceed together for the increased safety of all. Hassar had other motives as well. He was intrigued by the Christian slaves. As the hour grew later and the camaraderie warmer, he made an offer of camels and other goods for Horace. Seid, who claimed to personally own both the boy and Savage, began to haggle with Hassar.

This was an ominous and disturbing turn of events. When two Arabs begin negotiating, they expect to reach a deal. Asking the price of an item or making a counteroffer, as Seid did, commits one to a process in which two reasonable people acting in good faith should be able to arrive at an agreement. (This explains why a Westerner who casually asks the price of an object for sale in an Arab market often finds the merchant overly aggressive, and also why, when the Westerner suddenly breaks off a negotiation, the merchant is insulted.) Hassar now had a right to expect his offer to be either accepted or countered. When Riley realized what was taking place, he objected. Seid scoffed at him.

Only the influence and diplomacy of Hamet prevented Seid from closing the deal. Hassar, who had offered camels and merchandise for Horace, backed down calmly, perhaps figuring that if they traveled together, time was on his side. It was clear that Seid was eager to sell the boy.

Over the next two days, the group traveled north about forty miles, passing more camps and more stands of bushes. Hamet slaughtered another goat, feeding the sailors meat and entrails. Hassar's wife, Tamar, whom Riley called "an uncommonly intelligent woman," fixed them *lhasa* and talked to Riley in broken Spanish.

When she was younger, she had helped rescue some Spaniards whose vessel had wrecked on the coast. Her father had held three of the sailors hostage while she had accompanied the Spanish captain to Lanzarote in the Canary Islands to retrieve goods for their ransom. It was simply the way things worked on the Sahara. Tamar promised Riley that he and his shipmates would not go hungry in her company.

Near dark on the second day, they reached the mouth of a deep wadi, probably, though Riley did not name it, the Draa, a thousand-mile-long channel that drains the southern slopes of the Anti-Atlas Mountains. They descended to it by the sea and discovered an Arab camp on the beach. Hamet stopped to talk to the head of the camp. The man then took Riley aside and asked him in a patois of Spanish and Arabic, "Have you a friend in Swearah?"

"Yes," Riley answered in Spanish.

"Do not lie," the man warned. "If you do, you will have your throat cut. If you have told Sidi Hamet this merely to get off the desert and to get food, he will pardon that pretext and deception now, though he will sell you and your friends to the highest bidder. In a few days, you will reach a river of running water and houses, and if you persist in lying, he will kill you."

Riley did not hesitate. "I am incapable of lying to Sidi Hamet," he responded indignantly. "Everything that I have stated is the truth. He has saved my life, and he will be well rewarded by my friend and by our Almighty Father." Hamet listened as intently as the old man did and, Riley judged, with better understanding.

Hamet nodded. "You will see Swearah in several days," he said.

When they caught up with the others, the man and his young sons guided them across the mouth of the wadi. They waded through a hundred yards of hip-deep salt water. On the far bank, beneath a steep rise, Riley noticed that one of the man's sons had a pair of kerseymere pants that had belonged to Savage. The chain of theft and barter by which the pants had arrived there was likely long, but to the captain the only thing that mattered was that they go back to their rightful owner, who needed them. Riley begged Hamet and Seid to buy the pants. Seid traded a piece of blue cloth, which he wore as a shirt, for them, and gave them to Riley. He objected when Riley began to give the pants to Savage. "He is foonta," he insisted. "Give them to Clark or the boy." But Riley handed them to the second mate.

At dark Riley and Horace accompanied the Bou Sbaa to a *friq* by the sea. Here the Arabs gave them a pile of dried mussels, which they carried back to camp and shared with Savage, Clark, and Burns. That night, Hamet, Seid, and Abdallah slaughtered the remaining goats. After the Arabs battled over their shares of the entrails and meat, all stewed together in a pot, there was none left for the sailors. Their only sustenance came from the mounting evidence that they were at last about to leave the Sahara. But Hamet warned Riley that the region they were about to enter, the populated perimeter, was in many ways more dangerous for them than the desert itself. "Many robbers and bad men inhabit these parts," he told him.

The next day, October 16 — a date that would gain historical significance for Napoleon's arrival at St. Helena — they set out early on a slow, tedious passage along the rocky, eroded seashore, picking their way as inconspicuously as thirty people accompanied by livestock could. With guns drawn, the Bou Sbaa herded Savage, Clark, and Burns on the camels while Riley and Horace kept up on foot, walking and running. The sailors were never left alone now. If one had to stop, a Bou Sbaa stayed with him. As the day wore on, Horace's strength faded. The boy's frequent stops made the Arabs increasingly testy, and he bore the brunt of their frustration.

By sunset they had gone only fifteen miles. Afraid to stop in these parts, they continued on into the night. Around midnight, at the edge of a wadi, Riley and Horace swapped places with Savage and Clark, who fell back with the women and children walking mutely through sand drifts. It took nearly two more hours to cross the gulf. By the time they climbed up the far slope onto an inclined plane of more drifts, Savage could not keep up even with the women and children. Riley himself was fading in and out of wakefulness on his camel when Clark's cry jarred him awake. "They're flogging Mr. Savage!" he yelled.

Riley tumbled down from his camel and ran to the rear. Passing Clark, he found Seid and Hassar standing over Savage. He was unconscious, but Seid kept beating him with a goad. Hassar grabbed Savage's beard in one hand and pulled it to expose his throat. In his other hand he drew back his scimitar.

Riley took several determined steps, crouched, and butted Hassar hard, knocking him off his feet. He quickly grabbed and lifted Savage. "Water, please!" Riley begged. Enraged, Hassar climbed back to his feet, raised his scimitar, and lurched toward Riley. Just then Hamet arrived and spat out several harsh phrases of Arabic that stopped Hassar. The rest of the Arabs gathered around. Their enemies were near, and they believed that Savage was being purposely obstinate, heedlessly endangering them. They wanted to kill him.

Riley pleaded with Hamet. "Savage only fainted from exhaustion and illness," he explained. Hamet did not understand; to Riley's surprise, the Arab had no concept of fainting. But at Riley's insistence, Hamet had a camel brought up and water given to Savage. When he revived, Riley noticed tears in Hamet's eyes. The trader was clearly angry and fearful — it would have been costly for him to lose one of the sailors, whose ransom represented his only chance to appease his merciless father-in-law — but Riley sensed that he also felt some sympathy for the man who had almost been killed. Hamet ordered Clark and Savage to be put on the camel together to support each other and told Riley to ride another with Horace. "The English are foonta — you see even our women and children can walk and run," he gibed.

The insult nettled Riley. "I will go on foot," the captain insisted. He mustered the camels and began to drive them on. Hamet laughed at *el rais* the indignant, whose support of his men and boldness had enhanced his character in the Arabs' eyes, even Hassar's once he had calmed down. "Come and walk with me, Rais," Hamet said, beckoning Riley with his arm. "Leave the camels to the others. Good Riley, you will see your children again, inshallah."

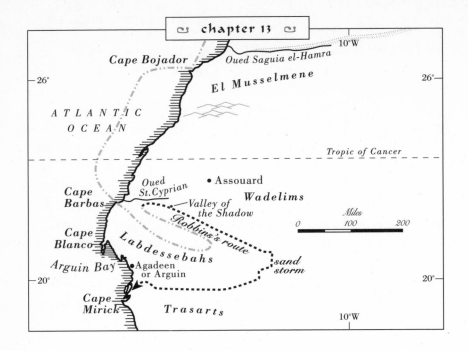

Skeletons

~~ From the Valley of the Shadow of Death, Ganus's little band — Sarah, Ishir, Muckwoola, his mother, the three children, and Robbins — had begun drifting to the southeast the day after Robbins had been accosted by the lone scimitar-wielding Arab. The man had raced up to him on the plain, brandishing his weapon and angrily demanding, "Soo-mook en tar?" — What is your name?

"Robbinis, Robbinis!" he had replied.

"Me-nane jate?" he asked, and Robbins pointed in the direction of his master's tent. "Ille-mein en tar?"

"To Ganus," Robbins answered.

"He seemed, by his conduct, to know my master, and said no more," Robbins noted, "but eyed me very sharply as I walked hastily from him." Rattled, Robbins returned to the camp, which had been abandoned now by all but a few families. Early the next morning, Ganus and his sisters had at last returned with water. The group left the valley that same day, riding off with another family — twenty Arabs and one American, with four tents and sixty camels.

For ten days they drifted southeast into the interior. One day they procured a camel head from a *friq* they passed. They baked it that night in a hole in the sand and ate regally. Then they turned due east into hillier country, where the grazing was better and where there were clumps of twisted acacia trees, one of the most useful plants on the desert. Though Robbins made no mention of it, the nomads extracted its resin to treat stomach ailments and eye problems and to improve blood clotting; they chewed its wood to relieve distress caused by drinking too much salty water; its berries they crushed for dye.

Here, "having retired to the most secret place," according to Robbins, they slaughtered a two-year-old *jmel*. "Before the skin was off, five or six Arabs came bounding over the sandy desert to partake of it," he recorded, as dismayed as Riley had been at the expansiveness of a Saharan feast. As they butchered the camel, they sliced off hunks of the hump, which Robbins described as "like the brisket of an ox," and ate it raw. The women carved off long pieces of lean meat to hang in the sun for drying. "Joy seemed to pervade every heart," Robbins observed, as they stewed the entrails in paunch water. He was not disappointed by his portion. For the first time since reaching the desert, he fully sated his appetite.

The following morning, Robbins assisted in preparing and preserving the camel hide, which they sliced into sections and threw into the fire. Once the pieces were dry and the hair had been singed off, they packed this jerky away for future meals. Vistors, some friends, some strangers, arrived periodically. Ganus and Sarah shared with them equally, cooking meat and serving *zrig*. Robbins could not but be impressed by their generosity. By American standards, it was prodigal. Tomorrow did not seem to exist for them until it arrived.

Among the callers was Hogan's master, with Hogan. The sailors embraced, much buoyed by the sight of each other. For a moment they could ignore the fact that they were being carried into the interior, farther from Mogadore. Hogan, who had put on some weight and regained his spirit, received a generous helping of the feast. "He tore off the meat from the hard, unyielding neck of the camel like a tiger," Robbins recalled. But before he had satisfied his hunger, Hogan stopped himself and stashed away a hunk for Deslisle, who had been left at camp. Then, summoned by his master, he went off, as quickly as he had come.

Robbins would never lay eyes on Hogan again.

Ganus now led his band south and west through a hilly, sandy wilderness. They were besieged by the *irifi*. At fifteen miles per hour, a desert wind picks up sand and dust and whisks it across the plain. At thirty miles per hour, it creates conditions of almost zero visibility. When the *irifi* reaches sixty miles per hour, as it is known to do, it blasts lentil-size grit through tents and clothes, hones sandstone hills smooth, and drives migratory birds to the coast, where many drink seawater out of desperation and die. Large mammals stampede before it as if from a forest fire.

For three days, the wind punished them, casting a demonic red glow on the horizon and making Robbins wonder if he was not at last approaching the gates of hell. More galling still was the fact that this same wind, gusting out over the Atlantic and carrying sand miles out to sea, was a part of the mariners' beloved east-to-west trade wind, the steady gale they relied on for crossing the Atlantic. It would have carried the *Commerce* on its homeward voyage.

"The atmosphere was as filled with hot sand as ours is with snow in a snowstorm," Robbins recalled. "The vertical rays of the sun beating upon a body almost naked — the sand filling the eyes constantly exposed — the feet sinking, ankle deep, into the sand at every step, made travelling all but destruction." They could not erect a tent for shelter either — the shifting sand would not hold pegs.

So they kept moving. With heads down, they rode or walked alongside the camels, constantly strafed from behind. Robbins's ears, nose, and sometimes his mouth filled with grit. He lived inside his own head as sight and sound, other than the monotonous roar of the wind, were virtually nil. As he walked, the clinging sand chafed his skin, rubbing him raw between the legs. His cracked throat plagued him. The sand obsessed him. During lulls in the wind, he tried desperately to rid himself of it, but without water it was impossible. Frantic, he caught his urine and washed his face and body with it.

On October 23, Ganus steered his band due south. The wind finally moderated, and at midday they stopped and pitched camp. Ganus's son, Elle, told Robbins that "Joe," the name the Arabs used for William Porter, was in a tent nearby and that he would show him the way. They set out immediately.

A few miles outside camp, they stopped at a tent where they found one of Savage's former masters, with Ganus and Porter's master, about to slaughter a camel cow. Ganus told Robbins to gather brush to feed the fire. With massive root systems for collecting the desert's scant nutrients, the bushes grew fifty feet apart. For three hours, Robbins gathered wood to feed the fire over which the Arabs stewed a kettle of entrails and meat. As a reward for this work, they tossed Robbins a fetus, the size of a rat, that they had found in the cow. Robbins was not in a position to reject any food, no matter how unappetizing. He roasted it in the sand and coals beneath the kettle of stew. Fearing that someone might take it from him, he soon dug it up and gobbled it down while it was still steaming hot. He noted later only that "extreme hunger made this a delicious meal."

Porter's master urged Ganus to let Robbins visit Porter, who was ailing. Ganus agreed, and at sunset, Robbins finally reached his shipmate, who, he discovered, had been suffering from, among other things, a massive headache for several days. Porter was also sandblind. The glare of the sun had begun to kill the cells in the outer layer of his corneas, the covering of the iris and pupil. With this condition, called ultraviolet keratitis but more commonly known as snow blindness, the dead cells create a stippling effect, and in severe cases, like Porter's, the cells mass and slough off, leaving the unprotected eye especially susceptible to airborne grit. Porter could now make out only things very near to him. His eyes were swollen and squinted.

As his sight had worsened on the desert, he had been unable to keep up with his master's family. One day in frustration, his master had beaten him into the dust, then left him behind. Porter lay where he fell for twenty-four hours, while the sun and the wind robbed him of his senses, just as they leach color from bones. He was left with only the agony of his throbbing head and thirst. All his sensations, some ebbing some flowing, seemed to be converging on the moment when his spirit would abandon his body to the jackals and his corpse would join the company of skeletons on the Zahara.

But before Porter's spirit could escape and he could be relieved of his miseries, his master's brother had returned on a camel to retrieve him. In an attempt to heal him, the Arabs had bled him from the head by making cuts in his skin with a *l'mouse,* or jackknife.

Gaunt and pale, Porter had sunk into a deep torpor and, it seemed to Robbins, had lost his will to recover. Although Robbins was loath to sound preachy, believing that the "cant of advising in such a case rather aggravates than mitigates sorrow," he realized that he himself was undergoing a spiritual transformation on the desert. He could think of no other way to urge Porter to buck up: "It is God's will that we suffer," he pleaded with him. "We must make the best we can of our situation, as wretched as it is." Robbins left Porter reluctantly, knowing that he might never see his friend again.

The next day, Ganus's clan packed up their tents and traveled southwest over deep sand. They had run out of water, and Robbins finally sensed urgency in their behavior. In the evening, they rested for a few hours and then set out again after midnight, hurrying along under a canopy of iridescent stars. At sunrise, they stopped only long enough to pray. Shortly afterward, they arrived at a plain that Robbins described as flatter than the sea in a dead calm. Even the dunes withered in an abrupt line before it.

Robbins called his first steps on this pocked, fossilized terrain "the most gloomy entry I ever made upon any part of the earth." Protruding stones made walking dangerous. Only the camels' hooves moved easily over the unyielding hardpan. No evidence of life appeared anywhere — no shrubs, no weeds, not even the meddlesome flies. In all directions, Robbins saw "the genius of *famine* and *drought*"; yet this disturbing view had its consolations. For a change, he did not feel like they were wandering aimlessly. He was sure Ganus knew where he was headed or he never would have entered such a place. Indeed, they raced across the desolate plain with a desperation Robbins found reassuring: he had reached the bottom, a place on the Sahara that even the Arabs found intolerable.

Just before sunset, to everyone's relief, they walked onto sand again. Several hours later they reached a fold in the surface with shrubs for the camels to graze on and stopped for the night. They had covered some ninety miles without drinking a sip of water.

At daylight, they set out to the west at a full rack. While the nomads showed no signs of weakness, riding even harder than they had the previous day, Robbins felt like he was dying of thirst. At noon, he found some relief at a tent, where they were given a drink of water and he found and ate a few roots and sprouts. As they continued toward the coast, the land gradually became less dreary, until they were winding past scrubby hillocks of sand, clay, and shrubs. After dark these grew denser. They threaded their way through a maze of mounds and stones, the only sounds coming from the complaining beasts. They finally stopped at midnight to eat and to let the camels graze. After sharing some meat, which though charred in the fire was as tough as leather, they set off again.

Night merged into wearying morning. The sun rose unobstructed, alone in the house of the gods, at their backs as they entered the east end of a promising valley surrounded by high rocky hills. Robbins could hardly believe his eyes when he saw in the distance what appeared to be a shimmering tower of smooth white marble. He believed they were approaching either a casbah for the defense of a city or the palace of a Moorish prince. As they advanced, he noticed approvingly the valley's grassy floor, which though strawlike from drought was the first groundcover he had walked on in Africa. At length, the white structure came into focus. Seventy feet high, a hundred long, and sixty wide — it was a block of stone.[1]

"I came to this astonishing monument — went round it — examined it as minutely as I possibly could, and could not discover upon it the least trait of human art," he observed. "My expectations were blown away by the wind that whistled round it."

Several hours later, around noon, Ganus located a *bir*. Robbins looked down through the well's triangular superstructure into the void. It was too dark to tell whether it held any water. As the well diggers had penetrated deeper into the hard earth, they had broadened the shaft at the top and added cross braces, which also served as ladders for users to clear sand from the bottom. Robbins shook his head in disbelief that the nomads did not bother to cover their wells with lids, which would have prevented this problem and cut down on evaporation.

In breathless silence, Ganus lowered the bucket, a wooden hoop with a tanned goatskin suspended from it. The pop of the stiff skin against water broke the tension. Amid their excited chatter, Ganus pulled up the bucket, holding about three gallons, and examined the liquid. It was green from stagnation and at the same time reddish from the dried camel dung that had blown into it. "It was with the greatest difficulty that I could force it into my throat, or retain it there when I had," Robbins said. They filled just two goatskins with the foul water.

Over the next five miles, as they exited the valley to the southwest, Robbins carried a bowl full of the water, deriving a small degree of comfort from determining for himself when to take a sip, no matter how disgusting. That evening, they used it to moisten their dried meat, which was so hard that after roasting it they had to grind it into meal to make it edible. Fortunately, the next day Ganus learned from a traveler of better water nearby. He ordered camp to be made and then took Ishir and Muckwoola with him to find the well.

The sisters returned the following day with skins of fresh water and some dried fish, but Ganus did not. In his absence, the women fed Robbins only fish skins and treated him with contempt as they wandered idly northwest in search of grazing for the camels. After four days, Ganus reappeared, to Robbins's relief, but with nothing other than a piece of tent cloth to show for his absence. Early the next morning, however, he awakened Robbins and they set out together with Ishir and Muckwoola, driving the camels to the west all day. Ganus had never taken him on his water runs before, which made Robbins suspect that something was up. They reached the coast as the salmon-tinted sun sank into clouds on the horizon, like a coin slipping into a bank.

With mixed emotions, Robbins gazed out on the ocean for the first time since being carried onto the Sahara. It was a month since he had been left behind by his shipmates. The Atlantic waves, which had thrilled his northbound shipmates with the promise of home, pierced southbound Robbins like a knife in the back. He had other worries too, but he barely had time to reflect on a fact of which he was now certain — Ganus was about to sell him — when the camels took their first tentative steps down the slope. Smelling the sweet vapors of the wells, the beasts launched into a headlong dash toward the bottom.

Robbins leaned back to keep from sliding onto his mount's craned neck. He clutched its shoulders in his legs, while with his hands he grasped at the saddle battering his tailbone like a buckboard. The lead camel, maddened by the presence of water, bolted maniacally toward the wells, and as the drove of twenty pursued it down a precipice just north of Cape Mirik, the front-runners — under Ganus, Ishir, and Muckwoola — kicked up sand like birdshot. Robbins saw blue sky, then black ocean, then his mount's wire-hair head. Then the whole cycle, a blazing blur, repeated with each jolt of the camel. The ground rose and receded beneath him. Obstacles surged up and vanished in a blink.

Robbins hit speeds he had never experienced before, not on horseback, not on a ship. He prayed that the camel knew what it was doing. He had no control over it. He cursed the refractory beasts. Even on a good day, they triggered conflicting emotions in him. He considered them "odious and deformed," yet he recognized their worth. On the desert, they were "noble" saviors. Their arrival with bags of *zrig* or water elicited "joy bordering on delirium." But while the Arabs believed camels were blessed and that anyone who fell from one was protected by Allah, Robbins did not share their faith. If he fell now, he would most likely break his neck and be trampled. If the camel stumbled at this speed, he could be crushed. He cursed the Arabs for not using a bit, a bridle, or stirrups. Somewhere in his lurching mind, he recalled the voice of Porter, who had witnessed his master's traverse of the bluff above the boat wreck: "An Arab on a camel can descend a precipice that will kill an American." As he raced down the slope, Robbins prayed that the magic was in the camel, not in the Arab.

Ganus's drove came tearing into the crowd below, "a great multitude of camels," and pulled up, frothing and growling. No one paid them any more notice than if they had just dropped in for tea. Around a number of wells, Arabs noisily watered their droves or restrained their beasts while waiting their turn. Others stood around, cooking, talking, or trading.

Trembling, Robbins made his camel kneel and dismounted, thankful to be on the ground again and unaware that he had reached a crossroads. He was closer both to freedom and to lasting servitude than he knew. Ganus had indeed brought him to the communal wells to sell him, as was the common practice among the Sahrawis. Yet just to the south was the territory where the coastal Arabs had a pact with the British to exchange all castaways for a cash reward.

At the plentiful wells, Robbins drank as much water as he wanted. He imbibed wholeheartedly, like a sailor in port for the first time in months, "for thirst past, thirst present, and thirst to come," as Melville would put it in *White Jacket*. That night, he, Ganus, Ishir, and Muckwoola slept under a large bush with other nomads near a fire. Ganus and his sisters rose early to water the camels, which drank deeply for the third time in five days.

Robbins had kept a keen eye on Ganus, but he had detected no overt signs that his master was trying to sell him. Now, however, Ganus showed unusual concern for his slave's filthy condition. He made Robbins remove his cutoff trousers and give them to Ishir and

Muckwoola to wash. Naked except for a section of the *Commerce's* American flag, which hung from his waist, Robbins tended to the camels while the sisters scrubbed his pants and hung them from a camel to dry. Then Ganus mounted his *jmel* and told Robbins to get on behind him.

They set out with a stranger at a fast clip to the south. Coming across fishermen on the coast with a fresh catch, Ganus bought and roasted fish for their breakfast. At midafternoon they reached a bluff over a sizable bay to the north of Cape Mirik, and they descended a trail to the beach at the head of the bay. Even this considerable body of water, which Robbins could not name, was unable to escape the dominion of the desert; low tide had pocked its dappled surface with peaks of sand.

From several shallow wells beneath the bluffs they tasted the water, which was so brackish only the camels could drink it. At last they reached a village of tents and lean-to huts, where they dismounted. As Robbins looked at the first fixed dwellings he had seen in Africa, he had a sinking feeling. Nomad camps were abysmal, both austere and disheveled, as unpleasant to the nose as to the eye, but this was worse. The stench of smoldering sewage permeated the place, and bone piles bespoke another age. At least with the nomads, every situation was by nature temporary. Life was miserable, but the next day it changed. The static squalor of this place struck dread in his heart.

The man who had accompanied them led Ganus off to a hut, leaving Robbins where he stood. In a trance, he gazed at the bay and at the point of Cape Mirik, which stretched out to sea. He studied the lean-tos around him, built of crotched branches hammered into the sand ten feet apart and supporting a horizonal beam. Other branches extended from the beam to the ground to form a roof, which was thatched with seaweed. "Lest they should blunder upon something that looks like the convenience and comfort of civilized life," observed Robbins, thoroughly cynical by now, "they are careful to make them so low that a human being cannot stand erect in one of them." Inside, they slept on beds of the same seaweed.

Soon, Ganus returned with several Arabs of the Oulad Delim

tribe, the purest of the Beni Hassan–descended bedouin tribes in the western Sahara. The Oulad Delim were feared warriors, "Sons of the Gun," a tribe with which the Bou Sbaa alternately traded and feuded.

Ganus had adopted a stern, rigid demeanor. He was no longer the relatively considerate master Robbins had come to know but a stranger. He prodded the sailor and told him to walk around. A Delim wearing a blue frock to his calves and a white haik examined him as he would an animal for sale. "I suspected he was about to open my mouth to judge of my age by my teeth, and examine my feet to see if I had been *foundered* by *high living* with Ganus," Robbins noted sardonically.

The Delim, Mohamet Meaarah, was better groomed than Ganus and seemed of higher status. He looked to be a little over thirty and had an open, ingenuous face, reassuring Robbins about his new circumstances.

Meaarah pronounced Robbins *bono*. A deal, the sailor now discovered, had already been struck contingent on his passing muster. With no further ceremony, Meaarah led him off to another hut, and Ganus rode away without so much as a good-bye.

Robbins believed Meaarah had come to the coast to buy fish, but he was probably collecting the *horma,* a tribute paid family-to-family by a *zenaga* tribe to a master tribe. Meaarah fed his bony Christian slave dried fish, which he got from the fishermen. It was then that it dawned on him that Robbins, wearing only a scrap of American flag and a rag of gazelle skin, was absurdly dressed. "Have you no other clothes?" he asked.

"No," Robbins replied, "this morning Ganus took my trousers and my shoes, which are worn out anyway."

"Ganus is foonta for taking them," Meaarah declared, angry at the Bou Sbaa's greed. "I will retrieve them." Though the trousers were long gone, Meaarah did return with the shoes. He did not indicate by what means he had gotten them. He gave Robbins a section of a haik to wear and then departed into the desert, leaving his new slave with an elderly *zenaga* fisherman. For the moment, Robbins was at rest. But he was not at ease.

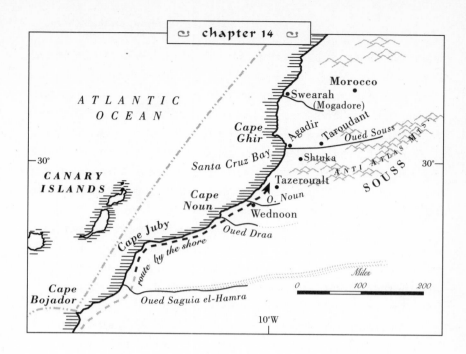

chapter 14

Wednoon
and the Atlas

◷❧ On the morning of October 19, three days after seeing the ocean, Riley, Savage, Horace, Clark, and Burns were roused from a brief, lethargic slumber. They had traveled fifty miles the previous day and through most of the night. Shortly after dawn they set out again, forcing their cold, weary bodies back into motion. Their path lay between the first and second banks from the sea, stone-pocked dunes sheltering a sloping groove of sand.

North of the Draa, they had entered Souss, on the shoulders of the Sahara, where the Anti-Atlas Mountains reached down from the northeast tentatively, like fingers touching a stove. In 1815, not only were Moulay Sulayman and the *makhzen,* or ruling class of Morocco, unable to control the Sahara, they were defied by this southern region of their would-be kingdom.[1] Two independent city states, Tazeroualt and Wednoon, had sprung up on the cusp of the great void, thriving on lawlessness, extortion of travelers, and the ransoming of Christian slaves who shipwrecked there or came up from the Sahara. The two states had also come to control the lucrative caravan traffic to the interior. Joseph Dupuis, who served as British vice-consul and agent for the United States in Swearah before the War of 1812, called the natives of Souss "more bigoted and cruel than even the remoter inhabitants of the Desert" (Robert Adams, p. 130).

As horizontal rays of sun spiked across the rocky eastern horizon, the five sailors made out vague saturnine shapes above the plain. With guarded enthusiasm, they nudged and whispered to one another. Unless this was another cruel illusion, the looming contours appeared to be proper hills, not dunes.

The sun climbed in the sky, and the sailors' imaginations brimmed. What lay behind those hills? Why not streams of icy running water? Fruit trees and onion fields that rivaled Wethersfield's? Civilized people?

Their path gave evidence of steady camel traffic. Around noon, they saw to the northeast the black tops of mountains. The sight bolstered their burgeoning confidence at a critical time. They had not slept for more than four hours in the past thirty. By this point, they had each lost more than half their original body mass. Riley, the biggest of them, would later find that he weighed less than 120 pounds. Savage, in particular, was barely hanging on.

Before nightfall they entered a deep valley heading south through bare black hills and then turned southeast in another valley on a well-trod path. They soon came to the banks of a river, where bullrushes and bushes resembling dwarf alders flourished, but the bright green water in the stream, which was about thirty feet wide and two deep, was brackish and undrinkable.[2]

Across the river, in another stream, a troop of men watered several dozen remarkably fine horses and a few camels. Hamet and his companions hailed these men and then crossed the briny stream to the good one, where fish surfaced and splashed. While the sailors eyed the fish hungrily, the Bou Sbaa ignored them. The horse riders bolted south along the river. After they had watered their camels, Hamet and Hassar led their group toward the sea, where Hassar's women pitched tents in the sand. Having traveled nearly ninety miles in two days, they cooked a goat and ate voraciously.

They left the sea the following day around noon and climbed up a path in a ravine between two slopes at the foot of what Riley described as "high mountains." As rough as the terrain still was, the sailors rejoiced at seeing the solid slopes of hillsides, with nooks and crannies where plants and trees grew. However, a growing sense of uneasiness pervaded the Arabs now that they had left the desert proper. When one of Hassar's young sons found a three-gallon earthen pot used for boiling and started lashing it to his camel as they might do with any found item on the desert, Hassar and Hamet rebuked him harshly and made him leave it. They had entered a zone where it was dangerous to give or even suggest offense.

That evening they camped in a farm clearing next to a heap of barley straw, a sight wondrous to the sailors in its very ordinariness. They had reached cultivated land at last. They celebrated by roasting a slab of goat that had been hanging from one of the camels for four days. "Some of my comrades, as if their taste had become depraved by the rage of hunger, declared that putrid meat was far preferable to fresh; that it wanted neither salt nor pepper to give it a relish, and that if ever they got home again, they should prefer such food," Riley wrote, granting that the aged meat was tender and flavorful. After eating, they made beds of fresh straw. Having slept on hardpan or sand for so long, resting their heads on nothing but their bony arms, they found the straw "softer and sweeter than a bed of down strewn over with the most odoriferous flowers."

In the morning, Riley, Savage, Clark, Burns, Horace, and their masters approached Oued Noun from the south. Although Moulay Sulayman, like many sultans before him, could not claim to control this region, the 550-mile river rising in the mighty Atlas Mountains east of Marrakech and terminating at the Atlantic did mark the southern frontier of his realm, as he perceived it, and of civilization, as he defined it.

The sailors had no expectations of what the Noun should look like and thus no disappointment upon reaching a shallow, fifteen-foot-wide stream. Nor did they care that the famous river, drained of strength by drought, petered out somewhere to the west, not in the Atlantic but in a dead-end dune. They had reached the end of the desert at a place where the pebble-bottomed Noun curled through a cultivated valley lined with date trees and blooming shrubs. Cows, sheep, and donkeys grazed on green grass, and the sailors reveled in sights that two months before they would not even have noticed. They plunged their heads into the cool northwest-flowing stream and drank until their bellies swelled. Afterward they sought the shade of the fig trees and slept for two hours.

They had almost reached Wednoon, a town on the wadi forty miles inland; in theory, they were just a week's travel from Swearah. Moreover, Sidi Hamet was now on familiar turf. His wife was from Wednoon, and he had twice journeyed from there to Tombuctoo. Wednoon was a magnet for northbound travelers off the Sahara, a place where the long deprived found provisions and the pleasures of society, where the naïve lost their djellabas, and even the wise were often outmaneuvered by the wise and also powerful. Many Christians being carried north for ransom had suffered heartbreak and a protracted stay at Wednoon after being bought by local middlemen or powerbrokers, who often worked the men until they were nearly dead before selling them for head money.

After roaming the desert in captivity for two years, Robert Adams of the *Charles* had reached the town in August 1812. His hopes of continuing on to Swearah ended when an Arab named Abdallah bel Cossim bought him and put him to work in his fields.[3] When Adams struck bel Cossim's cruel son, Hameda, in self-defense, he was beaten until blood dripped from his ears. When he refused to kiss Hameda's feet in apology, his master shackled him and barely fed him for two months. Bel Cossim finally sold Adams to keep from losing his investment to starvation. During his captivity in Wednoon, Adams saw one sailor-slave stabbed in the chest and murdered by his master. Two others lost hope and converted to Islam, the mark of circumcision changing their lives forever.

Hamet knew that if his presence were made known in the town, he would risk being coerced into selling the Christians to Sheik Ali, his father-in-law, or to Sheik Beyrouk, the ruler of Wednoon. Thus he decided to bypass Wednoon. In the late afternoon he woke the sailors and took them to a nearby hut, where he had bought a honeycomb. Hassar's hungry men had caught wind of the meal and loitered around, hoping to share in it. Balancing a bowl containing the hive on his knees, Hamet distributed sections to the sailors with one hand while holding his gun in the other in case Hassar's men abandoned their tenuous hold on self-restraint. The sailors attacked their portions like bears, swallowing along with the rich honeycomb the tender young bees that filled it. Tears rolled down their hollow cheeks as they ate the calorie-laden gold. They were so sated that they fell asleep again under a palm tree until dark.

At night, after the Americans had gathered the firewood as usual, the Arabs fed them a pudding made with argan oil, a dietary staple in Souss, the only place where the argan tree grows and where it was not unusual to see goats sitting in the branches of trees, like so many overgrown crows, eating the oblong green fruit. The goats passed the fruit's pits, which were obtained in this way, Riley observed, by the women and children, who cracked the shells with stones and pressed the meat inside for oil. Except for Riley, who was too full from the honey to eat again, the sailors downed this pungent food, which they found delicious, preferring argan oil even to butter. They slept outside the thornbush hedge surrounding a whitewashed and domed saint house, the mausoleum of an Islamic holy man. Riley mentioned only that they had "found a good shelter," unaware of the significance of saint houses to the inhabitants of the region, who left *kura,* round stones, on the ground around them to absorb the *baraka,* blessings from God, of the holy man. The *Kura* were later fetched when needed and applied to various body parts for healing. If the sailors heard the hooting of an owl that night, it came, according to local Berber belief, from the pained soul of someone who had not fulfilled his religious duties during life. A bee or a fly could be a soul leaving a body and heading for heaven, and a bird, a creature never shot near a cemetery, a soul returning to the tomb.

Throughout the next day the Bou Sbaa socialized with the Arabs and Moors who passed through camp, rough strangers engaging in demonstrative conversations and open fellowship — sharing food and drink, embracing heartily — in the way of the Sahara. Droves of camels rose up from the desert, while others with sacks of barley and salt, iron, and other goods headed toward the dunes. Bands of long-bearded soldiers on Arabian horses and armed with scimitars in silver-plated scabbards and ivory-inlaid muskets came and went. With all, Hamet acted as if he had nothing to hide and no one to fear; any other behavior would have invited suspicion and contempt. He did not shy away from exhibiting his sailors and recounting their tale of shipwreck and suffering. Riley pleased the proud horsemen by lauding their horses, saddles, and weapons.

One garrulous old man, who spoke fragmented Spanish and was traveling to Swearah by mule, questioned Riley about his alleged friend, assuring the captain that he knew all the consuls there: Renshaw, Josef, Estevan, and Corte. Figuring that Renshaw was the Englishman, Riley acknowledged him as his friend. The old man believed him and told Hamet that he would be willing to deliver a note from Riley to the consul. It would take him ten days to get there on the mule. The idea was shelved, however, when they could not find even a scrap of paper to write on.

Hamet was determined to strengthen his sailors before starting the strenuous and treacherous crossing of Souss, but he could afford them only one full day of rest, in addition to the calorie-rich meals. Before they set off, he purchased another beehive for the sailors. This time, Hassar's men played it smarter. Acting nonchalant at first, they rushed Hamet as he divided up the dripping hive, grabbed it, and gobbled it down. Furious but intent on keeping the unit together for safety, Hamet subdued his anger. He negotiated for one of the remaining but inferior hives and, with the help of the beekeeper and some strangers, managed to feed the sailors three pounds of honeycomb.

Together with Hassar's escort, the group now had to pass through territory guarded by Sidi Hashem, the notorious Berber who ruled the small state of Tazeroualt, north of Wednoon, and was an ally of Sheik Beyrouk's against Moulay Sulayman. Hashem drew his authority from the memory of his father, Sidi Ahmet ou Moussa, a marabout — a devout, saintly Muslim — revered for his justice and piety. Hashem's passion, however, was for lucre. From his seat in the town of Illigh, he controlled a narrow lane of north-south traffic between the Atlas and the sea and had grown wealthy and powerful by demanding tribute from traders and investing it in the caravan trade with the south. While his father's tomb attracted devout Muslims from all over Souss and the Sahara, Hashem's state was a renowned refuge for Moorish cutthroats and runaway slaves, particularly those fleeing from the *makhzen*. All who agreed to serve in his guard, some six hundred strong, lived in his state as free men off the spoils of war and banditry.

It was in one of Hashem's caravans to Tombuctoo that Hamet and Seid had nearly perished, expanding their bad luck on the Sahara.

By now, Hamet and Hassar knew, word of their company fresh off the desert with five Christian slaves had gone before them. The two clever Arabs divvied up their conspicuous company into three groups. Two men took the women and children and drove half the camels east on the well-traveled valley route. Hassar and all but two of the rest of his men drove the remaining camels, including all of Hamet's, off on a path to the northeast. Hassar's remaining pair, plus Hamet, Seid, and Abdallah, led the sailors on foot north along the bank of the Noun and then, to avoid being robbed of their slaves, ascended into the mountains to the east. They struggled up tortuous, steep slopes for four hours, hoisting one another over the most severe crags. From the top, they could see Hassar below, guiding the camels along an easier but longer and less secure route.

All day they climbed up and over ridges, eluding watchful eyes in the valleys and leaving no trail on the rocks. Hassar and his men shadowed them below, a simple band of traders for all to see, until near nightfall, when they rose up and joined Hamet's party below the ridgetops. In a small opening on a plateau, they discovered the fires of a camp with a dozen tents pitched in a semicircle. Hassar and Hamet's party approached to within about a hundred yards and sat down with their backs to the largest tent. Soon a bedouin woman from the camp brought them a bowl of water, followed by a bowl of fresh, slightly green dates. Hamet gave them directly to the sailors, bypassing his Arab compatriots. Hassar, Seid, and Abdallah indignantly grabbed handfuls. Though at that time they did not know what they were eating, the sailors found the dates delicious.

They set out early the next morning, but they did not get far before Hamet grew so ill with aching in his head and limbs that they searched for a place to stop. This was fortunate for Burns, who was also sick and too weak to walk. They descended through steep gullies to a hard, barren plain, which, though a hundred feet above the ocean, looked to Riley as if it had once been under it. Its gnarled bushes even resembled sea coral. Another gully took them down to a large group of tents on the beach. Both Hamet and Hassar seemed to know some of the twenty traders who were camped there with their families in the midst of transporting large sacks of barley south.[4] They placed Hamet in a tent and built a hot fire near his head to cure his ailment, which he diagnosed as "a stroke of the moon."

Seid heated a large knife until it was red-hot. He pressed the back of the blade against his brother's scalp, making his hair singe and crackle. He repeated this several times and then reheated the blade. Riley commented that his master came close to "roasting his brains out," but the treatment did little to improve his condition. Over the next hour, Seid branded his brother's arms and legs in four-inch intervals with the knife. Hamet writhed beneath the searing blade but never cried out. He instructed Seid to treat Burns too.

Seid pressed the scorching knife against Burns's flesh. Too sick even to tense, the sailor cried out, "God, have mercy upon me." Unable to watch this senseless torture, Riley begged to be allowed to go down to the beach to search for mussels, but Seid refused him and pressed the blade to Burns's flesh again, seemingly oblivious to his cries.[5]

After the treatment was over, the Arabs fed the sailors *lhasa* and allowed them to sleep under a tent. In the morning, Hamet and Burns were still weak. The honey gorging had left them all suffering from dysentery. Little understood at the time, dysentery, also known as bloody flux, caused inflamed intestines, griping pains, and diarrhea. It could be deadly, "especially if there be a malignant fever," wrote a contemporary medical expert, "and then it kills in seven, nine, or fourteen days." Bees would be identified as carriers of dysentery in 1816. But dysentery from drinking impure water would be the bane of most explorers of Africa. Among others, the Scotsman Hugh Clapperton would die from it in 1827 on his second journey to find the source of the Niger.

Perhaps the only thing worse than dysentery was the common treatment for it: "first to bleed, then to vomit with ipecacuanha, afterwards to purge with rhubarb, and last of all to give astringents." A cathartic, such as calomel or castor oil, and opium were often prescribed as well, along with various regional therapies. English soldiers suffering dysentery in Ireland were said to be cured by a "fungous substance between the lobes of a walnut" mixed with wine. In the East Indies, medics used an extract of saffron. Lacking any such substances, the Commerces were spared such regimens. They could only endure and worry that the painful voiding of fluids, including blood, might kill them by intensifying their dehydration.[6]

There was no chance to rest and recuperate. As they moved on, Hassar again traveled separately, taking most of the camels and attempting to divert attention from the others. The sailors, the Bou Sbaa, and a pair of Hassar's men set off along a section of coast frequently broken by sea-bound gullies, which they had to cross. Finally, they reached one so steep that it was impassable.

Before long they found a route down to the sea and a strip of beach, no more than ten yards wide, running north as far as they could make out. Heedless of the Arabs, Riley waded into the cold water and let it wash over him. It had been two months since he had bathed. Under the salt water, his skin, both scorched and new, and his flesh wounds roared back to life. Hamet, fearful of the undertow, shouted at him angrily to get out of the water and admonished him and the others to stay on land.

The sailors, on foot, followed the three Bou Sbaa riding camels up the beach. After about four miles, as they rounded a bend, four burly men with muskets and scimitars suddenly broke from the shadows of the bluffs and dashed in front of the camels. As they did, the Bou Sbaa drew their guns and dropped from their saddles.

Despite his illness, Hamet took the lead. He faced the bandits with his gun at his shoulder and trained on them. "Is it peace?" he demanded.

The bandit chief, a huge man, lowered his musket, sheathed his scimitar, and stepped forward. "It is peace," he said, with a foul-toothed grin, holding out his hand. Warily, Hamet took it. The bandit gripped Hamet's hand tightly, slowly increasing the pressure until it was crushing. He would not let go. As they glared at each other, locked together, he raised his heavy musket with one mighty hand, as easily as if it were a dagger, and wrapped his finger around the trigger. Before he could level it, however, Hassar's two men, who had fallen back, came running around the bend. Each had a musket raised and ready to fire.

The bandit leader saw them just before reaching the point of no return. Releasing Hamet's hand with a stage laugh, he made as if he were just pretending to give him a friendly scare. Not having an overwhelming force, Hamet pretended not to take offense.

After an awkward few moments, the bandits backed off, and Hamet's party continued up the beach. The bandits trailed them, watching for an opportunity, hoping to pick off a straggling slave. Hamet ordered Riley to keep his men tight on the heels of the camels and jockeyed into position between the bandits and the sailors. Without the benefit of surprise or overwhelming power, the bandits now did not dare directly start a skirmish. Instead, they stalked along the beach, hurling heavy stones, which Riley estimated at six to eight pounds, at them, shattering some against the cliff face.

When Hamet's group reached the end of the beach, they climbed to the surface of the desert. Hamet was shaken by the ambush and the manner of their escape, the last-second reprieve provided by Hassar's men. He had gotten out of tough scrapes by small miracles before, but never, he believed, had he seen Allah's hand at work so clearly. "Those were cutthroats," he said to Riley. "They would have murdered me and Seid, and they would have taken you to where you would have had no hope of ever seeing your homes and your families again — if Allah had not sent us the men." He paused. There was something else on his mind. "Would you fight to save my life?" he asked Riley.

"I would," Riley replied, in his usual direct way. "No one will kill you while I am alive if it is in my power to prevent it."

Hamet was not surprised by this answer. In fact, given what the captain had survived already, and his conduct toward his men, Hamet believed him to possess a certain *baraka*. "Good Riley, you are worth fighting for," he declared. "Allah is with you, or I would have been killed back there."

Near dark, as they marched on to their rendezvous with Hassar, they passed a man riding a donkey loaded with numerous large fish. The fish resembled the plump salmon the Connecticut River was famed for in those days, Riley observed longingly, and they weighed ten pounds apiece. As Phineus, whose food was spoiled by the Harpies, knew, having no food where there was none was painful, but seeing it and being denied it was torment. Riley asked Sidi Hamet to buy a fish, suggesting it would be good for Burns's health. Hamet agreed, but the man, probably a servant or else a provider for someone who would not be scanted, refused to part with even a single fish at any price, infuriating the Arabs nearly as much as it disappointed the sailors.

They soon arrived at Hassar's camp on a hill near the cliffs. This was a curious positioning. Camps on the Sahara, especially along the windy coast, tended to be made at the base of a hill, in a depression in the desert floor, or behind any other natural fortress that would shield them from the sandy wind and where there was more likely to be forage for the camels. The site Hassar chose seems to indicate that

the group was now more concerned about having a defensible position than going unnoticed, which was perhaps impossible anyway.
Hamet warned Riley that there were many brigands in the area and
that they should not wander from camp for any reason.

Not long afterward, Seid, Abdallah, and two of Hassar's men left
camp with their muskets. They were gone about two hours. Later,
when Hamet, Hassar, and his men heard footsteps approaching the
hill, they rose in alarm, taking up their weapons.

It was Seid and his companions. Smugly, they opened a blanket
revealing four of the large fish Riley had seen earlier. Despite the
fact that they did not eat fish, which some Arabs believed caused
lunacy, they had robbed the intractable fishmonger. "Riley, are these
good to eat?" Hamet asked suspiciously. Riley replied that they
were. "Take them and eat them," Hamet told him, "but be careful
not to choke on the bones."

Riley sliced up three of the fish, put them in a pot with water,
and made soup. Since none of the Arabs would eat the fish, the
sailors had all they wanted without worrying about their meal
being snatched away. The meal filled them and eased their dysentery, a relief for Savage particularly, who was in great pain and
nearly debilitated by cramps. But even the desert's purlieus seemed
to give nothing without exacting a price. That night the Americans
slept soundly within a ring formed by the Arabs and the camels,
but setting off just after daybreak, they found themselves desperately thirsty from the fish and with nothing to drink. Hassar again
took the women and children on one route, and the rest of the men
traveled together for speed and stealth off the main route.

Around noon Hamet's band came to a massive stone-and-lime
cistern. Riley estimated it to be eighty feet long, ten feet wide, and
about twenty feet deep. Covered by a vaulted top four feet off the
ground, it was supplied with water by aqueducts from the nearby
hills. The Arabs told the sailors that the cistern was the gift of a rich
and pious man. It could still provide water even after a year without
rain, water considered sacred and consecrated for the use of people
only. Camels were kept away, a thing unheard of anywhere else. But

Christians were not forbidden. Eager to slake their fish thirst, the sailors drank their fill.

They continued to journey along the coast, separated from the sea by a row of dunes, but here deep gullies from the now-dry mountain torrents blocked their route, adding frequent tedious ascents and descents. Though the going was slower, the sailors were encouraged to be entering settled regions. They were in the land of the Shilluh, or southern Berbers, ruled by Sidi Hashem, rich in cattle, wheat, and beeswax. Flocks of sheep and goats of the finest breeds grazed on remote mountain plateaus. Hashem's camels were renowned for their docility and endurance. These were the fruits of his thriving commerce with the south and an annual market in the village Hamet a Moussa that attracted traders from across the region and beyond.

At two walled towns, on hilltops surrounded by prickly-pear bushes and tilled land, men plowed fields of brittle dirt behind peculiar teams: one cow and one donkey. Women fetched the household goods, transporting bundles of wood on their backs and urns of water on their shoulders, all from some distance. Many carried children as well.

While Hashem's people were relatively well off, they showed none of the open generosity of the friendly Sahrawi tribes the sailors had encountered. They were inwardly focused and suspicious of outsiders. Dupuis made them out to be much worse, calling the Shilluh a people capable of "despicable treachery and murder, not merely against Christians . . . but even against Mohammedan travellers who have the impudence to pass through their country without having previously secured the protection of one of their chiefs" (Robert Adams, p. 183).

In the afternoon, Hamet's party came upon a walled village near the road. Outside its fifteen-foot walls, heaps of dried thornbush taller than a man protected a series of gardens. They hoped to get at least a drink of water, but the villagers would not open their gate. The band plugged on, at dusk entering a valley overlooked by two more walled villages. A stream irrigated an oasis of gardens.

Turnips, onions, and cabbages grew, protected by borders of thorn-bush, fig, and pomegranate trees and stone walls. These villagers shunned them as well, refusing even cursory hospitality to the travelers. Hamet, Seid, and Abdallah were stung by the irony that on the wild desert, where people had virtually nothing, they shared freely, but here, where resources were comparatively abundant, no one would offer them so much as a drink. They cursed the callous behavior of these unworthy Muslims.[7]

Certain that word of their arrival was rippling through the territory, they moved as rapidly as possible to keep ahead of trouble and considered themselves fortunate not to encounter any armed guard that day or the following morning. After crossing three dry river-beds, they reached another that was blocked by sand, forming a small pool. Berber villagers who had gathered there to fill skins and urns and to water livestock eyed the company of Arabs and white men with guarded curiosity and evident mistrust.

It was in the afternoon that they heard the first strains of danger. As ten horsemen raced across a plain to confront them, their spurs jingled shrilly on their stirrups. Their cries — "Hah! Hah! Hah!" — indicated that they meant business, and that it was urgent. They headed straight for Hamet and his ragtag band of travelers, who had added another member with two camels during the day, making six Arabs. As the riders neared, the six dismounted and drew their guns from the sheaths on their camels, five double-barreled muskets in all. Moroccan gunpowder was notoriously unreliable, and they reprimed their guns while forming a line in front of the sailors.

The riders came on at full speed. At ten yards' distance, Riley thought they were not going to stop, that they were going to simply ride right over them. Hamet and his men had their guns trained and their fingers pressed on the triggers.

Five yards from the group, the riders lurched to a halt.

"Who are you?" the lieutenant demanded of Hamet. "Where did you come from? What country are these slaves from? Where did you find them? Do you know Sidi Hashem?"

Hamet certainly knew Sidi Hashem. He had traveled in one of his caravans, a disaster to be sure. He answered with curt force and turned the tables, demanding the same information and inquiring by what authority the rider had stopped him and his slaves peacefully traveling on the road. It was a dangerous scenario Riley had grown all too familiar with on the high seas. The verbal sparring went on for a tense half hour. Finally, the riders allowed Hamet's company to pass.

When they were out of sight, Hamet's demeanor changed. He pushed his group relentlessly now, almost continually at a rack, with those on foot running to keep up. Finally he veered onto an open hilltop, where they stopped to rest. The view was both magnificent and significant. Far to the east, the peaks of the Anti-Atlas jutted into the blue sky; nearby, to the west and north, the ocean rippled darkly. With his mariner's eye, Riley soon made out what looked like a "high and distant island." Pointing there, Hamet said, "There is Swearah, Riley."

"How far is it?" asked the captain.

"Ten days, at our slow pace." He did not need to add that that was barring any further interruptions by the consorts of Sidi Hashem.

The sailors rode with renewed vigor. Traveling into the night, they covered fifty miles, outdistancing Hassar with the women and children. They continued on until they came to a camp of Arabs, who fed them dried mussels and barley *lhasa*. Riley, in turn, attended to their sick, examining a woman whose breast he described as swollen to an "astonishingly large" size. With each breath, the woman groaned in pain, and he feared the breast would rupture. He prescribed a poultice of *lhasa* and instructed them to change it frequently "until the swelling should subside or burst." The grateful woman gave him a drink of water and a handful of mussels and begged him to look at her brother's distended leg. Riley prescribed a "thick plaster of coarse salt to be bound round it," and his patient immediately swore that he felt relief.

This assistance made Riley uneasy about creating a demand for his services. The Arabs in this camp already wanted to keep Horace and aggressively pursued a trade. Against the wishes of Hamet, Seid negotiated with them, agreeing to a deal to be finalized in the morning. Hamet, who had borne the stresses of his illness and the trail with impressive calm, was disgusted with his brother. He snapped at Seid angrily, warning him not to sell the boy.

In the middle of the night, Hamet awakened the sailors, warning them to be silent as they rose. "I suspected some roguery going on," Riley wrote, "because we had never before started in the night." Hamet did not bother with an explanation, and they stole away without waking anyone else, including the Arab they had picked up on the trail the preceding day, though they took his two camels. Heading deceptively to the southeast through a mountain pass, they had gone only half a dozen miles when they heard pounding hooves and the unmistakable clinking of spurs on stirrups. Hamet and his Arab companions, including Hassar's two men, unsheathed their guns, but they kept moving at a steady rate as the riders approached.

Four riders passed them in a blur on the right-hand side. They swept around in front, and forced them to a halt. Hamet and his men dismounted and dashed forward, instructing the Americans to stay with them. The sailors followed as fast as they could in the dark.

Though these were not the same men who stopped them the day before, the scene was similar. Neither side having overwhelming numbers, they squared off and shouted at each other, all the time appearing to be on the brink of a bloody fight. The riders' lieutenant denounced Hamet for breaching their code of hospitality and demanded to know his name. Hamet made the same demand of him. They became ensnarled in punctilio until each revealed his name, Hamet first, followed by his rival, Ali Mohammed. The two continued to exchange barbs and accusations, jockeying for the moral high ground, but the argument would not be settled by debate. While the morning light gained strength, so did Ali Mohammed's forces: his footmen caught up to the riders, and as their numbers grew, Hamet's tone softened. Finally, the Arab who had been with them the day before came running up breathlessly. "You stole my camels!" he denounced Hamet shrilly.

Hamet did not deny that the camels belonged to the man. In a low voice, he asked Ali Mohammed to step aside with him and pleaded his case. "It was a mistake made in the dark of night," he argued. "I detest a robber and a thief. I am entirely innocent of intentionally driving off the man's camels. I am incapable of committing such an unworthy act. My character is all I have, and I will die before I let anyone accuse me of wrongdoing."

Ali Mohammed's forces now outnumbered Hamet's by two to one, but Hamet's men stood their ground. According to Riley, Ali seemed satisfied by Hamet's profuse rebuttals but even more so by his courage. "I am your friend," he told Hamet, "for you are a brave man." Ali made excuses for Hamet and abruptly released the group, silencing his accuser.

Around noon, they reached a plain and headed east. As they rode, Seid fumed over the confrontation with the troops, knowing that the chips could easily have fallen the other way, and they might have lost all. Aware that a storm was brewing, Abdallah and Hassar's men split off to the north and were soon out of sight in the bushes. This hasty exit was to be their last, for, in a quirk of Riley's account, he never mentions them again. Hassar and his fair wife, Tamar, are likewise abandoned on a parallel course without so much as a curtain call.

The sailors trudged behind Hamet's large camel at a frustratingly slow pace over the hilly terrain, "for," Riley said, "we were worn to the bones by our various and complicated sufferings." Suddenly, Seid ordered the men to stop.

Glaring at his brother, Hamet told them to continue. They listened to Hamet and kept walking.

Furious, Seid dismounted. His resentment had been growing ever since they had arrived in Souss. Unnerved by already having faced two guards of the local warlords, he insisted again that he alone owned Horace and Savage. Now all his complaints and doubts boiled to the surface. He did not believe the miserable slave Riley had a friend in Swearah to ransom him. Seid had decided to take his slaves and dispose of them as he pleased, not according to his brother's overly ambitious plan. He seized Horace and Savage.

Hamet vaulted from his camel. Not only had Seid toyed with offers for the two Christians on several occasions, he had squabbled with Hamet over other things as well. Hamet had been forced to humor and coax him; now he rushed upon his younger brother, pulling him away from the two sailors. The brothers grappled, trying to throw each other to the ground. After a struggle, they fell down in a bitter embrace. Seid, larger and heavier than Hamet, was on top, but Hamet, who was quicker and more active, struggled with the intensity of an older brother who would rather die than lose to his junior sibling. He fought himself free. They both sprang to their feet and went for their guns. Each retired a few paces, unsheathed his musket, and furiously primed and cocked it. Almost at the same time, they raised them and aimed them at each other's chest. "They were not more than ten yards asunder," Riley recalled, "and both must have fallen dead, had they fired."

Riley himself froze. He could not force himself to scramble to safety. "My God, have mercy on these unfortunate brothers, I pray thee, for our sakes," he cried out. "Suffer them not to spill each other's blood." As he shouted this, Hamet pulled the triggers of his double-barreled musket.

He fired into the air. Then he tossed down his gun and pulled open his haik, baring his chest. "I am unarmed," he called defiantly. "Fire! Your brother's heart is ready to receive your shot; take your vengeance on your protector."

Instead, Seid turned on Horace and Savage, who were quivering nearby. "Move and I will kill you," he threatened.

Hamet rushed over to Horace and sent him toward Riley. Hamet offered Clark to Seid in the boy's place. Seid refused, at the same time pushing Savage to the ground, clamping him there with a foot on his thigh. "Take Burns too," Hamet said. "Two men for one." Hamet ordered Riley to take Horace and follow the camels. "Savage, go too," he barked. Seid leveled his gun at Savage's head, telling him he would blow it off. Hamet ignored his brother. "Go, Savage," he said, pointing toward the others, who were already moving to the south.

Savage rolled free and bolted. When the second mate reached Horace and Riley, Hamet commanded them to stop. The brothers sat down on the ground. Hamet again proposed giving Burns and Clark to Seid for Horace. Seid shook his head. He would keep the slaves he had bought. "You will not separate him from his father," Hamet stated. "I have sworn to it."

"Then I will kill him," Seid vowed angrily, rising up and seizing Horace. Before Hamet could react, Seid lifted the boy into the air by his chest as easily as if he were a sack of grain. In a single motion, he flipped him over and threw him headfirst onto the ground. The crack of Horace's skull broke the silence like gunfire.

Believing the blow had killed the boy, Riley sank to the ground. "Go, Riley," Hamet bellowed, waving him away from Seid, who glowered nearby. Weak and disoriented, Riley rose, his emotions out of control. "I cannot leave the boy," he said. Then he staggered on a few steps.

His rage over, Seid backed away, believing he had foolishly destroyed his own property. Hamet rushed to Horace and gently pulled him to a sitting position. In a tender tone, he said to him, "Go to Riley." But Horace could neither speak nor get up. Riley went to the boy and held him in his arms. Horace's breath came fast and shallow. He moaned. Riley examined the ground around him, which was covered in stones, except where Horace's head had struck.

Seid and Hamet renewed the quarrel. Before it could heat up again properly, some strangers came into sight. The two brothers were suddenly brought to their senses. If they fought each other, they agreed, they would surely lose all. Hurrying on to avoid the strangers, the brothers decided to find a village where they could rest and seek a solution to their dispute. Riley cradled Horace on a camel as they went. At the top of a rise, they spotted a walled village and made for it. Entering through the open gate, they passed nearly to the other side before meeting an old man, an olive-skinned Moor who spoke some Spanish and whom Riley described as "respectable looking." The Moor welcomed the two Arabs while examining the ragged sailors. He could see that the boy was in need of care. Directing the visitors to a shady spot by a wall, the old man ordered his women to prepare food.

Two large bowls of boiled barley *lhasa* were soon set before them, one for the brothers and one for the sailors. "Kul, Rais," the old man said to Riley. Eating with their hands, the sailors filled their stomachs as fast as they could. Not until World War II, when concentration camp victims were nursed back to health, did scientists and doctors learn that the rapid intake of even normal amounts of food can incapacitate or even kill people who have long been kept on starvation diets. Contrary to popular belief, it is not the stomach but the small intestine that shrinks and must be allowed to reconstitute itself slowly by handling limited amounts of food. The sailors gobbled as much as they could as fast as they could, and they would pay for it later.

Afterward, on the Moor's advice, Hamet hired a guide, a sturdy young man named Bo-Mohammed with broad cheeks, hooded eyes, and a closely cropped beard to accompany them to another village. Not only would his familiarity with the terrain be helpful, Hamet hoped his presence would inspire the goodwill of his neighbors. He might also prove useful if Seid grew rebellious again.[8]

On the way to the nearby village, they discovered two bubbling springs beneath a rock shelf. The sailors drank the water but again suffered from crippling stomach cramps. This time it was not only dysentery that tormented them. They had gorged with such greed on the *lhasa* that some of them could hardly breathe, especially Savage. The group stopped in the dunes, waiting for the cover of dusk to resume their trek as well as allowing the sailors time to recuperate. Then they continued on to the intended village, a geographical watershed of sorts: they had reached the end of the land of tents and would see no more.

Amid the mud-walled houses, a pack of barking dogs besieged them until they were hushed by a stern-looking old man named Sidi Mohammed, who led the men to the walls of his compound. He told them to rest there while he gave orders for the preparation of

Bo-Mohammed of Shtuka
(from *Sequel to Riley's Narrative*, 1851)

supper. Then he had a mat placed near his walls and sat there beside Hamet and Seid. Soon he beckoned Riley to join them.

Mohammed lit a lamp and placed the glare of the light on Riley so that he could study his face. The old man peppered the captain with the litany of questions he had come to expect, but here, answering made Riley tense. Before, he had been playing an unreal game, in an unreal place, under unimaginable conditions, where accountability was a moot point. Now they were approaching reality. Mohammed was a knowledgeable man who was familiar with

Swearah and claimed to have visited the consuls. Riley worried that the old man would uncover his lie.

The captain breathed a sigh of relief when the arrival of hot loaves of bread brought the interview to an end. The sailors had not tasted this staple since the wreck, but despite their enthusiasm, they found they could swallow only a few bites of the heavy barley loaves after eating so much *lhasa* earlier in the day. Following the meal, the brothers washed their hands and feet and continued to consult Mohammed. When they had agreed to a plan, they called Riley over; Hamet told him that in the morning Hamet and Mohammed would go to Swearah. By traveling rapidly on mules night and day, they would reach the town in three days. Seid and Bo-Mohammed would guard the sailors and provide them with as much *khobs,* bread, and *lhasa* as they could eat.

"I have fought for you, have suffered hunger, thirst, and fatigue to restore you to your family, for I believe Allah is with you," Hamet told Riley. "I have paid away all my money on your word alone.

"Go and sleep till morning, and then you must write a letter to your friend, which we will carry," he continued. "If your friend will fulfill your engagements and pay the money for you and your men, you shall be free; if not, you must die for having deceived me. Your men will be sold for what they will bring."

On this matter, Riley did not doubt Sidi Hamet's word.

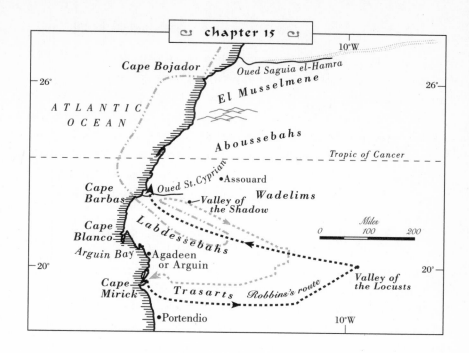

Valley of the Locusts

ᘛᘚ Archie Robbins supposed that marking the days with a knotted string had demonstrated some trifle of optimism. By it he knew at least roughly the date — it was the end of the first week in November — and the number of days of his captivity, fifty-nine. His crude calendar had served to remind him how long he had endured the ordeal but also that there would be an end to it. It had allowed him to live to a degree in the time frame of his former life, the one he had planned to return to just as soon as possible. But now, on the brooding, wind-whipped shore, time seemed to stand still. Living in the monotony and squalor of the seminomadic fishermen, his hopes of escape ceased, and he tossed his knotted string into the fire.

In the desert, he had seen only flies and scorpions, but wildlife teemed on the littoral. As the clear, cold Atlantic waters, rich in minerals and phytoplankton, upwelled in the tropical sun near the coast, they exploded into life. Fish of every imaginable sort fed along the shores on the abundant sea plants and creatures. Dogfish even hurled themselves onto the beach to scoff sand crabs and then wriggled back to sea. Pelicans, cranes, flamingos, and hundreds of other bird species converged on the sand islands to feed on the fish.

Compared with what was inland, the seaboard was a veritable garden, providing enough forage for the donkeys, mules, and goats, and an abundance of fish, or *l'hoot*, to eat or to trade with the Arabs, Berbers, and black Africans who came and went. Yet even with the traffic, it had a blind-alley feel about it, which terrified Robbins. With fish so plentiful they were even dried and used for firewood, this was a place one did not necessarily have to leave.

This stretch of rocky capes, sandy spits, and islets, now the northwest corner of Mauritania, was once an estuary when the Atlantic covered part of the Sahara. When the water receded, it left a fluctuating shoreline of mudflats and seagrass meadows next to a seabed only ten feet deep for fifteen miles out. To sailors, these shallows, called the Arguin Banks, were an infamous navigational hazard. Plenty of seamen had perished on them. Few ever saw them as Robbins now did, from the inside looking out.

"Stationary Arabs," Imraguen, and others inhabited the coast and fished on a semipermanent basis, with the greatest number present from August to April, when the schools of mullet came close to shore to feed. The Arab nomads abhorred the sea, and the dominant tribes forced submissive ones — those who had been defeated in battle or who had sought protection from their enemies — to fish for them, exacting periodic tributes of roe, fish-head oil, and dried fish, as well as livestock. This was a life of drudgery, without honor, for these vassals were not allowed to keep camels, the measuring stick of the Arab nomad. Nor did they have tents, the other essential possession of the Arab nomad, or guns, which were forbidden them. Instead, they lived in immobile lean-tos, defended themselves with knives and scimitars, and kept goats and donkeys, which survived on the seaweed and ragged bushes along the bay shores. The goats gave them milk, and the donkeys allowed them to haul fresh water from their wells to their huts.

They at least had the advantage of an ample food supply. Robbins's owner, Meaarah, passed him around to various of these stationary Arabs, who employed him in fishing. The first fed him plenty of *l'hoot*, the size of "mackerel, nearly the colour of our salmon trouts, of the most delicious flavor, and very fat," Robbins noted. For the first time since arriving on the desert, he found himself gaining rather than shedding pounds.

Several days after leaving the fishing village, Meaarah returned and questioned Robbins. "Soo-mook entar?" he asked. What is your name? Like Ganus, Meaarah pronounced it "Robbinis." "Where are you from?" Robbins claimed he was "Inglesis." "Is Inglesis better than Fransah?" his master asked. Robbins answered that they were both "bono."

Meaarah asked if he had a father and mother, brothers and sisters, a wife and children. Lying, Robbins replied yes to each, hoping to play on Meaarah's feelings, a feat that in the Arab world "cannot be more readily done," according to Robbins, "than by talking of wives and children."

"We will go to Swearah," Meaarah promised, but he did not say when.

Meaarah now attached Robbins to a group of fishermen heading to what Robbins called the outer bay, formed by the cape that made the inner bay and an island in the ocean close to the shore. There the fishing was even better than near the village.

Neither the Imraguen nor the Arabs had boats. They fished, as their ancestors had, along the shore with nets made of twined seagrass. The men started at low tide, crossing over the spit of land to the outer water, carrying with them their gear, mainly nets, firewood for cooking, and a skin of water. Loaded with the gear, Robbins labored across seven miles of deep, soft sand to reach the spit of land. Frequently sinking to his knees and stopping to rest, he became, he recalled, "an object of their scorn."

Each fisherman had as his prized possession his own tightly meshed seine with floats on the top and weights on the bottom. Any number of these nets were attached together to make one big net. Six-foot poles were inserted through the meshes at the ends, and two men walked together into the water to their armpits, holding the poles. They then moved in opposite directions, letting out the net as they went.

After they had extended the net fully, other men churned the water with threshing-poles, driving the fish into it as the two men holding the ends circled around and closed together. Their cohorts "then enter the circle made by the seine," Robbins reported, "and continue to thresh the water, until they suppose they have gilled all the fish." Afterward each man claimed his own net. The fish caught in it were his.

As the sun set, the men retired to their camp on the beach, cooking and eating their fill of fish. Robbins refused to learn the work of a fisherman's slave, feigning ignorance of the chores they tried to teach him, fumbling the tackle and tangling their nets. The fishermen despised him for his obstinacy and stupidity and "found," according to Robbins, "that the small benefit they derived from my labor cost more than it would fetch." As a result, he did not share fully in the mealtime bounty.

Returning to camp after two days, Robbins carried a load of fish. When he and the fishermen he was with saw a party of Arabs approaching them, they hid the catch. As they neared one another, Robbins could see that there was also a white man among them. To his astonishment, Robbins soon found himself embraced by James Barrett.

Both men had given up hope of ever seeing any more of their shipmates. Robbins was especially surprised at Barrett's appearance: he too had managed to put on weight. For the last three weeks, Barrett explained, he had been living at a fishing outpost about seven miles up the coast and eating as much fish as he wanted.

His master's brother had stolen him and taken him out onto the desert, but he had now been reclaimed and was on his way back to his master's village.

Robbins was elated to hear from Barrett that Williams, who had been near death when Robbins last saw him, was still alive. He had recovered to a considerable degree and was in good spirits again. Barrett's master also owned Williams, and, he told Robbins, despite his efforts, he was convinced their master would never sell either of them. "I cannot conceive why the cursed creatures want to keep me," he said. "I am not the least service to them."

"That is the great grounds of my hope too," Robbins told Barrett. "Be as useless as possible, ignorant and obstinate. This only will induce them to carry us to Mogadore."

The meeting was over in a short time. Robbins bade farewell to Barrett. He would never see him again.

Back at camp, the fish were slit open, gutted, "gashed . . . crosswise," and laid out to dry in the sun. In the arid heat of the Sahara, they needed neither salt nor smoke to preserve them. "The rays of the sun are so powerful," Robbins reported, "that fresh meat and fresh fish are dried so suddenly that putrefaction is always prevented."

Robbins was no longer starving, but after five days in the fishing village, he was despondent. The thought of remaining a fisherman's slave in the reek of drying mullet and the saline haze of seaside campfire smoke was more than he could bear. Worse, Meaarah was planning on leaving him again. Robbins pleaded with his master to take him with him. Meaarah agreed.

The next day, Robbins helped Meaarah pack his camel with fish, and they set off to the southeast at dawn. They traveled all day on the camel, passing from the littoral dunes to the small inland ones with scruffy, sparse bushes. Sixty miles from the fish camp, they reached Meaarah's tents. His family rushed out to greet them. His wife, Fatima, and daughters, Tilah and Murmooah, pawed Robbins affectionately, delighted that Meaarah had returned with a Christian slave. His son, Adullah, and brother, Mid-Mohamote, also tried to make Robbins feel welcome. Unlike the Bou Sbaa, these Arabs wore robes made of the finest cloth. The women's hair was braided with beautiful shells and wrapped in blue turbans.

In a festive mood, the Delim fed their new slave generous servings of fish and *zrig*, while they too ate as if the supplies were endless. Knowing all too well how they would suffer later after squandering this ration of food, Robbins became irritated by their profligacy. The nomad celebration also reminded him that it was nearly Thanksgiving in Connecticut, and his imagination wandered to his parents' home, a place as different from this as sod from sand.

In his mind he saw his friends and family gathered around the table laden with the bounty of the Lower Valley. "I could see the eyes of parents, beaming with benignity upon their visiting children, blessing heaven for the gift of them, as well as for the luxuries that loaded their hospitable board, rendering thanks that they had been blessed 'in their basket and in their store,' and that they had been preserved once more to form the happy family."

Nothing could have made him feel farther from home than the alien joy of these desert dwellers. "My heart," he said, "was near bursting at this recollection."

In the morning and over the next six days, Robbins learned much about these Delim. They were more advanced than the Bou Sbaa he had known. Compared with them, Meaarah was a wealthy man. His tent and the others in his *friq* were much more lavish, and his blankets were of a superior quality. A female slave from Guinea served them domestically. The women spent hours each day grooming their hair with needles and fish oil, fastening on the shells.

Meaarah supported a spiritual adviser and teacher, named Mahomet, who taught the children how to read and write using passages from the Quran. He was strict, and the lessons, which took place for three hours in the morning and three more in the evening, were solemn, since they dealt with sacred words. Robbins, who had seen no books at all among the Bou Sbaa, was fascinated by

Mahomet's ancient tomes, with their strange alphabet, and by the fact that they were written from right to left and read from back to front, epitomizing so singularly the gulf between his culture and theirs. Mahomet indulged Robbins's curiosity and never stopped proselytizing to the *kelb en-Nasrani,* urging him to join them in daily prayers. Robbins refused, having come to the conclusion that it was a "sacrilege to offer up worship to a prophet whose followers shew so little of humanity in their practice."

Fatima's brother, Illa-Mecca, and their mother, also Fatima, lived in a tent nearby. Meaarah owned sixty-eight camels, half a dozen of them in milk, and Illa-Mecca kept them. With so many to feed on scattered bushes in the hills and dunes, he needed all the help he could get. Meaarah appointed Robbins.

After the prayers, Robbins accompanied Illa-Mecca out to the drove of camels. While he performed his chores willingly around camp, he refused to be taught to tend the camels, just as he had refused to learn to fish. Anything that would enhance his value to them would, he believed, lengthen his servitude. The more useless he was, he reasoned, the sooner they would trade him, and the more likely he would be to find his way to redemption.

Not surprisingly, Robbins frustrated and angered Illa-Mecca. Finally, Meaarah, who while in this place mostly stayed in camp enjoying the pleasures of his tent, accompanied them out to the herd and tried to teach Robbins how to tend to the camels. They climbed to the tops of hills, spotted strays, and then drove them back in. Robbins ran beside his master like a faithful retriever, but when Meaarah instructed him to continue doing it on his own, he feigned incomprehension. Meaarah finally gave up, convinced that Robbins was incapable.

After six days, the family packed up their tents. They traveled to the east for eight days, at about forty miles a day, into the interior of the desert, crossing vast empty plains interspersed with rocky hills and shallow valleys of sand and stone. The region was similar to where Robbins had been before but more heavily populated. Encountering other nomads with large droves of camels, Meaarah and Fatima were treated with great deference as they shared news and sometimes a meal with other Arabs.

When they reached a vast stretch of dunes, the family was pleased, revealing their genuine affinity for sand.[1] To celebrate, they slaughtered a camel that night, gorged, and then dried the meat in the sun the next day. They turned northeast now, crossing the dunes, and four days later reached a small valley with a pool of fresh water from a recent rain. The pool had attracted nomads from all around. Tents belonging to both Oulad Bou Sbaa and Oulad Delim — "these two tribes, at this time, being at peace with each other," Robbins noted — surrounded the pool. Among the other group, Robbins discovered to his delight William Porter.

Porter had recovered from the headache and the medicinal bleeding that had made him so low. He had been given a steady diet of camel's milk and was looking strong again. His eyesight had improved too. In his memoir Robbins recorded little of their meeting in the deep desert other than the fact that Porter had lost track of time and was eager to know the date. Robbins, who had abandoned his calendar string, could only give him his best guess.

All sense of time and order now took a death blow anyway as a great tide of locusts, or *yerada,* as the Arabs call them, rolled into their valley, filling the sky with their whirring bodies and obscuring the sun. When they landed, the three-inch-long russet insects carpeted the land, devouring every bush and sprig of new growth from the recent rains and sounding, according to Robbins, like "small pigs eating grain."

To him, it was a nightmarish vision of Old Testament death and destruction. Though he was familiar with the biblical portrayal of these pests as the eighth plague, brought down on Egypt for refusing to let the Israelites go, he was perhaps unaware of a lesser-known passage from Leviticus, 11:22: "you may eat: the locust according to its kind, the bald locust according to its kind." In Matthew, John the Baptist lives on locusts and wild honey in the wilderness. But Robbins was stunned by the Arabs' enthusiastic reception for insects he associated only with calamity.

"From the days of Moses to this time, [locusts] have been considered by Jews and Mahometans as the most severe judgment which heaven can inflict upon man," he commented. "But whatever the Egyptians might have thought in ancient days, or the Moors and Arabs in those of modern date, the Arabs who are compelled to inhabit the desert of Zahara, so far from considering a flight of locusts as a judgment upon them for their transgressions, welcome their approach as the means, sometimes, of saving them from famishing hunger."

In the heat of day, the locusts swarmed from place to place in ominous waves, but the cool November nights stilled them, and the Sahrawis easily harvested as many as they wanted. The bugs were attracted to the pool of water, and at night everyone living with Meaarah except Fatima and the two youngest children eagerly collected them in sacks. Robbins, who was again living on a diet of *zrig* and snails, wrote that he "declined this employ, and retired to rest under the large tent." Whether Meaarah realized that he was too exhausted and weak to help, or all were in such high spirits over the ready food that Robbins's participation was optional, he does not say, but Meaarah's charitable attitude toward him was about to end.

Robbins called this place "the Valley of the Locusts." The family harvested fifteen bushels of the insects in one night. They cooked only live ones, first digging a deep pit and building a fire in the bottom. After the blaze heated the pit, they removed the coals. Then they emptied a bag of the insects into the earth oven, shaking the bag vigorously to get them all out, and gathering around close to toss sand on them to keep them from flying away. Once the pit was filled with locusts and sand, they built another fire on top. They roasted about five bushels in each pit, digging three pits one after another to cook them all while they were still alive.

When the locusts had cooled enough to touch, they pulled them out of the sand and spread them on tent cloth to dry in the sun for several days. They had to guard them continually during the day to prevent new swarms of live locusts from landing on the dead ones and devouring them.

Robbins and Porter learned to eat the insects, breaking off the head, wings, and legs and chewing up the body. Although the pair found the bugs unappetizing, they craved the nutrition; about twelve ounces of locusts would provide each of them with his daily protein needs, as well as vitamins A and D, phosphorus, calcium, and potash. For a few days, the Delim had an unlimited supply of locusts to eat, which was fortunate since it took about two hundred of them to add up to an edible twelve ounces, and Porter and Robbins had the previous months of deficiency to make up for as well. Most of the locusts were flattened and packed into bags and skins. These the Arabs would later pulverize in mortars and mix with water to make what Robbins called "a kind of dry pudding."

Despite this new source of nourishment, Robbins let his fatigue get the better of him at the wrong moment during the locust harvest. When Meaarah told him to carry a goatskin of water to the tent, Robbins hoisted the heavy skin onto his back and lugged it over. Swinging the bloated skin around to set it down, he lost control of it. The skin fell to the ground and burst. Meaarah erupted in anger. He had had enough of Robbins's incompetence. He grabbed an ax, cocked it back, and dashed at Robbins. At the last moment, Fatima stepped in front of him and deflected the blow. If she had not been there, Robbins believed, Meaarah would have taken his head off. The incident seemed to transform his master. From then on, Meaarah lost all sympathy for Robbins and began to treat him with "systematic cruelty."

At the same time, the teacher Mahomet began pressing Robbins all the harder to renounce Christianity, reviling him for being an eater of pork. He considered "a hog as possessed of the devil, and those who eat it as possessed of him also," noted Robbins. Mahomet tried to entice him to convert to Islam with promises of "wealth, and power, and wives upon earth, and eternal felicity and sensual enjoyment in paradise with the divine Prophet Mahommed," but Robbins resisted.

When the water in the basin ran out, the locusts vanished, and the Arabs began to do the same. Robbins had to say good-bye to Porter, a painful separation for both men. Meaarah now led his group to the northwest at a pace that reduced Robbins to the misery he had known under the Bou Sbaa. Walking and riding all day and sleeping under the stars at night, he lost weight and dehydrated. The chafing of his skin became insufferable. The coarse blanket he wore around his waist and hanging to his knees shredded the flesh on his legs, stripping them bare. Night offered him little relief. "After sleeping upon the sand for several hours, and rising upon my legs," Robbins wrote, "the blood gushed out of my excoriated and dried flesh."

Ten days after leaving the Valley of the Locusts, they crossed the St. Cyprian wadi, reaching the coast just north of Cape Barbas. Robbins had come full circle, in more ways than one. Neglected by Meaarah, he found his health had begun to deteriorate. It would continue to decline over the next month, until Robbins hit his lowest state since arriving on this shore in the longboat. His diet of hard-boiled blood and locusts made him severely costive. "I was completely dried up; and the skin was contracted and drawn tight around my bones," he said. The combination of his chafing clothes and sleeping on the hardpan had rubbed the skin and flesh off his hips so that he could touch his hipbones on both sides. He was "now literally reduced to a skeleton."

The end, one way or another, seemed near.

PART FOUR

A Slow Rush
to Swearah

chapter 16

Sheik Ali

❦ Was God with Riley? Or was that just a wishful conceit that he and Sidi Hamet shared? Clearly these two men from different cultures and different religions drew the conclusion that a divine power was watching out for the captain. Hamet had risked everything he owned on Riley and his men, when he could have already sold them at a profit with much less risk or hardship. Instead, he had fought even his own brother to secure the independence of this Christian, a man in whom he recognized great integrity and who he came to believe was blessed by Allah. Despite their differences, Riley and Hamet both believed in a higher being, whether called God or Allah, and found unity in his presence in their relationship. Still, they were engaged in a dangerous transaction for earthly rewards — freedom and fortune — and both dreaded failure.

Riley had, in fact, reached a physical, mental, and moral crisis. He spent the night before Hamet and the old man, Sidi Mohammed, were to depart for Swearah in "a state of anxiety not easy to conceive." Having bluffed his way this far north, he now had to produce real evidence that he had not been lying all along. "To whom should I write?" he fretted. "The Englishman Renshaw, who might or might not still be there? I know no one at Mogadore." And what should he say to procure the aid of whoever received the letter?

Riley recollected the vivid dream he had had the night the Arabs held a council to divvy up the sailors. To this point, the dream had proved true. He had survived all the hardships the desert had thrown at him. He had to keep faith: it was all he had.

Early in the morning, the Arabs woke the sailors and drove them inside Sidi Mohammed's gates. Riley was groggy from the sleepless night outside, but he was determined to persuade Hamet to allow him to go to Swearah too. "Come, write a letter," the Bou Sbaa enjoined him, handing him a ragged piece of paper, eight inches long and the width of his palm, and a reed with some inky black liquid.

Riley hesitated only slightly. He looked his good master in the eye. "Sidi Hamet, please take me with you," he said, "I beg you, sir. I will leave my son, whom I love with my whole heart, here as a hostage, as well as my three men." The boy was still recovering from Seid's abuse.

"I cannot," Hamet replied emphatically. "It is useless to plead." The decision had been made that he and Sidi Mohammed would travel on alone. Hamet had another serious matter to discuss, and he changed the subject. "Rais, the amount that you have agreed to pay is not enough," he said. "You must tell your friend, in the letter, to pay two hundred dollars for yourself, two hundred for Horace, and two hundred again for your mate Aaron. For your men Burns and Clark, one hundred and sixty dollars each. You have promised me a double-barreled gun, and you must give one to Seid too," he continued. "He is a hard man, but he has helped save your life."

Hamet's tone convinced Riley not to argue. He had learned that when two Arabs disagreed on a course of action, he could potentially affect the outcome in his favor, but when two Arabs agreed on a plan, there was nothing a Christian could do to change it. Hamet had obviously struck a deal with Seid and Sidi Mohammed and there was no reversing it now. Riley took the pen, steadied his hand, and began to scrawl the letter that would determine his and his shipmates' fate:

Sir,

   The brig Commerce from Gibraltar for America, was wrecked on Cape Bajador, on the 28 August last;

Suspecting that at best his letter would fall into the hands of an Englishman and not knowing what degree of assistance he might expect so soon after the war, he deliberately worded it so as to make his own nationality obscure. When the small crowd of Arabs who had gathered around saw him write Arabic numerals, they were amazed. Since Hamet and Seid denied teaching him, one of them suggested that Riley must have been a slave before, a smart and helpful one, and had thus been taught by his former master despite laws that forbade it.

With the Arabs gazing on intently, he continued:

myself and four of my crew are here nearly naked in barbarian slavery: I conjure you by all the ties that bind man to man, by those of kindred blood, and every thing you hold most dear, and by as much as liberty is dearer than life, to advance the money required for our redemption, which is nine hundred and twenty dollars, and two double barrelled guns: I can draw for any amount, the moment I am at liberty, on Batard, Sampson, & Sharp, London — Cropper & Benson, Liverpool — Munroe & Burton, Lisbon, or on Horatio Sprague, Gibraltar. Should you not relieve me, my life must instantly pay the forfeit. I leave a wife and five helpless children to deplore my death.

Eager to set off, Hamet looked over Riley's shoulder and hurried him. After establishing his commercial relations, Riley insisted on another scrap to write on. When it was produced, he saw that it was part of a Spanish bill of lading. He continued writing:

My companions are Aaron R. Savage, Horace Savage, James Clark, and Thomas Burns. I left six more in slavery on the desart. My present master, Sidi Hamet, will hand you this, and tell you where we are — he is a worthy man. Worn down to the bones by the most dreadful of all sufferings — naked and a slave, I implore your pity, and trust that such distress will not be suffered to plead in vain. For God's sake, send an interpreter and a guard for us, if that is possible. I speak French and Spanish.

James Riley,
late Master and Supercargo of the brig Commerce.

Riley folded up his note. He was unwilling to gamble on addressing it only to Renshaw. Consuls came and went. He could not risk
having Hamet think his friend was abroad, even temporarily. As for
the hope of finding an American representative there, it was
unlikely. America's poorly funded, extemporary network often
used merchants from other nations as agents, some of whom were
not even permanently based in the port they served. Unsure even of
which nations kept consuls in Mogadore, let alone who might be
present at the time, he addressed it to the "English, French, Spanish, or American consuls, or any Christian merchants in Mogadore
or Swearah."

Rightly figuring that they were in a race against time and fate,
Sidi Hamet and Sidi Mohammed sped off to the east on mules. Others more powerful than they had divined that the Christian slaves
were in the village and had begun scheming to take them. A steady
parade of curiosity seekers from the village — Moorish and black
Arabs armed with long knives or scimitars and their black slaves —
came to the yard where Seid and Bo-Mohammed kept watch. One
Arab, grabbing a button on Savage's pants, demanded, "Button, cut
it wit a nif," startling the Americans, who had not met an Arab who
spoke English, but it was all he could say in English other than a
few profanities. While the villagers sat on a mat observing them, the
sailors kept to the shade as far as possible, sitting in the unavoidable
manure of cattle, sheep, and donkeys. As promised, they were
allowed to drink as much water and eat as much as they wanted,
barley bread twice daily and *lhasa* once. Still, they remained weak,
all suffering from dysentery and severe hemorrhoids. "Our bowels
seemed to ferment like beer," Riley said, "and we were tortured
with cholics." While their skin healed in delicate patches, their wild
hair, bushy beards, and filthy clothes harbored lice, which became a
constant irritant.

The villagers tried to coax the sailors into helping with carpen-
try, shoemaking, and smithing, but Riley insisted that he and his
men had been raised as sailors since childhood and knew nothing
else. Previously, he had asked his men to cooperate to gain the best

treatment, but here he reached the same conclusion that Robbins had and warned them that showing aptitude in any of the crafts Christians were known for would only increase the chance of their being kidnapped or sold to a master willing to pay handsomely for skilled labor. When Riley was taken to frame a door at a new house, he pretended he could not understand the instructions for measuring the posts. He hacked at the timbers randomly with an adze, splintering the wood. The Arabs argued over Riley's incompetence. "By far the greater part of them were of opinion that a smart application of the whip would put my mechanical powers into complete operation," Riley observed. One who was not fooled fetched a cudgel, but Bo-Mohammed had no interest in seeing Riley beaten and stopped him.

At night, the sailors now slept in a dingy cellar, a crawl space beneath the floor of the house, which was supported by a mast, a boom, and other ship's wood. Seid and Bo-Mohammed turned a key in the iron lock behind them and slept outside the door with loaded weapons at their sides.

Riley soon learned how the villagers had acquired the ship's timber that some of them had used in their houses when a villager showed him official papers from the Spanish schooner *Maria* dated 1812 and 1814. Others produced clothing taken from her crew and repeated Spanish curses they had picked up. From what they told him, Riley pieced together the *Maria*'s story. The schooner had come to the coast to fish and trade. Sneaking alongside her in boats at night, the Arabs had climbed on board and killed her captain and three of her sixteen-man crew. After ransacking the vessel, they ran her on shore and made the crew dismantle her for the wood. One old man told Riley that five more of the sailors had died since that night and that the other eight had been traded off to the desert. Others claimed the survivors had gone to Swearah to be ransomed, but Riley believed the old man.

On the sixth day after Hamet's departure, an unexpected visitor hailed at the gate in the afternoon and demanded to be let in. Seid opened the door hastily, and a dark, six-foot Moor swaggered in on the back of a stout horse. From his saddle, Sheik Ali, Hamet's father-in-law, examined with obvious disgust the squalor around him and the scabby Christians lying about like beasts.

Ali's air of superiority as well as Seid's sudden transformation from sullen brute to obsequious servant indicated to the sailors the degree to which their fortunes had just changed. Ali promptly moved into Sidi Mohammed's house, imposing upon Seid and Bo-Mohammed to an extraordinary degree. His aura of command, Riley observed, surpassed even that of the most domineering sea captain. Sheik Ali was also beguiling and remarkably charismatic.

Ali's reputation was such that the villagers immediately began to seek him out to settle their disputes. His summary decisions were handed down with such authority and grace that neither party dreamed of protesting. He was at times, Riley admitted, the most eloquent man he had ever heard. "Open mouths seemed to inhale his honied sentences," the captain effused, explaining that Ali spoke with such "perfect emphasis" that the "elegant cadence so much admired in eastern oratory seemed to have acquired new beauties from his manner of delivery; his articulation was so clear and distinct, and his countenance and actions so intelligent and expressive, that I could understand him perfectly, though he spoke in the Arabic language."

But Ali's moods changed rapidly. Radiant and charming one moment, he was suspicious and conspiratorial the next, and then shouting furiously, terrifying Seid and Bo-Mohammed, who did everything possible to appease him. When he spoke, no one dared move or utter a sound.

It was inevitable that the sheik would turn his attention to Riley and his men, and when he did, looking them over and conferring in low tones with Seid, the captain felt an ominous chill. Ali summoned him and questioned him about his worth, his family, the shipwreck and the dispersal of its contents. He wanted to know how much money and what kind of goods the attackers at Cape Bojador had taken. "What crime was committed to induce these Moslemin to kill one of your men?" he asked.

It was clear that the sheik, to whom Hamet was in debt, was assuming an interest in their future and that his presumption knew no bounds. He examined their bodies carefully as if he were considering buying — or selling — them. Finding the cross tattooed on Clark's arm, Ali pronounced him a Spaniard and declared that he could not be ransomed. Clark, he announced, would go to the mountains and work for him. This was an unsettling verdict, given that, as Riley put it, "every thing that this man said seemed to carry with it a weight that bore down all opposition."

With Seid and the other Arabs, Ali cleverly began to plant the seeds of a dispute. He let it be known that he thought Riley was an "artful fellow . . . capable of any action either good or bad." One minute he was sure Riley was lying to Hamet about having a friend in Swearah; the next he was certain that the captain's friends could raise a great deal more money to ransom him than Hamet had demanded. Seid was only too happy to hear this. The calculating Ali decided that he would stay until Hamet returned.

On the seventh day came a new arrival. A dark, fierce-looking stranger, sporting a brace of horse pistols, a pair of knives, and a scimitar, and carrying a long musket, rode up to the wall on horseback. He hailed Seid by name and said, "Open the gate immediately." When Seid asked him who he was, he replied that he was Ullah Omar and that he had just arrived from Swearah.

As he led his powerful mount into the yard, no executioner could have looked more the part. Riley studied the formidable man, who wore a white turban, a haik, and yellow leather slippers with long iron spurs attached to them. In addition to the weapons, he had two powder horns and a leather pouch with musket balls slung about his neck. Sheik Ali knew him and shook his hand warmly. After greeting the others, Omar inquired which was Riley and approached him.

"I have seen your friend Sidi Hamet one day's ride this side of Swearah," he reported. "He told me that Allah had prospered his journey because of you. I hope that your friend in Swearah will be as true to you as Hamet is." Hamet, he suggested, might return as soon as the next day. But Omar had no more news. He addressed the

sailors, who could not understand him, but took heart in his attention and, when Riley translated, in the prospect of Hamet's immi-
nent return.

Seid served Omar a bowl of "cous-koo-soo," as Riley learned the
Moroccan dish was called, covered with slices of squash and well
peppered. "This dish," he added, "which is made of small balls of
flour, boiled with fowl and vegetables, looked (for I had not the
pleasure of tasting it) like a very nice dish." Ullah Omar, who carried a pipe and tobacco in his shot pouch, gave the sailors a handful
of good tobacco, seeming "exceedingly pleased to have it in his
power to administer comfort to such miserable beings." After his
meal and prayers, the cryptic messenger departed as suddenly as he
had arrived.

Riley could not sleep that night, buffeted by waves of panic.
Omar's presence had been reassuring to a degree, but Riley had
learned nothing material other than that he had maintained Hamet's
goodwill up to the gates of Swearah. The death sentence still stood,
and in a literal sense Riley was guilty as charged. He lay awake second-
guessing his pledge. It had been an easy decision — he and his men
would have traded their lives for a swallow of Connecticut water
then — but it did not look so clear now that skin covered his bones
again and he had shelter to hide in. On the Sahara, his life had not
been worth living. Now he was reminded of his family and former
existence.

"My desire to live kept pace with the increase of my comforts,"
he lamented. "I longed for the return of my master, and yet I antic-
ipated it with the most fearful and dreadful apprehensions . . . I
calculated on the moment of his arrival as decisive of my fate. It
would either restore me to liberty, or doom me to instant death."
Each arrival in the village and opening of the gate caused Riley to
shudder.

He prayed to God that he had not come so far to suffer death in
the animal filth of the courtyard, to widow his wife, to leave his
children without prospects, and to have his companions and his
adopted son shipped back out onto the hopeless blazing wasteland.

The Captain Has
Long Been Dead

⌒⌒ Striding in deep thought before the formidable walls and turrets of Swearah with minarets rising behind him, Rais bel Cossim nearly collided with the two dusty but dignified-looking Arabs entering the city's eastern gate. Bel Cossim, a Moorish sea captain and man of affairs, was struck with curiosity. Traders who had just crossed the desolate hills around Swearah would have brought goods, but these two had none. "Salem alikoom," he addressed the leading man, whom he recognized as an Oulad Bou Sbaa. "Where do you come from, Son of a Lion?"

"Alikoom salem," Hamet replied to the Moor, who he could see was a man of status and of some perception. "I have come from Souss and before that from the Sahara, a long way. I have come to see Sidi Consul."

"Tell me your business, friend," bel Cossim said, swallowing a laugh. "Perhaps I can guide you." Hamet told him that he had a note to deliver to Sidi Consul from an English captain who had wrecked at Cape Bojador.

"Come, I will take you to the man you wish to see," bel Cossim said, beckoning him with a wave. Swearah's port, customs house, government buildings, and central road and market were arranged on a neat, businesslike grid, marked by imposing gateways and towers. Beyond lay the mazelike medina where Swearah's commoners — the bulk of its thirty thousand Muslims and six thousand Jews — and the *abid al-Bukhari,* black Muslim soldiers, lived in segregated quarters. Bel Cossim led the two visitors through wide and relatively sedate and sweet-smelling streets among the four-story homes of the privileged Jewish traders, government administrators, and foreign consuls and merchants.

This was the inner sanctum, the casbah within the walled town, all built since Sultan Muhammad III had established the port in 1765 to tighten his grip on both foreign trade and the southern reaches of his dominion. The sultan had soon closed the port of Agadir to foreign ships and relocated its merchants to Swearah with its stone ramparts and massive turrets manned by two thousand heavily armed *abid al-Bukhari*. Here the imperial trade could be better watched, and private trade, where it could be better regulated and taxed. The reward, the sultan had promised all who would settle in this otherwise remote and dusty section of the Haha region, was that "he who comes poor, leaves rich." Within a decade Swearah, once a Phoenician trading outpost and possibly the lost "Cerne Island," which the Carthaginian Hanno colonized with thirty thousand people in 450 B.C., had become Morocco's principal maritime port.

Bel Cossim led them to the home of British consul-general William Willshire. Willshire was part of the small cadre of European merchants who, along with the local Jewish merchants employed by the sultan, lived in the casbah and conducted the foreign trade.

The visitors found him in, which came as little surprise to bel Cossim. Willshire, who was James Renshaw's successor and business partner, was a bachelor and a man who never seemed to tire of working. He lived in the British consulate's large — some would say lavish — house, where he had many servants and clerks and where on Sundays he conducted Anglican services for other Christian merchants.

Recognizing bel Cossim, Willshire's servants admitted him and the two Arabs. The young consul, a fastidious man of neatly cropped hair, fine features, and naturally pursed lips, received them in his office. As he examined the two scraps of paper one of the Arabs handed him, he felt his heart sink. Another merchant brig had been lost off the coast of the Sahara and her crew captured by the barbarous wandering Arabs.

Willshire looked up from the note. Rais bel Cossim was one of Willshire's most trusted Moorish intermediaries, a valuable man who spoke fluent Spanish and a smattering of English in addition to Arabic. With him stood two Arabs by the names of Sidi Hamet and Sidi Mohammed, who from their appearance had traveled a long way in a hurry. Willshire looked them over again. Hamet had a handsome, intelligent face, with the lines of wear and sorrow common to the tribal Arab. He stood before him without shame, despite the fact that he was there to ransom shipwrecked sailors.

"What can you tell me of this Captain Riley?" Willshire asked, examining Hamet's expression as bel Cossim translated.

A smile creased Hamet's cheeks. "Captain Riley is an intelligent and courageous man," he replied. As he spoke, his dark brown eyes seemed to swell a little, in what Willshire believed was a genuine look of affection. "He is an honorable man, with a wife and children. Allah is with him in all he does," Hamet continued. "My journey has been blessed by Allah for Captain Riley's sake. We faced many difficulties, but we passed safely through dangerous lands. His men, who are sick, have survived too. I have done the best I could for them."

Willshire reread the end of Captain Riley's note:

My present master, Sidi Hamet, will hand you this, and tell you where we are — he is a worthy man. Worn down to the bones by the most dreadful of all sufferings — naked and a slave, I implore your pity, and trust that such distress will not be suffered to plead in vain. For God's sake, send an interpreter and a guard for us, if that is possible. I speak French and Spanish.

Although he was genuinely alarmed for the writer's sake and for the crew of the brig *Commerce*, he was also puzzled and a little rankled. As consul-general, if only for a short time, he was already experienced at negotiating and raising funds to ransom shipwrecked sailors from the Sahara. He did not hesitate to make decisions and was willing to risk his reputation and his money. He refused to leave a man in captivity for a minute longer than necessary. This Captain James Riley listed reputable merchants in London, Liverpool, Lisbon, and Gibraltar as references. But several complications jumped out at him immediately. The fact that Riley did not state a nationality — though judging from the names listed, the crew was either British or American — raised questions of who exactly should handle this matter, and Riley had negotiated a larger than desirable sum for his ransom.

Willshire was commissioned to promote Britain's trade interests and to protect and assist her citizens. He was also, now that the war was over, once again an agent for America's consul in Tangier, James Simpson. Within certain limits, there were pools of money to draw from to ransom British sailors, namely from the Ironmongers' company, through the 1723 bequest of one Thomas Betton, which gave half his estate for redeeming British slaves in Turkey and Barbary. God bless him, thought Willshire; Betton had done more to relieve the worldly suffering of Christians than he would ever know.

Ready money was essential because by the time Western government officials could authorize expenditures for ransoms, it was often too late. The mistrustful Arabs raised their price with each meeting, requiring new authorizations, more delays, and eventually resulting in even loftier and more outrageous demands. He had seen men lost to this vicious cycle, either through their own despondency or from a complete breakdown in negotiations. America had no ready funds. Any ransom technically had to be approved by Simpson, who was loath to make a decision without the approval of the Secretary of State, James Monroe. Each round-trip trans-Atlantic communication took a minimum of eight weeks.

Willshire called an attendant. "Gentlemen, please excuse me briefly. Won't you enjoy a cup of tea in the drawing room while I attend to some urgent business?"

When his visitors had left, he turned to his tidy stack of back issues of the *Gibraltar Chronicle,* thumbed down to August, and began examining the weekly listings of port arrivals and departures. "There she is," he said to himself, as he checked the arrivals in the August 12 edition and found the *Commerce,* "40 days from New Orleans." She was an American brig, then, and captained by a clever man who must have suspected his letter would end up in the hands of an Englishman.

Willshire had a vested interest in seeing that Riley was not ransomed at the excessive rate he had negotiated. Not only Britain but other Western nations, especially the United States, desired to limit ransom payouts to $100 per man. Riley had agreed to pay double that for himself and two others and $160 apiece for two common seamen, as well as two double-barreled fowling pieces and various expenses. Willshire knew that paying this sum would set a bad precedent.

He considered stalling. It would take at least a month for him to receive word from Horatio Sprague, the Gibraltar merchant the letter listed, and probably weeks to hear back from Simpson. In the meantime, if he advanced the necessary funds, he would be out well more than $1,000 in specie and guns, for men whose trustworthiness and ability to repay him he could not be sure of. There were limits to what diplomats were authorized to spend in such situations and often labyrinthine systems for accessing the money, and there were limits to what even a fellow merchant could and should do. If Riley's promises turned out to be untrue, Willshire might well lose a tidy sum of money, at the same time he would be feeding the greed of the desert Arabs. Perhaps it would be prudent to tell the two men in the drawing room that he would need to write for authorization.

"Show Rais bel Cossim and the visitors back in," Willshire told one of his servants. The deliberations went on for some time, with bel Cossim interpreting. At last they agreed that Sidi Hamet would remain in Swearah as a guest of Willshire while Sidi Mohammed guided Rais bel Cossim south to see Captain Riley and his men. Willshire gave instructions to his servants to prepare a number of items to be sent with bel Cossim. Finally, he wrote a note to Riley and handed it to the dependable Moor. "Rais, Godspeed," he said. "Take your fastest mule and fly like the *irifi* to the house of Sidi Mohammed."

On the night of the eighth day since Hamet and Sidi Mohammed had left for Swearah, the sailors heard footsteps outside the wall. Seid went out to see who it was and returned with Sidi Mohammed and another man, a Moor from Swearah. The two men approached the sailors, who were sitting on the cold ground in the yard.

When they reached Riley, the dust-covered Moor spoke, startling the sailors with his English. "How de-do, Capitan?" he said. The sailors jumped to their feet. Certain that this man was bringing the news that would determine their fate, Riley at first could not speak; his heart seemed to rise in his throat. Finally he took the man's hand and blurted out his questions: "Who are you? What news do you have from Swearah? Is Sidi Hamet with you?"

"¿Habla español?" the self-possessed Moor asked calmly. Riley nodded. Then, speaking Spanish, the Moor introduced himself as Rais bel Cossim. "Your letter has reached one of the finest men in Swearah, an Englishman and a friend of mine. Mr. Willshire has agreed to pay the ransom," bel Cossim said. "He sent me straight away to deliver you from this place. I barely had time to kiss my wife good-bye," he added, "and then I rode night and day to get here."

Flushed with emotion, Riley told this news to the men. "Our souls were overwhelmed with joy," he reported, "and yet we trembled with apprehension lest it might not be true: alas! perhaps it was only a delusive dream, or some cruel trick to turn our miseries into mockery."

The Moor handed him a letter. Riley opened it, but he was too overcome by emotion to read it. His hands shook as he gave it to Savage to read out loud. Numb, Riley sank to the ground as Savage read by firelight:

Mogadore, October 25, 1815

My Dear and Afflicted Sir,

I have this moment received your two notes by Sidi Hamet, the contents of which, I hope, you will be perfectly assured have called forth my most sincere pity for your sufferings and those of your companions. . . .

I congratulate you most sincerely on the good fortune you and your fellow sufferers have met, by being in the hands of a man who seems to be guided by some degree of commiseration.

I can in some measure participate in the severe and dangerous sufferings and hardships you must have undergone; but, my dear Sir, console yourself, for, thanks be to God, I hope they will soon have a happy issue; for which purpose I devoutly pray the great Disposer of all things will give you and your unfortunate companions health and strength once more to visit your native land.

This letter will be delivered you by Rais bel Cossim, in whom you may place the fullest faith . . .

While Willshire commended the messenger, he went on to warn Riley to trust no one else. "I have agreed to pay the sum of nine hundred and twenty hard dollars to Sidi Hamet on your safe arrival in this town with your fellow sufferers; he remains here as a kind of hostage for your safe appearance."[1] Keep the transaction as secret as possible, he counseled, "for should the Moors suppose you able to pay more, they would throw difficulties in the way."

Then came the words that were almost overwhelming: "I have the most sincere pleasure to acquaint you, you will be at liberty to commence your journey for this town on the receipt of this letter." But Willshire begged them to "make what stages you please on the road" so as not to risk their health through "over-exertion and fatigue." He also instructed Riley to "write me an immediate answer, stating every particular relating to yourself, your crew, and vessel, as I have given orders to the Moor to forward it to me without delay."

Riley knew that his own letter had been a single flare fired into a dark night sky. Miraculously, it had been answered. As he and his men celebrated with the self-restraint dictated by their circumstances, they were sobered even further by the angry roar of Sheik Ali, who had now learned the facts of Hamet's negotiation from Sidi Mohammed. Ali railed at his fool of a son-in-law for ransoming the sailors at so low a price and for placing himself under the power of a "villainous Christian." "Riley," Ali bellowed, "will murder him, and steal his money as soon as he has these men in Swearah."

As the mercurial sheik worked himself into a froth, Rais bel Cossim, sensing the danger of his escalating rage, intervened. In what Riley called a "very firm, but eloquent and persuasive tone," the Moor addressed Ali, showing the quick thinking that gave Willshire confidence in him: "I bought the captain and his men with my own money," bel Cossim said, though this was untrue. "I paid Sidi Hamet before I left Swearah. Sidi Hamet remained there voluntarily as security against my safe return with the slaves.

"We are all of the same religion," bel Cossim soothed him. "We owe these Christian dogs nothing, and we have an undeniable right to make merchandise of them and use them as donkeys if we wish. That one," he said, pointing accusatorily at Riley, "he calls himself the captain, but he is a despicable liar. He has deceived Sidi Hamet and you. He was nothing but the cook on board the ship. The captain has long been dead."

Ali, a man well versed in the arts of subterfuge, glared at bel Cossim, smelling deceit. "If it were so, how could his note have convinced a stranger to pay so much money for him and the others?" he countered, despite having just claimed it was not enough. "No, he is a man of knowledge and standing. Perhaps you, though a Moslemin, have joined the Christians in a plot to rob and murder Sidi Hamet."

"No, by Allah! I am incapable of such a betrayal," bel Cossim declared. "Riley was indeed the cook. Look at him, he was stouter — fat, like a cook — and more able to endure. Look at the others. Give them paper, pen, and ink; they will show you they can write too, and better than Riley." Bel Cossim's gambit to downplay Riley's status and thus his monetary value put Ali on his heels.

While the two sparred, Seid quietly glowered. Sidi Mohammed, now reinstated as master of his household and aware that nothing good could happen at this late hour, broke up the proceedings, as was his right to do in his own home.

Bel Cossim insisted that his slaves would stay with him and would no longer inhabit the cellar. The others protested but to no avail. Bel Cossim reasserted that he had paid a lot of money for the captives and made it clear that he did not intend to lose any of them. Sidi Mohammed led all of his guests to a mule stable, which, even though recently used by the beasts, was an improvement on the cramped cellar.

At one end of the stable, the Arabs gathered on a platform that Riley believed was made of ship timbers. Here they talked and slept. At the other end, bel Cossim revealed as discreetly as possible the contents of his saddlebags and a pannier he carried. Willshire had sent shoes and hooded woolen djellabas, much needed now that they were in the hills with winter approaching. Willshire had also sent food and strong drink, which did even more for their souls than for their famished bodies. Out of the bag came hard biscuits, boiled tongue, tea, coffee, sugar, and several bottles of rum. They unpacked a teakettle, teapot, cups and saucers, all remarkable luxuries given that they had been eating — when they were lucky — with their hands from shared bowls since landing on the desert.

In the lamplight, Riley parceled out slices of tongue and biscuits, along with neat tots of rum. "We all felt as if new life was infused into our hearts," he recalled. They topped off this meal with a ripe watermelon.

Next the men slipped the soft leather shoes onto their toughened feet and wrapped themselves in the djellabas. Warmed inside and out, they lay down on the stable floor to sleep. But once again, even a moderate meal caused the sailors to writhe, according to Riley, with "such violent griping pains in our stomachs and intestines, that we could with great difficulty forbear screaming out with agony." In the clutches of cramps and nausea they were unable to sleep and lay awake contemplating the opening salvos in the conflict between bel Cossim and Sheik Ali.

Early the following morning, bel Cossim roused Riley and told him to make tea. Riley gathered some sticks, lit a fire, and boiled water in the teakettle. Word had spread that Sidi Mohammed had returned from Swearah with a Moor, and the locals, most of whom had never left the area in their lives, began to arrive to congratulate Mohammed on his return and to see the stranger.

In a loud and condescending voice, bel Cossim directed Riley in serving each visitor a cup of tea well sweetened with sugar, cleverly ingratiating himself with the poor villagers and confirming his position as master, not rescuer, of the Christians. None of the guests had ever tasted tea, which had only recently been introduced in Morocco and was far from being the ubiquitous drink it would become, or seen a teacup, and many drank it reluctantly, pleased, at the same time, to be the recipients of the northerner's gifts. Riley served all the guests until they left. Then he poured his men strong tea, which made their stomachs feel better. Bel Cossim turned to Sheik Ali and said, "I told you before that Riley was the cook, and now you see with your own eyes that he is the only one that can wait upon us."

Around eight in the morning, bel Cossim and the five sailors set off from the village. Their escort consisted of Sheik Ali, who insisted on accompanying them with two bodyguards, as well as Seid, Sidi Mohammed, and Bo-Mohammed. Bel Cossim had tried to buy mounts for all the sailors, but none had been available at any price. They would have to take turns on their insufficient collection of camels, mules, and donkeys. Horace had recovered enough to be steady on his feet. Only Burns was unable to walk and so occupied a mule the entire way.

As they traveled, Riley related to bel Cossim the story of their journey so far. At the end, bel Cossim responded: "Praised be the Almighty, the most high and holy, for his goodness. You have indeed been preserved most wonderfully by the peculiar protection and assistance of an overruling Providence, and must be a particular favorite of heaven: there never was an instance of a Christian's passing the great desert for such a distance before. Sidi Hamet is right. You are no doubt destined to do some great good in the world."

They passed first southeast through a dry, sandy terrain of sporadic cultivated fields. When they were separated far enough from Ali, bel Cossim answered Riley's questions about the sheik, whose presence alarmed them both. Ali was the chief of a tribe living in the hills to the south on the edge of the desert. "Sidi Hamet married one of his daughters but has since been at war with him," bel Cossim told Riley. "In the contest the sheik destroyed Hamet's town and took back his daughter but afterwards restored her again on making peace." The ruthless sheik, it was said, could muster ten thousand men when needed. Bel Cossim believed Ali was scheming against them but told Riley: "Allah could turn his evil intentions to our good. The power that has protected you thus far will not forsake you until his will is accomplished."

In the early afternoon, about twenty miles from Sidi Mohammed's village, the men were brought up short by a ghastly sight.[2] Not far from the path, around the breached walls of a silent village, the intermingled corpses of dozens of villagers and raiders lay sprawled on the ground. Most were little more than small heaps of dried bones picked clean by dogs and birds and bleaching in the sun.

Side by side, Muslim and Christian gazed out on a staggering scene of violent death beneath groves of unkempt date and pomegranate trees. No caretaker remained to prune their shaggy branches. No guard would ever again open the village's heavy wooden gate, which was still locked in its stone arch. Riley did not detail the futility he felt standing there on a plain before a medieval scene an ocean away from his family and home, his withered shipmates too exhausted to climb down off their kneeling camels. There were no words for it. Although Europe had been embroiled in two decades of bloody war and the British had recently burned Washington, this small-scale scene of annihilation, so far from the tracks of history and where so little — not even a grave — was to be gained by the ruin and suffering, felt even more tragic.

Finally, Sidi Mohammed broke the silence to tell the tale of his neighboring village, with bel Cossim translating his words into Spanish. Under Omar el Milliah (Omar the Good), a friend and benefactor of Mohammed's, the village of Widnah, built in 1775, had thrived. Upon Omar's death in 1813, his son Ismael had assumed control of the town. Ismael was a hedonist who put more effort into expanding his harem than governing and defending his subjects. Finally he grew so depraved that he snatched the betrothed wife of his own brother, Kesh-bah. Enraged, Kesh-bah fled south to the mountains and sought the aid of Sheik Sulmin, an old enemy of his father's, who lived there. Sulmin, eager to avenge past defeats, gathered an army of Arabs from the fringe of the desert with the promise of spoils of livestock, sacks of grain, clothing, virgins, and slaves.

The raiders had wheeled their siege machines right up to Widnah's unguarded fifteen-foot stone-and-mud walls without raising alarm. These two battering machines still stood next to the village's west wall, and Riley, whose profession was to command the most complex transportation machine of his day, examined them with a connoisseur's eye. Each machine consisted of a scaffolding built of tree trunks and logs and bound together by massive ropes made of braided thongs of camels' hide. From this, the attackers had suspended a boulder of several tons, which many men together pulled back with ropes, pendulum-fashion, and then sent crashing into the wall.

After they broke through, the carnage was great on both sides. The surprised villagers fought bravely, but the attackers, bloodthirsty and frenzied, prevailed, slaughtering every man and boy but two, who escaped carrying the alarm to the neighboring villages, and all the women and children, except for two hundred girls, whom they took alive.

Sidi Mohammed had been among those who had chased the fleeing attackers and caught up with them in the mountains the next morning. Sulmin sent his spoils on under heavy guard and fought the pursuit in a steep narrow pass, rolling boulders down the path on them. In a bloody, desperate fight, his wild men murdered or wounded half of those who had followed them. Mohammed pulled open his djellaba and showed a large scar where a musket ball had gouged his chest. Eventually the raiders dispersed on the Sahara, vanishing like the wind.

By the time the hunt for the enemy had been abandoned, Mohammed explained, the dead were too decomposed to approach and bury. "They had offended the Almighty by their pride, and none could be found to save them," he reasoned, trying to make sense of the tragedy with the fatalism endemic to the desert. "Thus perished Widnah and its haughty inhabitants."

Silently, the men headed east, mulling over the savage yet eerily tranquil scene. After three hours they reached a crooked northwest-flowing river in a five-mile-wide valley. As far as the eye could see, domed white sanctuaries garrisoned the arid banks of the river Riley mistakenly identified as Woed Sehlem.

In reality, it was probably Oued Massa, the area's only major northwest-flowing river, albeit reduced by five years of drought to a miserable trickle. At its broad, now empty mouth lay the town of Massa on what bel Cossim, a merchant captain in the grain trade with Europe, told Riley was the best harbor on the coast. It was five miles wide at the mouth and superior even to that at Cadiz, Spain's famous southern seaport. Bel Cossim had seen near Massa the ruins of a Christian town, which had been sacked long ago. Pieces of its walls protruded from the sand like gravestones.

Massa was also where British merchant James Grey Jackson once saw a pair of colossal whale jawbones arching up from the sand. A local informed him that they had always been there and that, when the whale had beached, a man named Jonah had emerged from its belly. Jackson laughed at the tale. His earnest informant responded only that "nobody but a Christian would doubt the fact."

Inland from the town where the patron saint of lost-luck sailors had allegedly been spewed from the whale, the Commerces discovered two fortified villages on the riverbanks. When the party paused to rest near an outlying house surrounded by vegetable gardens and ringed in dry thornbush, the hungry sailors furtively stole some of the prickly pears from limbs cascading over the thorn-bush. Fearful of being caught, they popped the fruit into their mouths whole. The punishment for this transgression was swift and excruciating. The needled skin of the fruit adhered to their tongues and the roofs of their mouths. The fine shafts broke off and their bases had to be painstakingly extracted, one by one.

The men crossed the shallow river where it was easily accessible for the camels and where villagers filled vessels and watered live-stock. As the party carried on toward the coast, the riverbed broad-ened, and they began to see bright green pools of stagnant water where the ocean tide had filled deep bends before being choked off by the sand. All was blighted by the lengthy drought and locust infestation, until they came to a village Riley identified as Sehlemah. Here, ditches from a hillside irrigated dark fields and borders of grapevines and date, fig, and pomegranate trees. Men and boys har-vested corn and barley in the fields, filling sacks and baskets and loading them onto camels and mules, which they drove inside the village walls. Trailing the harvesters, the villagers' thin and scruffy livestock, including oxen, cleaned up the chaff.

At dusk, Rais bel Cossim's party entered the village, which stretched for three hundred yards along the river. They made their way to a blacksmith shop near the gate. In one corner, a man worked large bellows made out of animal skins and attached to a charcoal-burning forge. Nearby sat a massive anvil, so squat that the smiths had to bend down to hammer on it. The sailors were given space on the shop floor while Sidi Mohammed and bel Cossim visited the vil-lage chief and asked for permission to remain overnight.

With Widnah still fresh in their minds, the sailors watched as the field hands filed in through the gates, bringing in their livestock and the pack animals with the day's last load of crops. The village's one-story flat-roofed houses featured ungainly iron locks on sturdy wooden doors, and each had only one small square window to let in light. Finally, the gates clashed shut, and guards secured them for the night with large wooden bars before mounting the massive twenty-foot walls to keep watch.

Bel Cossim gave the sailors dates for their supper. They ate while the village men and boys came and gawked and asked questions about their homes and their reason for coming there. Several villagers even spoke to Riley in Spanish, repeating "vile oaths and execrations," the meaning of which they clearly did not understand.

The following morning, October 30, the sailors and their escorts arose in the dark. A slender waning crescent moon on the eastern horizon sliced the inky night near the blazing planets Venus and Jupiter, marking the end of the lunar cycle. The travelers departed Sehlemah at dawn when the gates were opened. The Atlas Mountains loomed in the distance, delineating another world, and there was an urgency to their riding that stemmed from a variety of motivations. The sailors longed for a bath, a real bed, and a regular diet, but most of all an end to the pounding of the trail. Bel Cossim had sworn to deliver them to Willshire and was eager to do so.

Sheik Ali, on the other hand, had devised a plan for taking possession of the sailors. They would not reach Swearah if he had anything to do with it.

Unlike the day before, Ali was in a gregarious mood. He maneuvered alongside Riley and began an unctuous pitch: "Come with me, Captain Riley, to the mountains in the south, and I will make you a chief in my nation. You will marry one of my daughters." Ali was used to seeing his persuasive arts succeed, and finding Riley unmoved by his offers, he forced the group to stop several times while he pressed his case.

Near a copse of thorny argan trees, sagging under the weight of their ripe orbs, Riley, frustrated by the delays, picked up what he thought was a date from the ground. When he bit into it, however, he discovered that it was argan fruit. He spat out the bitter pulp, reminded that in this strange land little was as it appeared to be on the surface.

For several days, the sailors had viewed from afar the Atlas, whose snowcapped peaks ripsawed the northeastern sky. As they drew closer, they felt the mountains' presence in cold, brooding clouds that scudded down the northeast ridges. Increasingly frigid gusts buffeted them, and they privately thanked Willshire for his foresight in sending down the cloaks and shoes. The camels, mules, and two donkeys moved at a slower clip now, and Seid, Bo-Mohammed, and bel Cossim took turns running to stay warm. Yet even as the gloom worsened, Riley felt buoyed by this atmosphere, which more closely resembled that of his native Connecticut than the desert. He felt in his bones that he was approaching the border of the Empire of Morocco, the crossing of which symbolized freedom for him just as surely as traversing the Mason and Dixon line would for black slaves in the near future in the United States.

Thomas Burns did not share his captain's elation. His circulation was not up to warding off the cold, and numbness was spreading through his limbs. Suddenly, he tumbled off the back of his camel. Landing on his head and shoulders, he blacked out and lay unconscious for some time. After a while and with, according to Riley, "much exertion . . . on our part," he regained consciousness and was lifted back up onto the beast. He had no choice.

As they crossed the plain, they passed dozens of villages with increasingly sophisticated defenses that resembled old European castles. Crenellated walls, turrets, and sentry stations contrasted sharply with the wild Atlas foothills. In midafternoon, after traveling what Riley estimated to be fifty miles, they veered off the path and arrived at the turreted walls of Shtuka, a diamond-shaped town of about five thousand people.[3] Hungry and thirsty, they dismounted at a well outside the gate, but there was no bucket with which to draw the water. Sheik Ali and Seid entered the town, Riley believed, to get provisions. They soon beckoned bel Cossim and Sidi Mohammed inside, leaving Bo-Mohammed and Ali's two men to watch the sailors.

Despite the cold wind and dark sky heavy with mountain moisture, a crowd of men and boys poured out through the gate to see the Christians. Clark and Burns were so weak that they could not sit up even when pride and dignity called for it most. Riley, Savage, and Horace were little better. The Arab boys spat on them and threw dirt and stones at them while the fathers laughed at their sons' pluck. One kind man, however, retrieved a bucket, drew water, and served the tired sailors. After this relief, Riley assessed his bedraggled men. He doubted even the strongest of them could go on riding until dark again. Burns, bruised and shaken from his fall, certainly could not, unless he was strapped to a camel. Riley tried to rally them with the news that they were now just a day's ride south of Agadir and Taroudant, the southernmost towns controlled by the Sultan of Morocco, where they would be "out of the reach of the rapacious Arabs."

Riley need not have worried about whether his men could travel on, however. Ali had led them into a trap.

When the clouds burst, the crowd of Arabs prodded and pushed the Commerces to the town's rough-hewn stone gate. They sheltered beneath an arch in the walls, which rose twenty feet above and were five feet thick at the base. The rain, the first Riley and his four shipmates had seen in Africa, cascaded down. For two hours, they shivered in the damp chill across an alley from an uninviting warren of one-story pisé houses and wondered what was going on inside the town. To pass the time, Riley applied his engineer's mind to the architecture of the gate, noting that the opening was sealed by one stout door with "two folding leaves" and swung on the "ends of its back posts which are let into large stone sockets at the bottom and at the top." Four heavy wooden bars secured the door at night.

Inside the walls of Shtuka, Sheik Ali had worked himself into a paroxysm of rage, bellowing so forcefully that the sailors could hear him. He was laying out his case to the town's ruler, Moulay Ibrahim, whom he had known for many years and considered an ally. Other, more sober voices, bel Cossim's among them, also drifted out from Ibrahim's house.

At last, a frustrated Rais bel Cossim stumbled out of Ibrahim's meeting room accompanied by a number of thugs. Riley could see that things had not gone well. Bel Cossim's usually bright face showed indignation and telegraphed the result: Ali had prevailed. The Moorish captain took Riley aside and in a hushed voice told him that Ali had claimed him and his men as his property, on the grounds that his son-in-law owed him more than the value of five Christian slaves. Ali had also declared that Hamet was held hostage by a Christian in Swearah and that the slaves should not be allowed to move north of Shtuka until Ali was paid $1,500, and Hamet, the husband of his daughter, was set free. Seid, of course, had supported Ali.

"I have argued the matter every way, but all to no purpose," bel Cossim told Riley. "I promised to deliver them six hundred dollars as soon as we get to Agadir in the sultan's dominion. I agreed to proceed in company with the prince and sheik and to wait there for the return of Sidi Hamet, but they will not listen to reason."

The news came as a heavy blow to Riley. "It bereft me of my fortitude," he later reflected. "The fair prospects I had entertained of a speedy liberation from slavery, particularly for the last two days, were now suddenly darkened." He could not bear to relay it to his sodden men. Shaking him even further, bel Cossim said he had to leave them now and go to Willshire for instructions. He would be gone six days. "May the Almightly preserve you in the meantime from their evil machinations," bel Cossim beseeched.

As bel Cossim mounted his mule and prepared to depart, Sidi Mohammed brought him more bad news: "Moulay Ibrahim and Sheik Ali have determined that you shall not go to Swearah," he announced. "They fear you will cause a war to break out between them and the sultan." Mohammed volunteered to go in bel Cossim's stead, to carry letters to Willshire and remain as a hostage if need be. He promised Riley that because of his two wives, seven children, and property, he was an even more valuable hostage than Hamet. He also reassured him that Hamet, "your friend," would come down directly to help. "Allah is great and good," said Mohammed, who had embraced Hamet's belief in Riley's blessings, "and will restore you to your family."

Riley took the old man's hand and kissed it, addressing him, "Father, I hope the Almighty will reward you for your benevolence."

Before leaving, Mohammed joined the renewed debate over the sailors. The parties faced each other now in a ring outside the village gate. Supported by his elders, Moulay Ibrahim, himself seventy years old, a ruler enriched by nearby copper and silver deposits, listened as bel Cossim restated his position: He was the rightful owner of the Christians, for whom he had already paid an agreed-upon sum of his own money. Neither the prince nor the sheik had a right to stop him. This was a violation of the rules of hospitality and an affront to their religion, since they were all brothers under Allah.

Ali countered that Hamet and Seid both owed him a great deal of money, that he had an unquestionable right to their joint property and a responsibility to all three parties not to jeopardize that property or to let it be sold for less than its value. He was within his rights, he maintained, to hold the slaves in his territory until he was repaid. Ibrahim, a man Riley described as having a fairer complexion and softer features than many of the tough men of Souss, also listened patiently to the testimony of Sidi Mohammed and Bo-Mohammed, who supported bel Cossim.

Both principals prudently concluded by lavishing praise on Ibrahim, acknowledging his justice and virtue and agreeing — at least for now — that he should adjudicate the matter. Ibrahim's reply was swift and firm: "You, Sheik Ali, my old friend, and Rais bel Cossim, both of you claim these five Christian slaves as your own property, and each of you has some reason on your side. Yet, as it is not in my power to decide whose claim is the best founded, I am resolved, with a strict regard to justice, and without going into further evidence, to keep the slaves in my own city, carefully guarded, until messengers can be sent to Swearah, who shall bring down Sidi Hamet. It is only then that a just decision can be made regarding all the claims. Bel Cossim, you will be as a guest, not a prisoner, for as long as you stay in this city."

It was now dark out. Honoring their word that they would abide by Ibrahim's decision, Ali and bel Cossim swallowed their mutual loathing and ceased their recriminations. They were then ushered, Arabs and slaves alike, into the freshly scoured streets of the town.

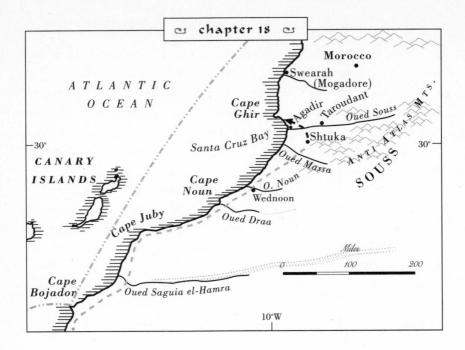

chapter 18

From the Mouth of a Moor

〰 Bel Cossim and Sheik Ali and his men took up quarters in a building next to Moulay Ibrahim's house. Joined by Ibrahim, they sat on a mat at one end of a large room and carried on a lively discourse through the night. At the other end, the sailors, vexed by dysentery, painful hemorrhoids, and lice, huddled in a corner among the saddlebags and luggage. Sentinels armed with muskets and scimitars attended the doors to the room and the building as well as the town gates. The sailors ate couscous out of a common bowl and, by Riley's admission, succumbed to their physical and mental distress: they sobbed like children.

In the morning, bel Cossim brought Riley a pen, ink, and paper. The captain scrawled a second note to William Willshire, apprising him of their arrival in the town of Shtuka and their current trouble.

William Willshire
(from *Sequel to Riley's Narrative*, 1851)

Bel Cossim, who could not write, dictated a note to a scribe. With these, Seid, Sidi Mohammed, and Bo-Mohammed set off for Swearah.

Vowing to return in four days, Sheik Ali also departed, giving Riley and his men some breathing room to recover their wits and their strength. After coming so close to regaining their freedom, the wait was excruciating. They could do little to help themselves but rest. Bel Cossim tried to buoy their flagging spirits. When Riley complained to him that he doubted he would live long enough to see freedom, as he was "extremely feeble and must soon perish," bel Cossim admonished him: "What! Dare you distrust the power of that God who has preserved you so long by miracles?" And he cajoled: "No, my friend, the God of Heaven and of earth is your friend and will not forsake you; but in his own good time restore you to your liberty and to the embraces of your family.

"We must say," bel Cossim added philosophically, " 'his will be done,' and be contented with our lot, for God knows best what is for our good. We are all children of the same heavenly Father, who watches over all our actions, whether we be Moor, or Christian, or

Pagan, or of any other religion; we must perform his will." The Moor's tolerant thinking humbled Riley. "To hear such sentiments from the mouth of a Moor, whose nation I had been taught to consider the worst of barbarians," he admitted, "filled my mind with awe and reverence, and I looked up to him as a kind of superior being."

Bel Cossim knew he must counterbalance Ali's advantage of prior friendship with Moulay Ibrahim, so he invited Ibrahim to come for a private talk in the great room he was sharing with the Christians. In these more relaxed conditions, Riley admired the intelligence of the prince's face and his mild but active character. Although he could not understand everything they said, he could tell from the Arabs' expressions and the tenor of the conversation that bel Cossim was artfully flattering him. Bel Cossim inquired about his family. The prince had one wife, who had no children. "Does she have tea and sugar?" he asked.

"No," Ibrahim replied.

After the meeting, bel Cossim quietly solicited the help of one of the prince's young black slave girls in acquiring some wood and water. He built a fire and brewed tea. When Ibrahim was out, bel Cossim gave the girl a lump of sugar and sent her with a cup of very sweet tea to the prince's wife.

The girl soon returned. Her mistress, she told him, thanked him for the tea and said she would keep the lovely cup and saucer, the likes of which she had never seen before. She asked what she could do in return. "Tell your mistress," bel Cossim said, "that I only want to be Moulay Ibrahim's friend. If she could influence the prince in my favor, I would be most gratified."

An hour later, Moulay Ibrahim burst into the room and demanded to know what bel Cossim had been doing with his wife. With great deference, the Moor explained the harmless nature of his interaction with her and that he was only trying to do her the honor she deserved as his hostess and the wife of a great prince. "You had no need to curry favor through her," Ibrahim responded. "You already have my friendship."

The maneuver was effective, even if Ibrahim saw through it. The two went to pray in the mosque, and when they returned hours later, Riley saw that they had grown more intimate. Now bel Cossim was truly being treated as a guest and not a quasi prisoner. Taking advantage of his liberty, bel Cossim dispatched a messenger to an old and wealthy friend, who lived within a day's journey, asking him to come to Shtuka and bring money, not as much as Ali had demanded but enough, he believed, to appease him nonetheless.

That evening, Moulay Ibrahim talked and prayed with bel Cossim. Afterward, the Moor told Riley that Ibrahim had given his "princely word that he will protect both me and my slaves." He had even promised an escort into the sultan's dominion.

Early in the morning on November 3, according to Riley's calendar, Moulay Ibrahim entered his guests' chamber carrying eggs and salt for their breakfast. He left and soon returned with half a dozen chickens. Ibrahim himself even carried in firewood and water, as Riley marveled. The sailors boiled the eggs, salted them, and ate ravenously. Meanwhile, bel Cossim slaughtered the chickens, deftly clutching the birds' wings in his left hand, turning to face the east, and crying "Besmillah!" as he cut their throats. The sailors cleaned four birds and put them in the pot with salt and the vegetables Ibrahim had also brought them: onions, green peppers, turnips, and miniature squash.

Riley allowed that the resulting soup would have been thought savory in any country. In an unusual show of respect to a Christian, Moulay Ibrahim invited Riley to eat from the bowl that he and bel Cossim were sharing.[1] While they ate, he asked the captain about his family, and Riley told him of the wife and five children awaiting his return.

From then on, Moulay Ibrahim made sure that the sailors received "all the relief and comfort in his power," according to Riley. Bel Cossim provided for them too. Late in the afternoon, his friend arrived with two mules loaded with couscous, eggs, and chickens. He handed bel Cossim the five hundred Spanish silver dollars he had asked for, but bel Cossim was now confident that Moulay Ibrahim would not succumb to Ali's reasoning or tricks. He told his old friend he did not need it. The old man insisted that he accept the food, and he agreed, he said, because it was a gift for Riley. The old man also stated that he would raise an army that day and use all of his influence to escort the sailors safely to Agadir, in the sultan's dominion. Bel Cossim thanked him but told him he believed he could count on Moulay Ibrahim's protection.

For three days they lived as well as they could wish on the old man's gifts. During that time, bel Cossim went to a fair in a nearby town. From there he proceeded to a shrine about fifteen miles outside Shtuka in honor of el Ajjh, "the pilgrim," a sharif famed throughout the region for his supernatural powers and feared and obeyed by all. At the shrine, bel Cossim had a vision. He returned to the fair and bought a small fat bull of the best quality. The butcher cut it into two sides. Bel Cossim sent a messenger with one side loaded on a mule to el Ajjh. "When you deliver the side and el Ajjh asks you who sent it," he told the messenger, "tell him a pious man who has lately come from Swearah, is now a guest with Moulay Ibrahim, and wishes to be remembered in his prayers."

Bel Cossim returned to Shtuka with the other half of the bull for the prince. Meeting Riley, he told him what he had done and that he was sure that if the sharif accepted his gift, he would visit them before sunset. Then he explained rather cryptically, "It is not so much the real value of the present that is important but the manner of giving it, which can put the receiver under such an obligation as to make him your friend forever."

Going out to pray near dusk, bel Cossim encountered el Ajjh, who had come to meet the man who had sent him so generous a gift. El Ajjh asked bel Cossim what favor he wanted that caused him to send such a gift. The Moor related the story of the Christian sailors to him, telling him that he himself had paid for them. He asked el Ajjh to intercede with Sheik Ali and persuade him to allow them to continue on to Agadir. El Ajjh promised that he would bring his influence to bear — even if that meant by force.

On November 7, Ali returned to Shtuka.[2] Confident of his alliance with Ibrahim, he arrived not with an army but with just a bodyguard. Bel Cossim sent an "express" messenger to inform el

Ajjh of the sheik's arrival. The holy man, who was also an old friend of Ali's, came at once to pay him a visit.

Insisting that his business was urgent, el Ajjh took Ali aside to speak in privacy. "Brother, I have learned that Sidi Hashem knows of the Christian slaves," he deceitfully warned the sheik, referring to Tazeroualt's powerful Berber ruler. "He has secretly tried to buy them and been rebuffed, and he is determined to take them for himself by force." Hashem would be setting out the next day, el Ajjh told Ali, who knew the resourceful warlord all too well. When the sultan had sent an army against Hashem, the Berber had cleverly abandoned his stronghold, sending the women and children into hiding in the mountains. The northern army sacked the town, torched their fields, and rampaged unopposed for a week. Hashem baited Sulayman's troops with fleeting raids, giving the impression that this was all the resistance he could muster. Then, when the time was right, Hashem unleashed his angry forces. They routed the sultan's army and pursued the fleeing troops north, hacking them down one by one. A few survivors staggered into the town of Taroudant, bringing news of the slaughter and burnishing Sidi Hashem's reputation for blood and terror.

With Beyrouk of Wednoon, Hashem controlled the Tombuctoo caravans. He would covet the Christians if for no other reason than to prevent them from reaching Morocco and falling into the hands of his enemy Sulayman.

"You must immediately ride north into Sulayman's territory," the sharif told a shaken Ali. "Hashem will not venture there merely for the sake of the Christian slaves. If you do not go, you will surely lose the slaves and at the same time engulf all of Souss in a war." Ali thanked el Ajjh for his guidance and rushed back to Ibrahim's house to meet with him. Bel Cossim, meanwhile, slipped away to the town gate, where el Ajjh informed him of his conversation with Ali.

When Ali appealed to Ibrahim to allow him to seize the prisoners that night and carry them away, the prince responded firmly that he could not break his word. He must keep them there until all parties assembled to settle the matter. Convinced that no amount of begging, cajoling, or arm-twisting would budge him, Ali then found bel Cossim. He took a friendly tack, conceding to the Moor that he considered him to be a trustworthy man meriting his friendship. To demonstrate his sincerity and to avoid imposing on Moulay Ibrahim any longer, he would consent to removing the sailors north to Agadir, a port solidly within the sultan's realm, in the morning. He would accompany them and wait for Sidi Hamet's arrival there.

Bel Cossim played his hand coolly. "Now that you have stopped me and my Christian slaves against the laws of justice and hospitality and kept us here this long," he told the sheik, "I have no desire to move them, until Sidi Hamet arrives and proves that you have done wrong in detaining us." Ali and Ibrahim insisted that the men would be safer and happier in Agadir, where they might find a doctor as well. Bel Cossim gradually allowed himself to be talked into the journey, consenting to it only under the conditions that a guard of Ibrahim's men accompany them and that Ali provide all the sailors with riding camels. Ali agreed and left to make arrangements.

Under the direction of bel Cossim, the sailors spent much of the night preparing for the journey. They killed the last chickens, boiled the remaining eggs, and packed these away. At daybreak, five camels awaited them, all with better saddles than any the sailors had used in the desert, as well as bags of barley and empty ten-bushel sacks made of tent cloth. This gave them both more padding and something to hold on to as they rode. Each camel was accompanied by his master, who would serve as a guide, leading the beast on foot for the entire journey.

As the camels stood up with their riders, first the hind legs rising, then the forelegs, in their awkward way, Riley was thrown head over feet off the backside of an enormous beast, nearly ten feet tall. He had the good luck to land on his heels, jarring but not injuring himself.

The guides helped Riley back onto his camel, steadying his legs as it rose and imploring him to hold on. His mount's owner told him: "Allah be praised for turning you over. Had you fallen upon your head, these stones must have dashed out your brains; but the camel is a sacred animal, and heaven protects those who ride on him! Had you fallen from an ass, though he is only two cubits and a half high, it would have killed you, for the ass is not so noble a creature as the camel and the horse."[3]

The group left Shtuka in a hurry, accompanied now by Moulay Ibrahim, heading northeast across a broad, fertile plain shaped like a long compass needle, with its base at the sea and pointing northeast between the Atlas and Anti-Atlas. The mountains towered above them at more than twelve thousand feet. Ibrahim had discreetly deployed two hundred men on horses along their route. The guard shadowed the caravan, only occasionally coming into sight.

Other than Oued Souss, with its mouth at Agadir, there were virtually no streams here. The land was dry but fertile. The party passed an increasing number of villages, which were supplied with water by deep wells tapping the subterranean flow from the mountains to the sea. These sat amid grain fields now being plowed, vineyards, and orchards. The argan trees were still green, the figs barren. Riley, who felt strongly the pull of civilization, reveled in the groves of date, almond, orange, and pomegranate trees.

After six hours, the guides running beside the camels the entire time, they came upon another scene of devastation. A mile southwest of the trail, an eerie still life of seven silent villages with breached walls and abandoned battering machines loomed on the plain. A family feud between two of the villages had engulfed them all in a ruinous monthlong war. Bel Cossim, who was from near Agadir, told Riley that feuds were common here. He knew many families in good circumstances caught up in them. "They were seldom finished until one family or the other was exterminated," he told Riley, "and their names blotted out from the face of the earth."

Despite this second scene of human folly, Riley found the increasing signs of commerce and cultivation encouraging. By midday the white walls of Agadir — a Berber word meaning "fortified granary" — came into sight at a great distance across the plain. Though much of the land was still barren and lacking in forage for livestock, they saw many people around the small villages busily plowing fields and sowing barley. They passed a continual stream of men in unsoiled haiks, who were refreshingly unarmed. Their droves of camels and asses carried salt, dried fish from the coast, and other merchandise for peaceful trading. A flourishing merchant class working under safe conditions, Riley knew, was a hallmark of all civilized nations during peace.

Still, the landscape — a battleground of the earth's surfaces — embodied instability, and there was something eerie about it. The arable land seemed temporarily borrowed from the craggy Atlas foothills, the snowcapped mountains, the sea that had once covered it, and the sand that still might. Human existence was elemental and tenuous. That afternoon, as they angled toward the coast, they encountered the grasping tentacles of the Sahara — massive sand drifts twenty miles from the sea. The walls and domes of aged saint houses still resisted the tide of "clean coarse beach sand" but only because the locals periodically pushed aside the drifts and tended to their walls. The company passed by the ruins of Rabeah, where Moulay Ibrahim was born. "It was a thriving place," Ibrahim told Riley, "until the sands toppled over the north wall and swallowed the town within a year."

They crossed a ten-mile band of high dunes and then came to the steep banks of a wadi that Riley identified as "el Woa Sta," but was probably Oued Souss or Oued Lahouar, since el Woa Sta, or Oued-i-Sta, lies much farther to the south. Nearly a hundred feet deep in places and perhaps four miles wide, the gorge accentuated the jagged mountains to the east and south of them buttressing the for-midable Atlas range towering on the horizon. Even without scien-tific evidence, from the signs that water once filled much of the lowland and on the grandeur of the mountain range, Riley sensed that this might have once been "one of the fairest portions of the African continent."

As dark fell on Agadir, Moulay Ibrahim, bel Cossim, Sheik Ali, the sailors of the *Commerce*, and the company of camel guides and servants quietly entered the lower town, a fishing port at the base of a mountain. A square-walled casbah on a conical hill dominated the bay. The sweet reek of bacalao, or codfish, assailed their nostrils, reminding Riley of previous visits to the Canary Islands, not far to the west of Agadir, where the fishermen sun-dried the catch on their decks. Locals were impervious to the stench, while foreign vessels, unable to bear it, anchored well away. Still, even foreign sailors prized the cod, which Riley praised as "extremely fat and delicate."

Fishing boats and nets sprawled on the beach, along a bay considered the southernmost anchorage on Morocco's Atlantic coast, with shelter from the east and northeast winds, though Riley quickly perceived that it was too open for a good winter harbor, when the winds would embay ships and drive them on shore. Masts of shipwrecks littered the beach in various stages of being consumed by the rising sand.

The town itself had a long history of boom and bust. The Portuguese had founded it three centuries earlier to tap into the riches of the Saharan caravans and had been driven from its shores by the Moroccans, who later abandoned it, moving many of its merchants north to Swearah. William Lempriere, who visited Agadir around 1790, observed that this former center of European habitation and international trade was then "a deserted town, with only a few houses, which are almost hourly mouldering to decay" (p. 714).

Lempriere might have exaggerated the town's decline. While the sailors took heart in reaching another milestone on the journey, Sheik Ali and Rais bel Cossim planned their next moves. Despite the cover of dark, the large company of men, including foreigners, could hardly go unnoticed, and the streets soon teemed with curious residents, fishermen and fishmongers, and the sons of fishermen and fishmongers, eager to see the Christian slaves or anything that would break the monotony of their daily lives. The Souassa, as people from the Souss region are known, spat on the sailors, heaved sticks and stones at them, and cursed them in Spanish. The greeting "¡Carajo a la mierda le sara, perro y bestias!" — You are lower than the dung of beasts! — stuck in Riley's mind. Bel Cossim, who was born near Agadir, spotted a man he knew. Taking advantage of the maelstrom of unwanted attention, he greeted him warmly in the Arab fashion and spoke to him in furtive tones.

Bel Cossim and the rest of the party made their way from the beach to the back of the town, where they pitched camp by a smithy. Some Souassa prepared baked and boiled fish and couscous for the Arab visitors and gave the leftovers to the sailors; the camels and mules were fed barley. Afterward, bel Cossim discreetly warned Riley to remain alert and told him that he would watch Ali, who he was sure was still plotting against them, and get information from his own allies in town. Despite bel Cossim's concerns, Riley calmly reassured his edgy men that they were now safe in the sultan's territory, just days away from liberation, and urged them to rest up for the final push. They lay down on the ground, curled up in the blankets they had been given, and went to sleep. Riley remained awake.

Just after midnight the Moor returned with bad news. "Sheik Ali has made a deal with the governor," he whispered to the captain. "They will seize you in the morning and make you pay the ransom Ali demands. If you cannot, he will be allowed to make off with you and return to his stronghold near the desert.

"You must get up now and ride out of town. If you are at least four leagues [about fourteen miles] out of Agadir by sunrise, I believe you will be safe," he said. "If not, the governor's men will overtake you and bring you back." Bel Cossim roused the cameleers, who were nearby, and instructed them to prepare the camels.

"The drivers know the road," he told Riley. "It is very rocky. Tell your men to hold on tight and to use their utmost exertions. In three more days you will be in Swearah with your friend, inshallah. I will join you as soon as I can."

The sailors mounted the camels, and the guides led them through the town, whispering soothing words to the animals to keep them calm. As they edged their way up along the northward path, the group had to pass right beside the fortress's lower batteries and the old Portuguese fort. For such large beasts, the camels were remarkably quiet on their padded feet. Often noisy growlers, none so much as bellowed or snorted now. Meanwhile, bel Cossim lay down in front of the door to the room where Sheik Ali slept. If the sheik stirred, he would know. Before drifting off, bel Cossim scripted the impending confrontation with Ali.

The sailors and the guides, now in the pay of bel Cossim, rounded Pointe Arhesdis, and rode north above a rocky beach, the crash of the surf below covering their escape. In a transcendent moment, the roar of the waves caused Riley to reflect on the "direful shipwrecks" that were sure to succeed his "and the consequent miseries of the poor mariner driven on this inhospitable coast." They traveled in silence for two hours, passing Oued Tamrhaght (the Wife's River, in the Tachelhit Berber dialect), a channel that when flowing carries water through a fertile valley and marks what is today the northern border of Souss. About nine miles outside Agadir, they heard the noise that they dreaded, the iron-on-stone clinking of horse or mule riders. While they were at an advantage in that their camels could not be heard at a distance, the hills had blocked out the sound of the approaching riders until they were very close. They had no time and no place to hide.

Suddenly, a large party of men appeared. Riley was momentarily confused, then relieved, then wary: these men were not pursuing them from Agadir but rushing toward it.

Riders at night meant urgency, usually trouble of one sort or another, men prepared to act first and ask questions later. It was too dark for either party to make out the faces of the other. Neither group wished to acknowledge or to be acknowledged by the other. The situation was so tense that a stumble, a sudden move, a glimmer of metal in the starlight could have started a fight. Every man with a weapon gripped it. But Riley, high on his tall camel, perceived something in the passing silhouettes.

On an impulse, he shouted out, "Sidi Hamet!"

"Escoon? Riley?" came the reply. Who is it? Riley?

Sidi Hamet had returned.

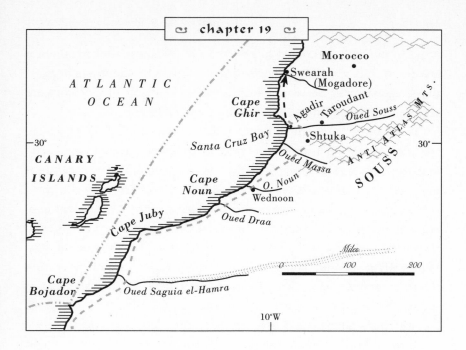

chapter 19

The Road to Swearah

The two parties lurched to a halt. Riley followed the sound of Hamet's voice, found him, took his hand, and kissed it. Hamet was equally glad to see the captain. He had spent many uneasy hours in Willshire's cluttered house and in the bustling streets of Swearah worrying about Riley, his son, and the other sailors. Nearby, Sidi Mohammed's ebullience indicated his satisfaction at reuniting with the men they had committed to saving.

As Riley recounted Sheik Ali's actions and warned of the current threat, Hamet shook his head.

"Ali is a bad man," he said. "He does not fear Allah."

Hamet told Riley that the sailors must continue on toward Swearah. He would settle affairs with his father-in-law either in Agadir or on the trail. At the least, he would do his best to slow down Ali's pursuit of the sailors. They wasted little time in conversation. Riley met Bel Mooden, another emissary of Willshire's, a short, stout, neatly dressed gray-bearded Moor, who spoke Spanish fluently and listened intently as Riley gave him news of bel Cossim. Without ceremony, Bel Mooden took possession of the sailors and in turn presented the ransom money, entrusted to him by Willshire, to Sidi Hamet.

The camel guides, uncertain of allegiances, remained on guard throughout the midnight meeting — even within these small parties, alliances could shift with the momentum. Under strict orders from bel Cossim, the cameleers urged the party to continue on. As they parted ways once more, Hamet promised Riley that he would see him again. Bel Mooden refused to return to Swearah while his colleague bel Cossim was still within the grasp of Shiek Ali and went with Hamet.

The sailors continued north with the camel guides and with the three muleteers and mules brought by Bel Mooden to help carry them back. Once again, they found themselves in the awkward position of having handlers who could not speak their language, no one who could interpret their problems without a laborious conversation, no one to reassure or encourage them. Having had their hopes raised and dashed more than once, the sailors remained leery of their circumstances. Without Rais bel Cossim or Sidi Hamet, who would defend them if they were confronted by armed Moors or Arabs now?

Three of the sailors mounted the mules, whose shuffling gait they preferred to the pounding of the camels. Covered by straw-filled blankets, with bulky panniers made of palm leaves slung across their backs, the mules offered a broad seat best for sidesaddle riding. But the mules' easy pace lulled the exhausted sailors toward a sleep they could not afford. When Burns drifted off, he toppled from his mule, struck his head on the rocky path, and lay unconscious. It was the second time in a matter of days that he had been knocked out, and try as he might, Riley could not fully revive him this time. The muleteers lost patience. Burns, semiconscious, was hoisted onto a mule, and a muleteer mounted behind him to hold him on. They continued as fast as they could through the night.

Agadir marks the southern end of a coastal strip where the High Atlas joins the sea. Swearah, their destination, marks the northern end. In between lies a spiky stretch rougher than anything they had seen since the desert: gullies, boulder-strewn riverbeds, craggy mountainsides, cliffs. James Grey Jackson said it was a three-day journey from Swearah to Agadir. Lempriere commented wryly that while a seventy-six-mile journey generally should not take three days, the way was not over the "level turnpikes of England" (p. 413).

In the cold night mist rising from the sea, the Commerces and their guides traveled numbly toward Cape Ghir, only eighteen miles by sea northwest of Agadir but twice that on the tortuous land route. The path took them along the coast, sometimes dropping onto the beach. Where a strip of sand ended, they climbed nearly vertical faces on what Riley described as "a winding kind of zigzag road that seemed to have been cut in the rock in many places by art." The route descended into deep valleys with these broad natural stone stairs covered in tricky scree, demanding all the concentration of beast and rider. Rocky bluffs pinned them to the coast.[1]

Slowly up and slowly down, the sailors clung to their mules, thankful to no longer be pounded by the camels but now beaten by their own profound drowsiness. As their nodding heads jolted them awake again and again and their arms and legs flailed reflexively to help them regain equilibrium, they feared they might hit the ground like poor Burns or, worse, tumble to the sea.

Dawn broke on a dramatic panorama. The sailors could see the Atlas foothills on one side of them and the sea on the other. Towering inland, Jebel Tazenakht, nearly 4,430 feet high, fifteen miles east of Cape Ghir, marked the western end of the Atlas chain. They were northing another milestone.

At dawn, Sheik Ali nearly stumbled over Rais bel Cossim, asleep at his threshold. Unaware that he had been outmaneuvered, Ali suggested that they pay their respects to the governor. Bel Cossim insisted disingenuously that first he would have Riley make them coffee. Ali agreed.

When they entered the place where the sailors had slept and discovered them missing, bel Cossim feigned shock. He erupted in rage, accusing Ali of having stolen the slaves during the night. "I will have you arrested and sent before the governor," he shouted, "and you will be condemned by the laws of Islam."

Awakened by the shouting, Moulay Ibrahim, who knew of bel Cossim's deception and had, in fact, watched over the sleeping Ali the previous night as bel Cossim sent the sailors off, rushed in, and joined bel Cossim in castigating Ali. "I can no longer hold friendship with a man who is capable of committing such an act," he declared. "This is one of the worst breaches of faith that ever disgraced a man of your supposed high character!"

The tactics put Ali uncharacteristically on the defensive. He admitted that the night before he had discussed having the party detained until the matter could be settled but insisted that he had had no part in the disappearance of the slaves. He begged not to be denounced to the governor, urging bel Cossim, instead, to leave a small gift for the governor and to proceed immediately to the north, the direction in which the slaves must surely have escaped.

"I am in your power, and will go on with you and my friend Moulay Ibrahim, without any attendants, to prove to you that I am innocent," Ali conceded, "and that I place the greatest confidence in your friendship."

They rode north together, bel Cossim and Ibrahim trusting that the sailors' seven-hour head start was enough to put them beyond reach of their search. Not long after they had arrived on the plateau to the north of Agadir, they encountered Sidi Hamet's party traveling south. Sheik Ali now resorted to righteous indignation, accusing Hamet of reneging on his lawful debts. He and Seid owed him four hundred dollars, he declared, which they were obligated to pay him upon their return from the desert. They had, instead, passed three days through his territory without informing him of their return, "without even calling on me to eat bread," he complained, bitterly. This was disrespectful and dishonorable. He was their patron and would have accompanied them with a guard safely through Sidi Hashem's territory. "But you wished to cheat me of my money, as you did of my daughter," he accused Hamet.

Hamet did not take the bait. He could only lose a shouting match with the older, more powerful man. He replied calmly but firmly to the tirade, "It is better for us to settle our disputes than to quarrel. For the goods that you consigned to us to sell on the desert, Seid and I owe you exactly three hundred and sixty dollars, though, in fact, the merchandise was not worth half that much. To settle this matter, however, we agree to pay this amount, but no interest on it."

After some discussion, Ali accepted these terms. Hamet counted out the required number of silver pieces from the ransom money that Willshire had sent and handed them to Ali, who agreed that the matter was settled. Rais bel Cossim presented Moulay Ibrahim with a gift for his hospitality and justice. They swore lifelong friendship and prayed together. Ibrahim, whose secret betrayal of Ali had gone undetected by the sheik, now returned to the south with him. Ibrahim could rest soundly knowing that he had done the right thing, averting a large-scale conflict and not materially harming the sheik. The rest of the party headed north again.

Around ten o'clock, Hamet, Seid, bel Cossim, and Bel Mooden caught up with the sailors. Riley asked bel Cossim what had happened to Sheik Ali and Moulay Ibrahim. "They have set out for their homes," he replied. The group stopped nearly at sea level beside a well that gave them good water, and over a breakfast of biscuits and butter, bel Cossim told Riley about the meeting that had settled matters between Hamet and Ali.

With the recent arrivals and the muleteers and camel guides, the sailors were now in the hands of a strong, heavily armed company of men. The group again followed a path along the beach where there was enough firm sand and, where the beach terminated, headed up the bluffs on tight switchbacks. To reach Cape Ghir they faced either a lengthy inland trek around insurmountable peaks, which would take them through possibly hostile passes, or a direct route across an exposed cliff face. They chose to attempt the latter, on a narrow, storied ledge above the sea.

The Jews' Leap was a path so wanting that once you started on it with beasts, there was no turning around. Slightly less than a half mile long, it had earned its name when a chance meeting between six Jews heading north from Agadir met a company of Moors heading south, resulting in catastrophe. It was customary for travelers in both directions to make sure the path was clear by checking it from an outcropping at either end built for that purpose or by calling loudly and listening for an answer. But it was after dusk, and both parties, being in a hurry and assuming no one else would be crossing at that hour, failed to take the usual precautions.

The two groups of men, all mounted on mules or other beasts, met in the narrowest section about halfway across, where it was impossible to pass each other or to turn back. The Moors were outraged and threatened to throw the Jews down. The Jews, though by necessity submissive in Morocco, would not sacrifice their mounts without a fight. The Jewish leader vaulted carefully over the head of his mule with a large stick raised for fighting. The first Moor did the same but with a scimitar, forcing the Jew back and knocking his mule off the ledge. The Jew's stick was soon hacked to a nub. Faced with being stabbed or pushed off, he lunged for the Moor's arm, grabbed hold, and leaped over the side.

Another Moor and two more Jews followed, along with eight mules, before the rest could flee on foot. Eventually, relatives of the dead Moors hunted down and murdered the three remaining Jews, completing the tragedy.

In one stretch, the trail narrowed to just two feet. Any slip by mule or camel meant a hundred-foot plunge into the sea. "It is, indeed, enough to produce dizziness," Riley observed, "even in the head of a sailor."

They continued on to Cape Ghir, on a path undercut by the sea, so that huge chunks of the coast were lying in the churning surf below them. Riley was certain that where he stood would soon follow. Inland lay "an inclined plane . . . covered with pebbles and other round smooth stones that bore strong marks of having been tossed about and worn by the surf on a sea beach." This was topped by "cliffs of craggy and broken rocks," in all, a 1,200-foot promontory, around which mariners have frequently reported treacherous shifting winds.

North of the cape, the party stopped at a wadi, which Riley identified as "el wod Tensha" and is now called Oued Tamri. Not crossable for twenty miles inland during the rainy season, the wadi had been reduced to a stagnant pool. The company ate more biscuits and butter. Bel Mooden shared some dried figs, dates, and nuts. Then they crossed over the massive sand dam to the north bank of the Tamri.

They rode fast toward the highlands in the east. Having passed no dwellings, only saint houses, since leaving Agadir, they now began to see hilltop casbahs again. For two hours, they climbed up one slope, reaching the top as dark fell, and traveling down through an ancient groove in the limestone, sometimes fifteen feet deep and wide enough for only one beast to pass at a time. In the narrowest stretch, they had to remove the mules' panniers. After descending for three hours, they reached a plain on which they rode until midnight. They camped on the flat roof of a long stone cistern outside a walled town. Barking dogs aroused the inhabitants, and a contingent emerged, greeting the strangers with the traditional "Salem alikoom, labez," as if it were the middle of the day and they were expected. They fed the Muslims couscous, while the sailors ate dates and figs.

After traveling for twenty-four hours straight and not having slept for half again as long, the sailors were nearly delirious. "The night was damp and cold," Riley recalled, "and this, with my fatigues, rendered it impossible for me to sleep." Three hours after they got settled, the sun rose, and they set out again.

Even now that they were in the sultan's realm, they were not just any Westerners. Once relegated to slave status, Christians were at the mercy of the sultan, who could still detain them indefinitely if he so chose, waiting for gifts from government emissaries for his "hospitality." At this point, though, the race to freedom was increasingly against physical and mental collapse. The men were so weak and run-down that they could barely stay on their mules. After sunrise, they could see that they had reached a richer land, though, like the rest of the region, stressed by the recent drought. They passed compounds, villages, and fields enclosed in stout walls of stone mortared with lime. The plowed fields awaited rain and barley seed. Cattle, horses, donkeys, and camels gnawed on shrubbery for want of grass, and the goats fed on the bitter shells of argan nuts.

Now they began to ascend once again. At the top of a hill, one of the Moors pointed out to the sailors their path. It lay over two mountains, the farther being twenty miles away. They climbed to the summit of the nearer of the two, where they had an expansive view of the awesome chain of snowcapped High Atlas peaks knifing through the clouds to the northeast. The mountain they stood upon marked the border with the region known as Haha. As they descended into the first valley of Haha, they passed camels and mules packed with salt and other goods. The men with them wore caftans under their haiks, turbans, and daggers or scimitars in scabbards, hanging on red wool cords from their shoulders.

Here again villages with lime-mortared walls and turreted casbahs, all designed to harbor livestock at night, occupied the knolls. As elsewhere, the valley's normally fertile fields had been devastated by drought and locusts. No one would sell the travelers barley for their animals. As they passed, whirring locusts scattered before them like a parting sea.

The men zigzagged up another slope beside a roaring stream that irrigated terraced fields, worked by men and boys, and then vanished into the sand before reaching the valley below. On a plateau near the summit, they discovered peaks of a different sort: heaps of salt. Standing in a patchwork of red clay pans, dozens of workers raked red-tinted crystals into great piles. "To see marine salt in such quantities on the top of a mountain, which I computed to stand at least fifteen hundred feet above the surface of the ocean," Riley commented, "excited my wonder and curiosity." It was the biggest salt operation in all of Morocco.[2] A saline spring filled the pans, which gleamed like a mirror, until the sun evaporated the water, leaving salt. Hundreds of piles awaited loading onto four hundred donkeys, mules, and camels.

The party stopped near the operation, and bel Cossim paid off the camel guides, who had extended their escort this far in order to load up with salt to take back and trade in the south. Meanwhile, the curious salt mine workers broke to examine the Christians. They gave them raw turnips, which the sailors gladly accepted. Riley deemed them "the sweetest I had ever tasted, and very refreshing."

After parting with the cameleers, the rest of the group descended the gentler north side of the mountain onto a level plain of argan groves. Shortly after dark they came to a walled village and entered a large livestock pen on the eastern side of it. The sound of the village men chanting evening prayers at a mosque on the north side of the village filled the plain as the travelers settled near one of the pen's stone walls for protection from the night wind. More weary than hungry, they gnawed on hard biscuits and drank water. According to Riley, they too "thanked God for his goodness" and then lay down and slept.

Several hours later they woke suddenly, choking on dust. Their reeling minds tried to cope with the braying, bellowing, and staccato grunts that surrounded them. The hardpan trembled as thirty Arabs drove dozens of camels, mules, and donkeys into the pen, heedless of the current occupants. Irritable from their journey, the camels growled as they collapsed beneath their heavy loads, lurching backward and forward to the ground. After the Arabs had unpacked the beasts and lain down wrapped in their haiks to sleep, bel Cossim and Hamet quietly roused their party, and they continued on their way.

As the sun rose, they saw some Berber dwellings. Riley begged bel Cossim to buy milk to soothe their stomachs and to give them energy to keep them going, but the Berbers, who had little to spare in the drought and wanted nothing to do with the night-traveling band, refused to sell them any. "Keep up your spirits, Captain," bel Cossim told Riley, seeing that he looked desperate. "Only a few hours longer and you will be in Swearah if Allah the Almighty continues his protection."

"I was so reduced and debilitated," Riley recalled, "that I could not support even good news with any degree of firmness, and such was my agitation that it was with the utmost difficulty I could keep on my mule for some moments afterwards." Sidi Hamet had ridden ahead, so Riley knew they must be getting close. But after waiting eight weeks for a moment that until very recently he had despaired of, Riley could not comprehend the fact that they would reach the town in only a few hours. Each step felt like it could be his last.

Around eight o'clock in the morning, they came upon another set of large dunes. As the mules plodded stoically up the side of one, the sea came into sight. There before them, at last, lay the stone walls and towers of Swearah, on the shallow peninsula of Mogadore. Near the town rode a brig flying the Union Jack. Ten months earlier, the sight of Britain's colors would have raised the Americans' ire. Now it brought tears of joy.

Riley looked at Horace with fatherly affection. The boy's grin pushed back the dark lines on his face like ripples on the surface of a pool. He had been through so much in the past months and borne it well. Some stumble into manhood, some fight it, but few earn it as he had. Truly, he was a man now. Riley was proud to be his adoptive father.

Burns and Clark perked up for a moment, but their slack faces soon returned to the gloomy, wasted cast they had assumed and would not shed without the passage of time. Savage's eyes flashed. As turbulent as his mind had been, there was still fight in him. Riley looked upon him with sorrow, but he would hold no grudges.

Impatient with the excruciatingly slow pace, Bel Mooden and Sidi Mohammed now raced ahead to the town, leaving the sailors with bel Cossim. "There is a vessel to carry you to your country and family," announced the Moor, suddenly garrulous. "Inshallah, you will soon see the noble Willshire, who will relieve you from all your miseries." Bel Cossim prayed out loud in Arabic, and then in Spanish declared his own wish: "May it have pleased Almighty Allah to have preserved the lives of my wife and children!"

About two miles southeast of Swearah, they stopped beside an imperial palace, a square-walled enclave with thirty-foot towers, capped by green tiles, at each corner. Nearby, a stream flowed into

"[Riley's] and his men's first interview with Mr. Willshire, with a distant view of Mogadore." (from *An Authentic Narrative of the Loss of the American Brig Commerce*, 1817)

the bay, across which rose the walls and minarets of Swearah. The mules grazed while the men relaxed and gazed out past the many small fishing boats on the water at the impressive town, a view that, Riley declared, "infused into my soul a kind of sublime delight and a heavenly serenity that is indiscribable, and to which it had ever before been a stranger."

Then suddenly, to their astonishment, the American flag rose above the town.

"At this blessed and transporting sight, the little blood remaining in my veins gushed through my glowing heart with wild impetuosity," Riley exclaimed, "and seemed to pour a flood of new life through every part of my exhausted frame."

William Willshire approached on horseback. Bel Cossim met him and prepared him for the sight he was about to encounter. As they rounded the corner on foot, Riley heard bel Cossim say only, "Allá están" — There they are.

Willshire had seen captive Englishmen just off the desert before, but he was staggered at what now met his eyes: five men so ragged and wasted that he was momentarily repelled. Then he strode forth to greet them.

Now it was Riley's turn to be stunned. This young man, not yet twenty-five, dressed in an immaculate riding coat with tails, concern etched in the fine features of his face, was the same tall, trim youth he had seen in his dream on the desert, the dream that had buoyed and propelled him to this point.

Heedless of his formal attire, the flesh-and-blood Willshire embraced the musky, bearded captain, half clad in a filthy haik hanging from one shoulder. "Welcome to my arms, my dear sir," he said. "This is truly a happy moment." Tears trickled down Willshire's face as he took the once powerful seaman's hands. He winced as their frail old-man bones shifted in his grip.

"Come, my friends," Willshire said at last, "let us go to the city."

～ Homecomings ～

As soon as Riley and the sailors entered the town, attracting a great crowd, the Bashaw of Swearah summoned them to appear before him. After examining them, he pronounced them free, subject to the sultan's approval. At Willshire's house, barbers sheared their lice-ridden hair and beards. Servants gingerly washed their ravaged skin and rubbed them down with oil.

The date was November 7, though they certainly did not know it when they entered Swearah. For the first time in more than two months, the sailors felt clean clothes against their bodies. They ate well-seasoned beef kebabs, wheat bread with butter, and pomegranates, an unforgettable meal cut short, alas, by the sailors' nausea. A Russian Jewish doctor administered "physic" for their ailing stomachs. Riley credited this man's continuing care during the following weeks with restoring their health.

On his first night of freedom, Riley broke down. He was delirious with symptoms of what we now know as post–traumatic stress disorder. This was not an unusual reaction for sailors recently emancipated from the desert, who tended to be "abject, servile, and brutified," according to British vice-consul Joseph Dupuis. "If they have been any considerable time in slavery," he elaborated, "they appear lost to reason and feeling, their spirits broken, and their faculties sunk in a species of stupor which I am unable adequately to describe" (Adams, p. 130).

Regarding his sudden collapse, Riley was, as usual, forthright.

"My mind, which (though my body was worn down to a skeleton) had been hitherto strong, and supported me through all my trials, distresses, and sufferings, and enabled me to encourage and keep up the spirits of my frequently despairing fellow-sufferers," he said, "could no longer sustain me: my sudden change of situation seemed to have relaxed the very springs of my soul, and all my faculties fell into the wildest confusion." Riley cowered in the corner of the room he shared with Savage, frequently crying, trembling when anyone approached, convinced that he was about to be carried back to the desert. Willshire himself attended to him, taking him for walks in the house's gallery during his more lucid intervals.

As the men slowly regained their equilibrium, Willshire insisted that they be weighed. Riley, whose normal weight was 240, weighed less than 90 pounds. Clark and Burns, who had been the sickest, had dropped to levels "less than I dare to mention," reported Riley, "for I apprehend it would not be believed, that the bodies of men retaining the vital spark should not weigh forty pounds."[1]

Willshire sent as far away as the city of Morocco, a hundred miles, for hearty food to supplement the sometimes meager rations available at Swearah. A Captain Wallace of the English brig *Pilot* even brought the Americans salt pork, split peas, and potatoes, reasoning that sailors needed ship's mess to restore their health.

Now Riley received a letter from Horatio Sprague. The Gibraltar merchant told him that he had written Willshire to guarantee that "your draft on me for twelve hundred dollars, or more, shall be duly paid for the obtainment of your liberty, and those with you." Sprague told Riley in this letter, dated November 13, that he hoped to soon have "the happiness to take you by the hand under my roof again." In his rush to meet Riley's obligation to the Arabs, Sprague had delivered the two double-barreled shotguns — including his own, a finely crafted weapon — to Willshire. Riley's risky promise to Hamet and Seid, who had remained as guests in Willshire's house for two weeks, was at last fulfilled.

Having received their coveted guns, the brothers prepared to leave. Hamet was eager to return to his family but promised that afterward he would set off with a strong party to find the rest of the crew of the *Commerce*. The following morning, the Americans saw the brothers off. Though Riley could never fully understand Hamet's ways, the Arab had earned not only the captain's respect but his admiration. True, he had profited through a corrupt system involving the ransoming of human beings, but by his own standards and the standards that Westerners in this place had no choice but to accept, he had done nothing immoral. In the end, he had saved the sailors from slavery; he was a humane and trustworthy man. Grateful at being rescued, Riley did not regret the bargain he had made, only the circumstances that had made it necessary. Now that he was dressed as a Westerner again and among powerful friends, he would not turn his back on Hamet, a man who had seen past their differences and trusted him, in a place where trust among strangers was a rare thing.

At their departure, commensurate with his means, Riley gave Hamet a small present, which he did not name, and Willshire gave him some fine gunpowder and other tokens of his gratitude. Riley noted with confidence that Hamet again swore, "by his right hand, he would bring up the remainder of my crew if they were to be found alive, and Allah spared his life."

Savage, Burns, Clark, and Horace embarked on a Genovese schooner under the British flag for Gibraltar on January 4, 1816. Riley stayed behind. He had promised Archie Robbins to do all that he could to send assistance, and he would be true to his word. After an emotional departure from Willshire, who would later tell his colleague James Renshaw, "I shall always reflect with pleasure on the day that made me acquainted with Mr. Riley," the captain crossed Morocco by mule to meet James Simpson, the American consul-general in Tangier, to ensure that arrangements were made to rescue the remainder of his crew.

Clark and Burns returned to the United States from Gibraltar on board the Massachusetts ship *Rolla*. At the end of January, Riley himself reached Gibraltar, where Horatio Sprague received him with "demonstrations of unfeigned joy." Riley, Savage, and Horace sailed on board the New York ship *Rapid,* reaching New York City on March 19 after a forty-four-day passage.

Reunited with Phoebe and his children in Middletown, Riley could not rest long. "Our meeting was one of those that language is inadequate to describe," he noted. "I spent only a week with them, our hearts beating in unison." He was bound for Washington to lobby for his urgent causes: finding his shipmates and repaying Sprague. He was received by many congressmen and introduced to Secretary of State James Monroe, who, Riley said, "received me in the most kind and feeling manner." The administration agreed to pay the $1,852.45 needed to cover the ransom and expenses and assured Riley that funds to liberate the rest of the crew would be made available. But Willshire wrote Riley on March 10 to say that he had neither heard from Sidi Hamet nor received the "least information" respecting the rest of the crew.

Like Robbins, William Porter had been carried south to the coast, where he continued to have problems with his eyesight. Heading north again, he went completely blind, and his master had to carry him in a basket on a camel. When a February rain rejuvenated their camels, his master instructed him to bathe his eyes in camel's milk and water several times a day. This treatment, Porter believed, restored his sight.

Around the beginning of March, eight traders with the same number of loaded camels entered the camp of his master's tribe and bartered with them for four days. At the end of that time, Porter discovered that the traders had bought him. The leader, a man named Hamet, informed him that they would take him to Swearah, where his captain had arrived safely. Hamet fed him dried figs, dates, and biscuits.

After traveling north for a month, the band of traders left the desert. Three days later, they encountered a company of fifty men on foot who appeared suddenly before them and brought them to a halt. The men on foot did not have firearms or even swords. Each had a leather bag on his left side, suspended by a belt slung over the opposite shoulder, filled with stones. They demanded that the traders give them the white slave. Hamet refused. The robbers, with their overwhelming numbers, would not back down. The traders fired a volley, dropping a number of their foe, but the rest immediately began to pummel them with fist-size rocks thrown with amazing strength. When the furious battle was over, Hamet and his seven men lay dead. The stone throwers stripped them of their clothing and arms and fled south to a walled village with the camels, the goods, and Porter. About a month after the attack, Porter was taken to Wednoon and sold to Abdullah Hamet, a wealthy merchant who treated him well.

In March 1816, to Porter's great surprise and joy, he was reunited with Robbins, who suddenly arrived in Wednoon. Having nearly been starved to death, Robbins had been treated by Meaarah with the hot knife and fed meat. Meaarah then sold him for five camels and two blankets to Hamet Webber, an Arab trader of the Oulad El Kabla, which, Robbins said, was a splinter of the Oulad Bou Sbaa but "more warlike as a tribe, and less cruel as individuals than any Arabs I had seen." Life with Hamet Webber was good. Robbins thrived as they wandered a great distance northeast and then northwest. Three days outside Wednoon, Webber had sold Robbins to Abdallah bel Cossim, not the bel Cossim who rescued Riley but the same man who had previously owned and brutalized Robert Adams of the *Charles*. Robbins was put to work harvesting barley, tobacco, and other crops and building a mud wall around a field.[2]

In April, Willshire received a scrap of paper from Wednoon with William Porter's signature scrawled on it. In a second note, the nearly illiterate sailor managed to inform him that Robbins was in Wednoon also. Six months later, Willshire ransomed Porter for $163 and informed Riley in a letter that he had negotiated a ransom for Robbins. Porter arrived in Boston in December and reunited with Riley in New York shortly thereafter.

Riley, who included an update of Porter in the second edition of his memoir, listened intently as the sailor told him about his journey to Swearah. He was most interested in the man named Hamet who was killed while transporting Porter north. When Porter told him that the Arabs had biscuits (a Western food that could only have

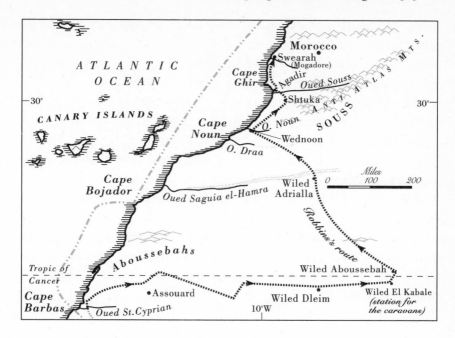

come from Swearah) and that each carried good double-barreled guns, Riley felt certain that this Hamet was his Sidi Hamet, who was "under a most solemn oath to do his utmost in endeavouring to prosecute the redemption of the remainder of [the] crew." Riley was sure that Sidi Hamet had died trying to keep his word. He mourned the news, not only because he considered Sidi Hamet a good man but also because he knew that the crew's best chance for rescue had perished with his Arab friend.

Meanwhile, Robbins, like Robert Adams before him, suffered under bel Cossim's cruel son Hameda and was brutalized by bel Cossim, who one day threw a heavy stone at him, hitting him in the side and leaving him in pain for two months. Robbins began to give up hope. The Muslims of Wednoon, he wrote, "had often urged me to espouse the faith of a good Mussulman — relieve myself from slavery — take an Ishmaelitish wife, and become great. I cannot tell what increasing misery might have driven me to." Finally, he was bought by an emissary of a wealthy Berber named El'ajjah Mahomet and taken to his house 130 miles north of Wednoon. From there he wrote Willshire and eventually was taken to Swearah. In March 1817 Robbins finally arrived there, as he described it, "clad in an old woollen frock shirt, as my whole apparel; my hair had grown at random in every direction; and my beard presented one evidence of a Mahometan." Willshire treated Robbins with the same kindness he had his shipmates. Soon thereafter, Robbins set sail for home, arriving in Boston in May.

In Swearah, Willshire had told Robbins that two Christian slaves were on an island near an Arab fishing camp far to the south. He had sent an emissary "to find them, if possible, and bring them to him that they might be redeemed." Robbins knew that these two men had to be James Barrett and George Williams, but neither was ever rescued. No verifiable news of the remainder of the crew of the *Commerce* — Dick Deslisle, John Hogan, and Antonio Michel — was ever received.

To honor the two men who helped save him and his four shipmates, the captain renamed his two youngest sons Horatio Sprague Riley and William Willshire Riley. At his request, Congress voted to formally thank William Willshire for his role in rescuing the Commerces. This acknowledgment was delivered to Willshire through the U.S. consulate at Tangier. President James Monroe also sent a letter via the British government thanking Willshire for his services.

Riley's account of the voyage of the *Commerce* and the captivity of her crew on the Sahara, published in 1817, was encouraged by Monroe and many congressmen and endorsed by New York statesman and abolitionist DeWitt Clinton. Aaron Savage wrote in an open letter printed in the book: "I do hereby certify that the narrative up to the time of our separation in Mogadore, contains nothing more than a plain statement of facts, and that myself, as well as others of the crew, owe our lives, liberties, and restoration to our country, under God, to [Riley's] uncommon exertions, fortitude, intelligence, and perseverance."

Riley's memoir became legendary, propelling him to national and international fame. It was published in England that same year;

French and Dutch editions followed during the next two years. Riley's son William Willshire Riley later claimed that it had been "read by more than a million now living in these United States." Although this figure is an exaggeration that has been amplified by careless scholars, Riley's narrative did make a widespread and deep impact. Abraham Lincoln, for one, read the book as a boy and never forgot Riley's graphic tale of captivity.[3] One well-known nineteenth-century Ohio historian was named Consul Willshire Butterfield, and a South Carolina man named his son Sidi Hamet.

The book remained in print through the end of the nineteenth century. Walking along blustery Cape Cod beaches and imagining himself on the desert, Henry David Thoreau thought of Riley's narrative, "notwithstanding the cold," as he stated in his collection *Cape Cod*. Anecdotal evidence of the *Narrative*'s impact and long popularity can be found in an 1876 history of education in Ohio:

> One pupil read from the family Bible, another from Poor Richard's Almanac, while still a third read thrilling passages from some highly prized volume, such-as Captain James Riley's Narrative of Shipwreck and Captivity among the Arabs. If the reader of the last chanced to possess some elocutionary power, the whole school, teacher included, suspended operations and with open mouths and eyes listened intently to the interesting narration.

Riley's son William would claim that "no private citizen of this country, whose name has been altogether unattended by any official station to give him consequence in the opinion of the world, has made himself so extensively or so favorably known as has Capt. Riley" (*Sequel*, pp. iv–v).

Riley's book made the survivors of the wreck of the *Commerce* celebrities of sorts in their communities and in their travels, though this did not necessarily help them materially. The brutal conditions of captivity had left a lasting mark on each of them. They suffered from various health problems, and two died within seven years of returning home.

James Clark was plagued by swellings in the neck and chin, which were diagnosed as scrofula, or tuberculosis of the lymph glands, and deemed incurable. Dr. Felix Pascalis examined him in November 1816 and in a letter described a broken man with kidney pain, incontinence, depression, and a swelling in the neck so painful that Clark begged him to cut open his glands. "He was emaciated, of a pale, sallow, and dark spotted appearance," Pascalis observed. "His weakness was extreme; he could not move without difficulty, as if his joints were stiff; and his thinking powers seemed also slow or suspended." Under Pascalis's care, which included alkaline baths and poultices, applications of potash to his glands and sores, and the use of ammonia, phosphate of soda, opium, bark, and wine, Clark made a remarkable recovery, but he lived only a few years longer, dying in 1820, at age twenty-nine, in New Haven.

Shortly after returning to East Haddam, Thomas Burns remarried, to Jane Lord, who soon gave birth to a daughter, Agnes. The family eked out a living on a rented farm, though Burns, who had suffered from two concussions in Morocco, exhibited questionable behavior. In November 1818, under rather odd circumstances, he shot twenty-three-year-old Ezekiel Fox. "Burns having been annoyed, as he says, by a *white Cat,* loaded his gun, and went out in the evening for the purpose of shooting it," the *Connecticut Courant* reported. "Perceiving something moving, as he supposed, along the top of the wall, which he thought to be the white cat, he fired and shot the young man dead on the spot." Burns claimed that Fox's white vest and cravat had fooled him. He was apparently never prosecuted. Five years later, Burns, then forty-nine, his wife, and daughter all became ill and died. The *Courant* obituary identified Burns simply as "one of the unfortunate sufferers with Capt. Riley, on the great desart of Sahara."

Aaron Savage married Martha Edwards of Middletown Upper Houses in 1817 and died in Stonington, Connecticut, on May 16, 1831, at the age of thirty-six. In 1842, his daughter Margaret married Captain Riley's son William. They gave their child Sarah, born the following year, the middle name Willshire.

Nothing else is known of William Porter's life except that he died in Stow, Ohio, on September 11, 1847, at age sixty-three.

After returning to Connecticut, Archibald Robbins published his own narrative recounting the shipwreck and his captivity, which lasted the longest of any of the survivors'. In matters of fact, Robbins's work largely confirmed Riley's, the fate of Antonio Michel being the chief difference between the two, along with Robbins's omission of the theft of the bottle of wine. Like Riley's book, Robbins's was an immediate sensation and went through twenty printings by 1830. Robbins remained a mariner and became master of a brig in the West Indies trade. He was later captured by Spanish pirates, who plundered his vessel and tried to extort more money from him by hanging him upside down until he was nearly dead. Eventually, they released him. In 1823, he earned a large profit ferrying workers up the Hudson to dig the Erie Canal. That same year, he married George Williams's niece Almira, and they gave their first son, William, born in 1826, the middle name Riley. Robbins, judiciously, left the sea to become a storekeeper and postmaster. After Almira died, in 1835, Robbins married her sister Elizabeth. They moved to Solon, Ohio, where Robbins, a father of nine, died in 1860.

In 1825, Horace Savage became master of the Hartford schooner *Spartan* and the following year of the *Albion*. He eventually moved to Mexico, where he lived and traded for some years. Despite his urging, his wife, Lavinia, refused to move there from Wethersfield, where she remained with their daughter, Jane. Horace later returned to Wethersfield, where in 1882 he died, the last known survivor of the *Commerce*, at the age of eighty-two.

His book sales notwithstanding, Riley's Sahara ordeal left him broke and battling chronic arthritis. In 1818, he went west on horseback, hoping to improve his health and find new opportunities. He worked as a government surveyor in northwest Ohio, a low-paying job in wilderness so fierce that in one swamp the ravenous flies killed his horse. Yet Riley saw promise in these wilds. He bought

360 acres on the St. Mary's River, settled his family there in a log cabin, and established a town, which he named Willshire. "My object," he wrote with his defining zest in a letter to his friend John F. Watson in New York, "was to Establish mills, to build up a town, which would be likely to perpetuate the Name of *my benefactor,* to Establish my children in a new Country, where with proper industry and energy and good conduct they might rise with the Country." His hope was that by river and canal, he would be able eventually to establish trade with the East Coast.

But Riley was still pursued by his personal demons, memories of his captivity on the desert and anxiety over the fate of his shipmates left there. "Overcome by this crowd of sensations which torment me almost incessantly," he wrote in a letter in 1819 to Ohio governor Ethan Allen Brown, "I endeavour to shake them off by sleep, or laborious employment, but all in vain; if sleeping, my agonized soul is harrowed up by phantoms."

But if Riley was forever troubled by his experiences in Africa, he was also improved by them. He became an outspoken advocate for abolition. "When the subject of slavery is brought forward — every nerve & sinew about my frame is strangely affected . . . my whole body is agitated," he wrote in the letter to Brown, protesting the admission of Missouri to the Union as a slave state. Having suffered "cruelty & religious intolerance and bigotry," he now cherished freedom and religious tolerance and could not accept the enslavement of black Africans, "who have been snatched & torn from their native country . . . by professors too of moral & political freedom & christian benevolence.

"Men though covered with a black skin are not brutes," he concluded. "The hypocritical advocate of slavery shall be detested by all mankind."

The arduous life of a pioneer suited Riley. He thrived and was elected to the General Assembly of Ohio in 1823. But wolves, mosquitoes, isolation, and recurring illness often made life miserable for his family. In 1826, weakened by fever, Riley suffered an attack of what was then called phrenitis, an inflammation of the brain now known as encephalitis. He suffered from painful swelling of his throat and neck and partial paralysis. Finally, he had to be trans-ported to New York heavily dosed with opium.

Riley's doctor told him he should return to the sea, where the air would do him good, and during a short passage off the coast he found his health wholly restored. After more than a decade on land, he decided to resume the life of a merchant captain. Three years later, he was joyfully reunited with Horatio Sprague in Gibraltar. Since the time of his captivity, Riley had spoken out on a number of causes, and now he suggested reforms to strengthen America's international trade.

In a long, lucid, and impassioned letter to U.S. Senator John Forsyth, he argued that the nation's consular system was outmoded and needed to be revamped. Among its shortcomings was the fact that it employed many foreign nationals whose commercial interests conflicted with those of the U.S. merchants they were supposedly serving and who sometimes did not even reside in the port where they were consul. At the same time, Riley made an appeal for Sprague, a "feeling, liberal, talented, honorable and independent" American citizen, to be named consul at Gibraltar.

Because of his widely read book and his outspokenness, Riley was well known in Washington. Although he remained an outsider there and something of a gadfly, several times failing to receive promised political appointments, his letters to top government offi-cials were often heeded. On April 30, 1832, much to Riley's satisfac-tion, the senate approved President Andrew Jackson's appointment of Sprague as American consul at Gibraltar.

The following June, Riley returned to Swearah. He was too late to see Rais bel Cossim, who, having remained close to Willshire — con-ducting other missions for him and often inquiring about Riley — had died suddenly in 1825. Willshire had written to inform Riley of the news, saying, "By the Boston and other newspapers, you will most probably hear of the death of your liberator, Rais bel Cossim," indicating, by the suggestion that the press would report the Moor's death, the extent to which Riley's story had become known.

Willshire, now a married man with young children and graying hair, welcomed Riley to the place the captain associated with liberty and rebirth. The Englishman captured their relationship in a letter to his namesake, William Willshire Riley:

> A long series of years has made no abatement in the gratitude your good father has always expressed towards me, and made known to the world by the publication of the narrative of his shipwreck and sufferings: And I assure you, that the mention of my name in such honorable terms, has proved a passport to me wherever I have traveled; and has given me a stimulus to emulate and deserve the character given me — far as I fall short of the description, I have studied to deserve it.

Riley returned to the United States with a cargo of goatskins, gum, wool, and almonds. He and Willshire had become business partners and remained so until Riley's death.

In 1836, nearly three decades after the seizure of his ship the *Two Marys* with all its cargo, Riley and his associates received partial war reparations. While no amount of money could have compensated Riley for the misfortune that had turned the momentum of his career and caused his family so much distress, it was at least a moral victory.

In March 1840, on a voyage from New York to St. Thomas, Riley fell ill and died at sea on board the brig *William Tell*. He was committed to the deep. Later that year, the *William Tell* sank off Gibraltar with all hands but one.

Four years later, William Willshire lost his fortune. When a French squadron bombarded Swearah, destroying its batteries and igniting chaos, Berber fighters there to protect the town looted it instead, brutalizing and robbing Jewish and foreign merchants. Two of Willshire's houses were pillaged in the process, and Mrs. Willshire even had the stays of her corset searched for hidden gold. Leaving everything he owned in Africa, Willshire fled with his family back to England, thus bringing to an unceremonious conclusion his remarkable thirty years' service to his nation and to sailors of all nations in Morocco.

∾ Appendix ∾

The Publishing of Riley's Narrative

∾ After putting the finishing touches on his manuscript, begun in Morocco, Riley took it to the printer William A. Mercein on Gold Street in Manhattan. There he was greeted by a young Thurlow Weed, who would go on to prominence as a political journalist and backroom manipulator. Weed, an apprentice, read the first chapter. "I ventured to suggest that it was carelessly written and needed revising," Weed wrote in his memoirs, noting that Riley seemed annoyed at first but, nonetheless, took it away and "availed himself of the services of a school-teacher, who improved the whole narrative in its style and grammar." Riley acknowledged two men who assisted him. New York City lawyer and man of letters Anthony Bleecker revised the manuscript and suggested explanations. In one instance he recommended deleting a section sharply critical of the Jewish merchants of Swearah. Josiah Shippey, Jr., also a New Yorker — presumably the schoolteacher — whom Riley described as a close friend, suggested improvements "both in point of diction and grammar." Shippey's wordsmithing is evident throughout the manuscript.

Now in the collection of the New-York Historical Society, Riley's bound manuscript of irregular-size sheaves of paper is largely written in one rather polished hand. Only a small number of pages, including the last three with a description of and speculation on African geography as well as the news of Porter's ransom, match up with the handwriting in Riley's letters before and after the shipwreck. A comparison of the handwriting in Bleecker's letters to that in the manuscript shows that he was not the person who took down Riley's story. I was unable to locate any samples of Shippey's handwriting, but he would have been the most likely amanuensis, though the possibility remains that Riley dictated the book to his wife, Phoebe.

Bleecker was an early supporter of the New-York Historical Society. Riley joined the society and presented its head, John Pintard, with his manuscript on February 20, 1817.

The second edition of Riley's narrative, published in Hartford by the author in 1817, has a map showing a modified route of Riley's Sahara crossing. It also contains a postscript, from New York on June 25, 1817, in which Riley gives news of Porter and Robbins, both of whom had recently returned from Africa, and of Clark's flagging health.

In a note to an 1818 third edition published in New York by Collins & Co., Riley states that "care has been taken to correct some errors which had crept into the former [editions]." Some versions of the third edition also include Judah Paddock's account of his own shipwreck and captivity on the Sahara, which had not been published before. In a letter printed in the book, Paddock called Riley "a man of veracity and strict integrity."

A British edition, titled *Loss of the American Brig Commerce*, appeared in London in 1817 and a French edition, *Naufrage du Brigantin Américain Le Commerce Perdou Sur la Côte Occidentale d'Afrique, au mois d'août 1815,* came out in Paris the following year. Both carried a testimonial letter from James Renshaw, the former British consul-general to Mogadore, saying that Riley "has given a very accurate description of what he has seen. Judging, therefore, from that part of his travels which accords with my own personal observations, it is I think fair in me to conclude that the remainder is described with equal veracity." Renshaw noted that Mr. Green, His Majesty's consul-general at Tangier, considered Riley "a very intelligent and well informed man" and that William Willshire had informed him that not only did Riley possess the "ability" to produce a valuable work on the region but his "very considerable influence with his own government" had already gained for James Simpson, U.S. consul-general in Tangier, "extensive limits to redeem American shipwrecked citizens" in Morocco.

New editions appeared in the United States in 1820 and 1823. Andrus and Judd, of Hartford, Connecticut, published a revised edition of the narrative in 1829, and this stereotyped edition was reprinted many times up through the Civil War. Most recently Riley's narrative has appeared from Clarkson N. Potter (1965) and the Lyons Press (2000). The slightly abbreviated edition published by these two presses unfortunately contains many often confusing typographical errors.

∾ Glossary of Arabic Terms ∾

baraka	The virtue of a holy man and the healing, miracle-making, or magic powers associated with him.
bedouin	An Arab of the desert.
besmillah	A frequently used blessing meaning "In the name of Allah."
bir	A well deeper than forty feet.
chorfa	A religious tribe that traces its ancestry to Muhammad, often spuriously.
djellaba	A long-sleeved, hooded woolen cloak.
erg	On the Sahara, an area of shifting sand dunes. *Erg* covers about a tenth of the Sahara.
foonta	Bad, worthless.
friq	A tribal subgroup of half a dozen or fewer families, a unit large enough for mutual protection but small enough for effective grazing of the animals; their camp.
geddack	A wooden bowl used for cooking and eating.
ghazu	A tribal raid for booty.
haik	A long piece of cloth, usually about six yards by two yards, that Arabs wrap around the head and body for protection from the sun and sand.
hammada	Plains of wind-stripped rock, similar to *reg* but generally higher in elevation.
inshallah	"If it is God's will." A frequent invocation of Arabic speakers.

irifi	A hot, dry desert sandstorm created by powerful winds blowing from the south or southeast. The *irifi* kills plants, hones the landscape, and creates sand drifts.
jmel	A male camel.
Kabyles (or Qabila)	A Berber people of North Africa who are largely agricultural.
kelb en-Nasrani	Christian dog or dogs. A curse.
kul	Eat.
lhasa	Semolina or barley mush.
l'hoot	Fish.
makhzen	The Moroccan government; the ruling class in Morocco.
moulay	A title roughly equivalent to "lord," originally used for the descendants of the Prophet Muhammad and later taken by many sultans and princes.
oued (or wadi)	A riverbed, dry except in the rainy season, often a rare place of vegetation in the desert.
rais	Captain or chief.
reg	Hard plains covered with boulders and stones, lower than the *hammada,* including depressions in the desert floor caused by wind erosion. Caravans usually prefer to travel on the *reg.*
salem (salaam) alikoom	Peace be with you.
selaï	A large wooden bowl used for watering camels.
sharif	A descendant of the Prophet Muhammad through Fatima, his daughter.
shesh	A long, thin rectangular cloth wrapped about the face and head for protection and ending in a coil.
sidi	A term of respect used for an Arab male, comparable to "Mr."
zenaga	A lesser tribe that must pay tribute to a master tribe.
zrig	Sour camel milk, often mixed with water.

∾ Notes ∾

∾ The events in this story are taken from the memoirs of Captain James Riley and seaman Archibald Robbins. In order not to interrupt the narrative, I have not cited quotations from their books. These passages are usually easy to find because the chronologies are essentially the same. At times I have created dialogue for conversations implied by Riley or Robbins. I have occasionally elaborated on scenes based on my study of the time period and my travels in the region. For the most part, I have retained Riley's and Robbins's renditions of Arabic names and language, though many of them would be transliterated differently today.

Regarding religion, it is almost universally acknowledged that Christians, Jews, and Muslims worship the same God. In other words, the God of the Old and New Testaments and the God of the Quran are one and the same. All three faiths trace their roots to Abraham. Although Muslims call Christians and Jews "infidels," the Quran nonetheless holds them in higher regard than those they deem to be pagan — giving rise to the traditional term Muslims use for Jews and Christians, "People of the Book." It was for this reason that in places long under Islamic control by the time of Riley, there were often prominent and thriving Christian and Jewish communities.

Prologue

1. Captain James Riley reported in his *Narrative* that before heading into the desert, the caravan "cut wood and burned coals for the camels, for the caravans never attempt to cross the desert without this article." He was confused in this, however, perhaps through a poor translation of Sidi Hamet's account or perhaps because the actual substance resembled charcoal, or both. In explaining this mistake, Riley's French translator cited

British Consul-General to Swearah James Renshaw, who had observed the Arabs of the Moroccan Empire using the fruit of the argan in the way described here. The balls of argan pulp resembled charcoal.

Chapter 1: A Good Yankee Crew

   1. The original name of the Rileys' fourth child is unknown. He was renamed Horatio after his father's 1815 voyage to Africa.

   2. The wording of Riley's petition is found in *Sequel to Riley's Narrative,* page 392.

Chapter 2: Omens

   1. Under the wrong conditions, this was a treacherous spot for mariners. Riley later wrecked the brig *William Tell* here in April 1831. His vessel was pulled off the reefs by salvagers, who wanted half the value of the brig and its contents as their return for about six hours' work, during which they never left their crafts or were endangered in any way. Riley fought these claims in court, where a compromise was struck.

   2. Though they did not know it, the *Commerce*'s Archie Robbins and his cousin Horace Robbins, a drifter whose life made a seaman's look sane and stable, were possibly in New Orleans at the same time. Having left the Lower Valley as a trader six years earlier, Horace had landed in Mexico and ended up on the wrong side of a battle between the Spanish Republican Army and the Spanish Royalist Army. After surviving a crushing defeat at San Antonio, he fled with four Americans and a Spaniard into the mountains, where they survived for seventeen days on tree bark, rodents, and snails. He lived closely watched among Indians for a year before Indian traders helped him to escape. Making his way to New Orleans, he had joined Andrew Jackson's army but being away on duty missed the Battle of New Orleans. By the time Horace ventured back to Connecticut from New Orleans five years later, his relatives, having heard a report of his demise, had erected a tombstone in his memory.

   3. The entrances and clearances records for the Port of New Orleans at the National Archives and Records Administration in Washington show that the *Commerce,* Master Riley of Middletown, entered the port on June 1, 1815. No reference to the *Commerce*'s departure can be found. Both Riley and Robbins, who in 1817 published separate accounts of their journey, agree on the June 24 departure date. Curiously, the thrice-weekly *Louisiana Gazette* carried advertisements for the *Commerce* through the July 28 issue, at the rate of a dollar for the first day and fifty cents for each additional appearance. The "ship news" list in the June 29, 1815, issue, does not list the *Commerce* under its heading "cleared, June 24."

4. The August 12 *Gibraltar Chronicle* notes the arrival of the *Commerce*, "40 days from New Orleans," in its list for August 5 to 11.

5. Riley wrote that Clark, Porter, Barrett, and Hogan were in the boat, but Robbins's narrative contradicts this, saying that it was he and three others who crewed the craft. I have placed Robbins in the boat, and as Clark and Porter were of equal rank to Robbins, I have removed Clark, reasoning that Porter seemed to be of a willing nature and a good friend of Robbins's and that the two might have chosen to do the duty together. The material point here is that Robbins was indeed in the craft and provided some of the details of this description of the incident.

Robbins's account also contradicts Riley's in another way. He says Captain Price's schooner was embayed and that they had assisted the schooner in beating out of the bay.

Chapter 3: Shipwreck on Cape Bojador

1. The English and Americans called the peso, or Spanish piece of eight (eight reales), which was widely circulated in Africa and the Mediterranean, the "Spanish dollar." It was roughly equivalent in value to the American dollar. Depending on location, the value of the Spanish dollar and the American dollar ranged from four to five to the pound sterling.

Chapter 4: A Hostile Welcome

1. Under attack from skeptics who doubted the veracity of his own book, Riley published Paddock's memoir, *A Narrative of the Shipwreck of the Ship Oswego, on the Coast of South Barbary,* in 1818. Paddock's account corroborates many of Riley's observations regarding the desert and the Arabs of the western Sahara. The passage quoted from is found on page 176.

2. "Sahrawi" is the collective name of the inhabitants of Western Sahara regardless of race or tribe. Although it was not coined until 1976, when Spanish Sahara became Western Sahara, I have used it as the most succinct way to identify the people of the region at the time of this story.

3. Riley certainly exaggerates when he says he "could not but imagine that those well set teeth were sharpened for the purpose of devouring human flesh!!!" A little more subdued, Robbins writes that the man had "gnashing" teeth. Both were playing to their audience's fear of cannibals.

4. The passage criticizing the avarice of Americans appears only in Riley's manuscript, which is in the collection of the New-York Historical Society. It was removed by his editor. Riley was presumably aware of the change.

5. In his *Narrative,* Riley writes it "Allah K. Beer," explaining that he knew "Allah" was the Arabic name for the "Supreme Being" and that he guessed "K. Beer" meant "our friend or father."

Chapter 5: Misery in an Open Boat

1. Oddly, neither Riley nor Robbins mentions the subsequent actions of the tribe that attacked them. Since the captain ordered a single unarmed man — Porter — ashore, he must have felt certain they were not hiding nearby. That the Sahrawis would have simply abandoned eleven potential Christian slaves, who represented a small fortune to them, is hard to explain. The news of a shipwreck on the Sahara usually attracted tribes from hundreds of miles away, and fighting over the spoils often resulted: perhaps this band felt it more important to secure the silver they had already taken than to wait around and risk a fight over the unsubmissive sailors.

2. Writing in the October 1817 *Monthly Review, or, Literary Journal* (and unaware of the contradiction between Riley's letter and memoir), one London critic dodges the question of Riley's moral culpability, noting of the incident that he "attempts to justify it on more pleas than one, the strength of which we leave to be decided by the learned in moral casuistry."

3. This sailor's oath is found in Noah Jones's *Journals*. Early European and American mariners usually practiced hazing inspired by ancient pagan seafaring rites when crossing the Tropic of Cancer. In modern times, sailors often perform similar ceremonies when crossing the equator.

4. Riley's and Robbins's chronologies do not coincide exactly, which is not surprising given that neither was able to keep a written account at the time and both recorded the events after considerable and eventful delays. Their calendars of the boat voyage differ by two days. Both say it began on August 29, and both say they turned back to the coast on September 2. Robbins believed they reached land on September 5, while Riley says September 7. To complicate matters, in an open letter published in the March 26, 1816, *Connecticut Courant,* just after his return to New York, Riley said they returned to the ship on August 30 and reached land again on September 8. Riley's chronology contains other inconsistencies, which I have tried to reconcile. When his and Robbins's accounts differ, I generally deem his to be more accurate, given that as captain he was used to keeping a detailed log and that he recollected the events a good year in advance of Robbins.

Chapter 6: Purgatory

1. In his manuscript, Riley originally recorded that the urine had passed through their bodies twenty times. Upon reflection, he reduced it to twelve.

2. We seem to remain as conflicted as McGee was in assessing the value of drinking urine. Opinions vary so widely that while a U.S. Marine Corps desert operations manual advises Marines never to drink urine even

in survival circumstances, some natural health faddists recommend a daily regimen of urine consumption for nutritional and medicinal purposes.

3. Robbins gives the date as September 6.

4. Although Riley mentions finding only locusts, Robbins reports that while they were traveling below the cliff that day, they came across the tracks and dung of wild animals; that night, they heard howling in the dark. He also writes that the next day they saw a leopard, which was actually probably a wildcat or a cheetah.

5. Riley says they also had sticks they had carried with them from the boat, but he does not mention these sticks earlier when he describes the digging of wells. These inconsistencies are typical of his account. It and Robbins's differ in minor ways. The sailors discovered the tracks of a camel and the footprint of a man, and Riley says they determined them to be "old"; Robbins maintains that they were "recently made," adding, "indeed they must have been, as the blowing of the dry sand would soon have filled them up."

Chapter 7: Captured

1. Was the fact that Riley stole from the cook, the only black man, an act of racism, happenstance, or something else? In survival situations, people tend to cluster around, protect, and seek protection from those most like them, whether by family relation, race, religion, or nationality. This was perhaps most profoundly demonstrated in the wreck of the *Méduse* in 1816, when the 150 men, women, and children set adrift on a makeshift raft factionalized by race, nationality, and even profession as they murdered one another in a desperate struggle to survive. Théodore Géricault portrayed the tragic scene in his epic 1819 painting *Le Radeau de la Méduse,* now hanging in the Louvre. Riley might have picked Deslisle because he was most conveniently located, or perhaps because Deslisle, being a black man and one of the lowest-ranking in the crew, was the most different from him. Nevertheless, as events progressed, Riley showed that he was above many of the baser instincts, in a way that seemed to transcend both his religious upbringing and his role as captain. He showed moral strength based on common sense and his own fortitude, and for a man of his day, he seemed remarkably free of bigotry.

2. While it is common knowledge that a severely malnourished stomach should be filled slowly, it takes more than common restraint for the owner of that stomach to do so. Rescued from a gale-wrecked schooner in the Gulf Stream off Virginia in 1830, Captain Charles Tyng warned his crew that drinking too fast would make them sick. In the cabin of his res-

cuer, he found a pitcher of water. "I thought I would just take one swallow," he related, "but when I put it to my mouth I could not take it away until I had nearly emptied it of its contents." Tyng paid for it with racking pain and vomiting.

3. For further reading on rehydration, see E. F. Adolph and associates' landmark 1947 work, *Physiology of Man in the Desert,* incorporating much research on the subject from World War II.

4. In various parts of the world, the saddle on a dromedary, or one-humped camel, sits in front of, on top of, or behind the hump, each position having its advantages. In front of the hump, the rider has the most control over the camel and can reach farther forward when fighting. Behind the hump, he has more freedom of movement, and the pounding is less severe. On top of the hump, on a platform or raised saddle, the ride is smoother, but the rider has the least control of the camel.

Chapter 8: Thirst

1. Lempriere, p. 725. Nigritia, also then known as Soudan, was a large region of sub-Saharan central Africa.

2. My experience riding camels while tracing parts of Riley's route and attempting to cover more than twenty miles a day corroborates the sailors' pain. On the first day I rubbed a hole bigger than a plum through the flesh of my backside. At the end of that day, even our guide, a camel-racing instructor, fell off his mount and writhed on the ground with leg cramps. Later in the journey, another guide became so sore while riding that he strapped a Land Rover cushion on top of his saddle and blankets. Fast speeds were untenable for long distances while riding in front of the hump. Behind the hump was only slightly better and required us to cram shoes and empty water bottles beneath the backs of our saddles to keep from being bounced off the camel's rear end.

3. In his memoir, Robbins rarely approaches Riley's objectivity. His account is largely bitter and lacks empathy for the Sahrawis, though he does acknowledge Ganus's kindness to him.

4. According to *The U.S. Army Survival Manual,* a man working moderately in the desert in ninety-five-degree heat needs to drink about two and a half gallons a day.

5. Robbins's account of this meeting is, as usual, less detailed than Riley's. Among the contradictory details they give, Riley places the meeting on the evening of the second day of their captivity, but according to Robbins, Ganus led him out of camp and on a five-mile march to the council on the morning of the third day, and then they left it around three in the

afternoon. They do not agree on which sailors were there, Riley pointing out only that Porter and Burns were not there, while Robbins remembers seeing Burns. Neither mentions Savage by name. Robbins recollects that there were about twenty nomads present, typical of the many tribal gatherings he saw during his captivity, while Riley describes a much larger group.

6. Although, like many Westerners of his day, Riley uses the terms *Arab* and *Moor* interchangeably, the Moors are generally considered to be specifically the descendants of the Arabs who occupied Spain for eight centuries, beginning in 711, and who then inhabited the cities of the Empire of Morocco.

7. Robbins believed that Riley was using the stones to negotiate a ransom price, an easy mistake on his part since neither he nor the other men understood Riley's conversation with the Arabs.

Chapter 9: The Sons of the Father of Lions

1. The tribe's name has appeared in numerous forms in the West. Brisson calls them the Labdesseba, placing them on a 1792 map of his and Saugnier's routes to the southeast of Cape Blanco and dubbing them "a ferocious nation." Mungo Park's 1798 map also places the Labdessebas in this vicinity. Riley does not name them, but the map of his route published with his *Narrative* indicates regions belonging to the "Labdessebahs," near Cape Blanco, and the "Abdoussebahs," to the north, which he apparently did not realize were branches of the same tribe. Robbins calls his captors "Wiled Lebdessebah" and places them near Cape Blanco on his map. He marks an area to the north as belonging to the "Wiled Aboussebah." Joseph Dupuis, who annotated *The Narrative of Robert Adams* (1817), calls them the "Woled Aboussebah" and notes that "there are various branches of it, who consider themselves wholly independent of each other, yet all calling themselves the 'Woled Aboussebah.' " Some of these names may actually be variations of the more generic term for the peoples of these regions, l'Abd al-Siba, or "those in dissidence." Adding to the confusion are twentieth-century renditions of the tribe's name. In his book *Spanish Sahara* (1976), John Mercer calls them simply "Sba." One of the most detailed descriptions of the tribe is in Pazzanita and Hodges's *Historical Dictionary of Western Sahara* (1994). They use the modern French transliteration "Oulad Bou Sbaa," which I have adopted and often shortened to "Bou Sbaa," as is common.

2. Riley never actually gives the name of his third master, instead calling him "my old master" to distinguish him from his sons, Riley's "young masters." From Riley's references to Arab names, I have taken "Sideullah,"

one of the few that did not belong to any of the other sailors' owners, as the name for this third master.

Chapter 10: Sidi Hamet's Feast

1. When Muslims accept a gift or a serving of food or drink, they often say "Besmillah" — In the name of Allah. Riley would have picked up on this often-repeated Arabic word and used it as an American would use "Thank you."

2. In his seminal 1928 book *Le Sahara,* the French anthropologist E.-F. Gautier observes that among the Tuareg tribe, bathing in water was almost taboo. He theorizes that it was not due just to the scarcity of water but also for fear of adversely affecting the sweat glands and causing overheating. But, he adds, rather poetically, that for a human body "exposed almost naked to the desert wind for an entire lifetime, the rites of cleanliness are superfluous; the eternal wind, charged with sand, scours the human skin and keeps it as clean as it does the slabs of naked rock on the tops of the plateaus" (p. 16).

3. Today a standard English translation of the Shahadah is "I bear witness that there is no God except God. Muhammad is the messenger of God."

4. According to Knut Schmidt-Nielsen et al., in "The Question of Water Storage in the Stomach of the Camel" (1956), "the fluid that can be drained from the rumen contents is like a green soup and it seems rather repulsive to the normal person. However, to the desert traveler who is out of water, any fluid is attractive, and he will even drink his own urine. In this situation the rumen fluid would be quite helpful because of its relatively low salt content" (p. 10).

5. The details of this argument over Hogan come primarily from an account by Robbins, who heard about it from Hogan. Robbins calls Hogan's master "Mahomet" and does not point out that he was also Riley's first master, who claimed Dick Deslisle and the captain at the outset. Riley calls him "Hamet." To avoid confusion with Hamet, the Bou Sbaa trader from the north, I have used the full name and more standard spelling "Mohammed."

6. Robbins actually writes "kellup en-sahrau" (more properly, *kelb es-sahrawi*), which means "desert dogs." It is used as an insult because the dog is considered one of the lowest forms of animal on the desert. Here and later, he translates it, however, as "Christian dogs" — *kelb en-Nasrani* — which makes more sense in context.

7. Riley recalls in his memoir that they were in the process of departing, already walking up the dune, when Robbins appeared. If the fire was

still burning, then Robbins probably smelled either the lingering scent of camel grease, which had saturated the area, or some vestige of a meal the tribesmen were trying to concoct from the stripped carcass.

Chapter 11: Is It Sweet?

1. Riley repeats the date September 28, thus throwing his chronology off by a day. He does it again on October 2, putting him two days behind in his account.

2. Robbins writes that the Arabs prayed four times a day, but the Quran actually prescribes five daily prayers: at dawn, noon, midafternoon, sunset, and twilight (bedtime).

3. Riley's water calculations show that he was not very precise in his math. He guessed that the big pool had "not more than fifty gallons" and that the smaller pool held much less. Yet the large camel alone drank sixty gallons all at once. Three other camels and all the men also drank, and they filled up two skins. Even if the smaller camels drank half as much as the large one, they still would have consumed more than Riley estimated was there, and it is unlikely that the spring would have replenished itself so quickly.

Chapter 12: Honor Among Thieves

1. In the manuscript of Riley's narrative, unlike the published book, the word *savage* is capitalized and underlined, further suggesting that the culprit was the second mate.

2. I tried to identify this herb root while I was in Western Sahara. As I described the substance, my trusted guide nodded his head to indicate he knew what I was talking about. He returned from an unseen kiosk in Laayoune with a six-inch sheep-shinbone pipe still adorned with wool and a bag of a sweet-smelling brown substance that he called *menajie*. Smoking it was like smoking tobacco, and, in fact, I was told by another guide that *menajie* was a blend of tobacco from Mauritania.

3. Riley calls *lhasa,* the Arabs' semolina or barley mush, "lhash" or "l'hash." Robbins calls it "laish."

Chapter 13: Skeletons

1. Roger Key, a senior mapping geologist at the British Geological Survey, who recently completed a remapping project of the area west of Atar, Mauritania, has suggested that what Robbins saw might have been a large reef of vein quartz, which can reach tens of yards high. There is no marble in the area.

Chapter 14: Wednoon and the Atlas

1. Riley spells the name "Moolay Solimaan." In the nineteenth century, the state was generally referred to as "the Empire of Morocco." A sultan is the sovereign of a Muslim country; the title "Moulay" is often translated as "king" or "emperor." (Morocco's chief ruler has been officially called king since 1957.) *Moulay* is the French, and most commonly used, transliteration of the Arabic title, which is also seen as *mulay* and often today as *mawlay*. It roughly translates to "lord," and was originally used for the descendants of the Prophet Muhammad. In Morocco, most sultans took the title before their name, even if they were Berber and thus unrelated to the Prophet.

2. By "dwarf" alder, Riley probably meant the black alder, or alder buckthorn, a berry-bearing European shrub, once believed to be related to the alder tree.

3. "Bel Cossim" is the transliteration that Riley and Robbins (as well as S. Cock and Joseph Dupuis, who edited Robert Adams's narrative) use for this surname, a fairly common one in northwestern Africa. Today, it would appear as Belkaçem (the preferred French spelling) or, in English, Belkassem. In a postscript to his narrative, Riley uses "bel Cafshim."

4. It is not surprising that two men like Hamet and Hassar, used to traveling and trading in the region, seemed to know people everywhere. In a place where there was little outside news, a man's reputation and that of his family radiated far. Tribal, family, and village ties carried great weight, as did the bond of Islam, with its tradition of hospitality. Naturally expressive and not overburdened with distractions, the people of this region still make friends quickly. As I traveled across a broad stretch of the Sahara with a loquacious guide named Mohammed el Arab to research this book, he seemed to know everyone we met. In one memorable encounter, a man who looked like the grim reaper in his hooded djellaba appeared on the horizon just as we climbed off our camels and sat down for lunch near a remote salt flat. I watched as the walker crossed the ridge in front of us and his path arced like a rolling steel ball diverted by a magnet toward us. This stranger was soon embracing Mohammed like a long-lost brother. He drank tea and shared our meal. They exchanged news and cigarettes, gesticulating warmly and laughing frequently. Afterward, the stranger disappeared over the horizon again.

5. This procedure was painful for Riley to recall and seemed almost unbelievably crude even in his day. But cauterization with smoldering wood or heated metal is still practiced as a popular cure-all on the Sahara today, as I discovered from my guide Achmet, who bore scars on his neck and shoulders from a treatment for a recent illness. He told me he had been

very ill and that the branding saved his life. He has used the same technique to treat the illnesses of his young children.

6. The original Encyclopaedia Britannica, published in Edinburgh in 1771, gives reliable treatments for dysentery on pp. 117–18. Yet more than a century and a half later, in 1930, on the return leg of a grueling journey through Souss and the Saguia el-Hamra to see Smara, the young French adventurer Michel Vieuchange was brought down by the disease. He died at Agadir.

7. From this point on, Riley grows increasingly confused about the passage of time. Here in his narrative he telescopes events between October 23 and October 25.

8. This physical description of Bo-Mohammed is based on the illustration on page 329 of *Sequel to Riley's Narrative,* which calls him Bo-Mohammed of Shtuka, though he joined Riley before Shtuka.

Chapter 15: Valley of the Locusts

1. Modern Sahrawis share this affinity with their ancestors. Some, now forced to live in cities to earn a living, fill their terraces with sand, on which they pitch tents and prepare tea at various times during the day. In a remote part of the Saguia el-Hamra, where I was camping during my research for this book, I saw other city-dwellers who had ventured out from Laayoune to spread blankets and have tea on the dunes. One of my guides told me that they did this because they missed the sand.

Chapter 17: The Captain Has Long Been Dead

1. On page 217 of his narrative Riley writes that Rais bel Cossim told him Willshire "had paid the money to [Sidi Hamet] immediately," but according to this letter from Willshire to Riley, which Riley reproduces (apparently from memory) on page 218, Willshire agreed to pay the sum only upon the safe arrival of Riley and his men in Swearah.

2. At one point in his narrative, Riley says that they traveled for about five hours at the rate of five miles an hour. Several pages later, he says they traveled for five hours at about four miles an hour. I have chosen the more conservative estimate.

Robbins placed the village of Widnah just north of the Oued Sehlem, instead of three hours south of it, where Riley positioned it. Both Riley and Robbins seem to have mistaken Oued Massa, another northwest-flowing river, for Oued Sehlem, which lies farther to the south.

3. Riley says they had traveled for ten hours at this point, "from four in the morning till two in the afternoon." Previously, he says they had left Sehlemah "as soon as it dawned" and the gates were opened. Dawn occurred there around 6:30 on October 30, 1815, which was more likely their time of departure.

Chapter 18: From the Mouth of a Moor

1. Even today, this intimate sharing of a meal from the same bowl is a common act of friendship and hospitality. Strangers might well do it upon meeting for the first time, but for a Muslim to do it with a Christian is more unusual. While I was on the Sahara tracing Riley's route, it was only after we got caught too far from camp one night and had to set up an impromtu bivouac with our camels that I shared a bowl with three of my guides. Our heads nearly touching as we leaned over the large, flat bowl, we ate using bread and our hands after a long day on the trail.

2. Riley says November 4, but he has lost track of the dates. He makes reference to the fourth day after Seid's departure. Even if November 2, the day Seid and Ali left, is counted, that would make this the 5th. Yet he calls the next day the 4th, and the day after that he calls the 4th as well. Later, he makes reference to "October 6," intending "November 6." At this point, he abandons date-keeping altogether, until December 1.

3. Riley goes on to observe that he found this belief that the camel was a sacred beast to be prevalent throughout the region. My experience as I traced Riley's route in 2001 substantiated this observation. On my first day on a camel, as we were running on the beach, my saddle began sliding to the side, eventually dumping me on the sand — not far, I might add, from a long stretch of rocks that could well have "dashed out" my brains. The first thing Mohammed el Arab, a camel-racing instructor and my guide, said to me was "That was your fault. Why didn't you jump?" Shaken and incredulous, I did not respond at first. He then quipped, good-naturedly, "It doesn't matter. Those who fall from camels never get hurt."

Chapter 19: The Road to Swearah

1. Writing earlier than Jackson and Riley, Lempriere explains that the coastal path was through "one continued expanse of wild, mountainous, and rocky country. . . . Our progress indeed could be compared to nothing but the continual ascending and descending of a series of rough and uneven stone steps. At one place in particular the descent was so steep, and the road so choaked [sic] up with large pieces of stone, that we were all obliged to dismount and walk a full mile and a half with the utmost caution and difficulty, before we could mount again" (pp. 713–14).

2. Salt pans can still be found today in the hills between Agadir and Essaouira (Swearah). Techniques and conditions have changed little in two hundred years. Families live in windowless earthen huts on the perimeter

of the pans; men, women, and children all work in some part of the salt extraction process.

Epilogue: Homecomings

1. In an October 1817 review of Riley's *Narrative,* the London literary journal *Monthly Review* states that "we do not see any reason to discredit the general story: it containing nothing to impeach its own veracity, but much to corroborate it; and it is externally supported by the printed correspondence of those individuals who procured the author's redemption," but the critic notes that the "description of their sufferings, indeed, exceeds any thing of a similar nature which we recollect to have read; and they seem to be more than any human beings could inflict or any endure." The drastic loss of weight Riley reported, the writer adds, "makes us almost doubt the author's accuracy, though we do not suspect an intentional error." Modern physicians would agree that while it is possible for a 240-pound man to lose 150 pounds over time, to have done it in less than three months is improbable. Riley was convinced of it, however, and willing to risk his credibility on it.

2. Riley mistakenly reports that Porter was owned by bel Cossim in Wednoon; Robbins says Porter was owned by a different wealthy man.

3. William Riley's claim that "more than a million" Americans had read Riley's narrative (*Sequel,* p. iv) has often been misconstrued to mean that one million copies were published. The error can be traced at least as far back as Gerald McMurtry's article "The Influence of Riley's Narrative Upon Abraham Lincoln" (*Indiana Magazine of History,* 1934). Even if William Riley's bold estimate of a million *readers* was accurate, the number of *copies* purchased would have been far smaller, especially when library copies are taken into account. In trying to accurately assess the numbers printed as well as to determine the impact of Riley's book, historian Donald Ratcliffe cites nineteenth-century library records showing a high rate of readership for the title in certain regions, anecdotal evidence of Riley's fame, and the great extent to which his narrative saturated the public. Ratcliffe concludes that even the claim of a million readers was overstated, though that many people may have read some version of Riley's story either in his book or in various periodicals.

In the only biography authorized by Abraham Lincoln, John L. Scripps's *Life of Abraham Lincoln,* Scripps wrote that after the Bible, Aesop's Fables, and *Pilgrims's Progress* in Lincoln's early reading "came the Life of Franklin, Weems's Washington, and Riley's Narrative" (p. 3).

∽ Selected Bibliography ∾

Adams, Charles Collard. *Middletown Upper Houses: A History of the North Society of Middletown, Connecticut, from 1650 to 1800, with Genealogical and Biographical Chapters on Early Families and a Full Genealogy of the Ranney Family*. Facsimile of 1908 ed. Canaan, N.H.: Phoenix Publishing (for the Ranney Genealogical Fund), 1983.

Adams, Robert. *The Narrative of Robert Adams, An American Sailor, Who Was Wrecked on the Western Coast of Africa, in the Year 1810, Was Detained Three Years in Slavery by the Arabs of the Great Desert, and Resided Several Months in the City of Tombuctoo*. Edited by S. Cock and Joseph Dupuis. Boston: Wells and Lilly, 1817.

Adams, Sherman W. *The History of Ancient Wethersfield*. Edited by Henry R. Stiles. Vol 1. Facsimile of 1904 ed. Camden, Me.: Picton Press, 1974.

Adolph, E. F., and associates. *Physiology of Man in the Desert*. New York: Interscience, 1947.

Africa Pilot: Volume 1, Comprising the Arquipélago da Madeira, Islas Canarias, etc. 13th ed. Taunton, England: Hydrographer of the Navy, 1856.

Al-Bukhari, Sahih. *The Translation of the Meanings of Sahih Al-Bukhari*, 9 vols. Translated by Muhammad Muhsin Khan. Chicago: Kazi Publications, 1979.

Alig, Joyce. *Ohio's Last Frontiersman: Connecticut Mariner Captain James Riley*. Celina, Ohio: Mercer County Historical Society, 1997.

Allen, Gardner W. *Our Navy and the Barbary Corsairs*. Hamden, Conn.: Archon Books, 1965.

Allison, Robert J. *The Crescent Obscured: The United States and the Muslim World, 1776–1815*. New York: Oxford University Press, 1995.

American Mercury. May 24, 1815.

Baepler, Paul. "The Barbary Captivity Narrative in Early America." *Early American Literature* 30 (1995): 95–120.

———, ed. *White Slaves, African Masters: An Anthology of American Barbary Captivity Narratives.* Chicago: University of Chicago Press, 1999.

Brett, Michael, and Elizabeth Fentress. *The Berbers.* Oxford, England: Blackwell, 1996.

Briggs, Lloyd Cabot. *Tribes of the Sahara.* Cambridge, Mass.: Harvard University Press, 1960.

Brisson, Pierre Raymond de. *An Account of the Shipwreck and Captivity of Mr. de Brisson; Containing a Description of the Deserts of Africa, from Senegal to Morocco.* Translated from the French. London: J. Johnson, St. Paul's Church-yard, 1789. See Saugnier for a better translation of this work. All Brisson quotations have been taken from that book.

Bulliet, Richard W. *The Camel and the Wheel.* Cambridge, Mass.: Harvard University Press, 1975.

Cochelet, Charles. *Narrative of the Shipwreck of the Sophia on the 30th of May, 1819, on the Western Coast of Africa, and of the Captivity of a Part of the Crew in the Desert of Sahara.* Translated from the French. London: Sir R. Phillips and Co., 1822.

Cooper, J. Fenimore. *The History of the Navy of the United States of America.* Paris: Baudry's European Library, 1839.

Decker, Robert Owen, with Margaret A. Harris. *Cromwell, Connecticut, 1650–1990: The History of a River Port Town.* West Kennebunk, Me.: Phoenix Publishing (for the Cromwell Historical Society), 1991.

De Villiers, Marq, and Sheila Hirtle. *Sahara: A Natural History.* New York: Walker, 2002.

Duncan, T. Bentley. *Atlantic Islands: Madeira, the Azores, and the Cape Verdes in Seventeenth-Century Commerce and Navigation.* Chicago: University of Chicago Press, 1972.

Edholm, O. G., and A. L. Bacharach, eds. *The Physiology of Human Survival.* London: Academic Press, 1965.

Elting, John R. *Amateurs, To Arms!: A Military History of the War of 1812.* Chapel Hill, N.C.: Algonquin Books, 1991.

Fabian, Ann. *The Unvarnished Truth: Personal Narratives in Nineteenth-Century America.* Berkeley: University of California Press, 2000.

Gautier, E.-F. *Sahara, The Great Desert.* 1928. Reprint. Translated by Dorothy Ford Mayhew. New York: Octagon, 1970.

Grant, Ellsworth S. *Thar She Goes!: Shipbuilding on the Connecticut River.* Lyme, Conn.: Greenwich Publishing Group, 2000.

Hodges, Tony. *Western Sahara: The Roots of a Desert War.* Westport, Conn.: Lawrence Hill, 1983.

Huntress, Keith, ed. *Narratives of Shipwrecks and Disasters, 1586–1860.* Ames: Iowa State University Press, 1974.

Jackson, James Grey. *An Account of the Empire of Morocco, and the District of Suse: Compiled from Miscellaneous Observations Made During a Long Residence In, and Various Journeys Through, Those Countries; to Which Is Added, an Account of Timbuctoo, the Great Emporium of Central Africa.* Philadelphia: Published by Francis Nichols. Fry and Kammerer, printers. 1810.

Jewitt, John R. *A Narrative of the Adventures and Sufferings, of John R. Jewitt, Only Survivor of the Crew of the Ship Boston, During a Captivity of Nearly Three Years Among the Savages of Nootka Sound: With an Account of the Manners, Modes of Living, and Religious Opinions of the Natives.* Facsimile of 1815 ed. Fairfield, Wash.: Ye Galleon Press, 1967.

Johnson, Judith E., and William H. Tabor. *The History and Architecture of Cromwell.* Middletown, Conn.: Greater Middletown Preservation Trust, 1980.

Jones, Noah. *Journals of Two Cruises Aboard the American Privateer Yankee by a Wanderer.* Reprint: New York: Macmillan, 1967.

King, Dean, and John Hattendorf. *Harbors and High Seas: An Atlas and Geographical Guide to the Complete Aubrey-Maturin Novels of Patrick O'Brian.* 3rd ed. New York: Holt, 2000.

Lawrence, T. E. *Seven Pillars of Wisdom: A Triumph.* 1926. Reprint. New York: Anchor Books, 1991.

Lempriere, William. "A Tour from Gibraltar to Tangier, Sallee, Mogadore, Santa Cruz, and Tarudant, and Thence Over Mount Atlas to Morocco." 1793. In *A General Collection of the Best and Most Interesting Voyages and Travels in All Parts of the World.* 17 vols. Africa. Edited by John Pinkerton. London: Longman, Hurst, Rees, and Orme, 1808–14.

"Loss of the Brig *Commerce.*" *Monthly Review, or, Literary Journal* 84 (October 1817): 127–39. London: R. Griffiths.

McKee, Alexander. *Wreck of the Medusa: The Tragic Story of the Death Raft.* New York: Signet, 2000. Originally published as *Death Raft: The Human Drama of the Medusa Shipwreck,* 1975.

Mackenzie, Donald. *The Flooding of the Sahara: An Account of the Proposed Plan for Opening Central Africa to Commerce and Civilization from the North-West Coast . . .* London: Sampson Low, Marston, Searle, & Rivington, 1877.

Maclay, Edgar Stanton, with technical revisions by Roy Campbell Smith, U.S.N. *A History of the United States Navy from 1775 to 1901.* New and enlarged ed. in 3 vols. New York: D. Appleton, 1904.

McMurtry, Gerald R. "The Influence of Riley's *Narrative* upon Abraham Lincoln." *Indiana Magazine of History* 30 (1934): 133–38.

Mansour, Mohamed el. *Morocco in the Reign of Mawlay Sulayman.* Outwell, England: Middle East and North African Studies Press, 1990.

Martin, Margaret E. *Merchants and Trade of the Connecticut River Valley, 1750–1820.* Northampton, Mass.: Department of History of Smith College, 1939.

Mercer, John. *Spanish Sahara.* London: Allen & Unwin, 1976.

Ming's New-York Price-Current. Various dates, 1815.

Ohio State Teachers Association Centennial Committee. *A History of Education in the State of Ohio: A Centennial Volume.* Columbus: Gazette Printing House, 1876.

Paddock, Judah. *A Narrative of the Shipwreck of the Ship Oswego, on the Coast of South Barbary, and of the Sufferings of the Master and the Crew While in Bondage Among the Arabs; Interspersed with Numerous Remarks Upon the Country and Its Inhabitants, and Concerning the Peculiar Perils of That Coast.* New York: Published by Captain James Riley. J. Seymour, printer, 1818.

Pazzanita, Anthony G., and Tony Hodges. *Historical Dictionary of Western Sahara.* 2nd ed. Metuchen, N.J.: Scarecrow Press, 1994.

Purdy, John, ed. *The Colombian Navigator, or, Sailing Directory for the American Coasts and the West-Indies.* London: Whittle and Laurie, 1819.

Ratcliffe, Donald J. " 'Captain Riley's Narrative': A Forgotten Antebellum Bestseller?" Paper delivered at the American Antiquarian Society, December 14, 1998, revised and expanded.

———. "Selling Captain Riley: North African Slavery and American Readers, 1817–1859." Paper presented to the BrANCH conference, the annual meeting of the British American Nineteenth Century Historians, Madingley Hall, Cambridge, October 5, 2003.

Riley, James. *An Authentic Narrative of the Loss of the American Brig Commerce, Wrecked on the Western Coast of Africa, in the Month of August, 1815. With an Account of the Sufferings of Her Surviving Officers and Crew, Who Were Enslaved by the Wandering Arabs on the Great African Desart, or Zahahrah; and Observations Historical, Geographical, &c., Made During the Travels of the Author, While a Slave to the Arabs, and in the Empire of Morocco.* New York: James Riley, 1817.

———. *An Authentic Narrative of the Loss of the American Brig Commerce.* 2nd ed. Hartford: James Riley, 1817.

———. *An Authentic Narrative of the Loss of the American Brig Commerce.* 3rd ed. New York: Collins & Co., 1818.

————. "Captain Riley's Narrative." *Connecticut Courant*. March 26, 1816.

————. Letter to Ethan Allen Brown. December 24, 1819. Ethan Allen Brown Papers, Ohio Historical Society, Columbus.

————. Letter to Benjamin Silliman. July 19, 1810. Manuscripts and Archives, Yale University Library.

————. Letter to John F. Watson. July 3, 1824. Rutherford B. Hayes Presidential Center, Fremont, Ohio.

————. *Loss of the American Brig Commerce, Wrecked on the Western Coast of Africa, in the Month of August, 1815, With an Account of Tombuctoo, and of the Hitherto Undiscovered Great City of Wassanah.* London: J. Murray, 1817.

————. *Naufrage du Brigantin Américain Le Commerce Perdou Sur la Côte Occidentale d'Afrique, au mois d'août 1815.* Paris: Le Normant, Imprimeur-Libraire, 1818.

————. *Sufferings in Africa: Captain Riley's Narrative.* Gordon H. Evans, ed. New York: Clarkson N. Potter, 1965.

Riley, William Willshire, ed. *Sequel to Riley's Narrative; Being a Sketch of Interesting Incidents in the Life, Voyages, and Travels of Capt. James Riley, from the Period of his Return to His Native Land, After His Shipwreck, Captivity, and Sufferings Among the Arabs of the Desert, as Related in His Narrative, Until His Death. Compiled Chiefly from the Original Journal and Manuscripts Left at His Death in Possession of His Son, W. Willshire Riley.* Columbus, Ohio: G. Brewster, 1851.

"Riley's Loss of the Brig Commerce." *Monthly Review, or, Literary Journal* 87 (October 1817): 127–39.

Robbins, Archibald. *A Journal: Comprising an Account of the Loss of the Brig Commerce, of Hartford (Conn.), James Riley, Master, Upon the Western Coast of Africa, August 28th, 1815; Also of the Slavery and Sufferings of the Author and the Rest of the Crew, Upon the Desert of Zahara, in the Years 1815, 1816, 1817; with Accounts of the Manners, Customs, and Habits of the Wandering Arabs; also, a Brief Historical and Geographical View of the Continent of Africa.* 1817. Reprint. Hartford: S. Andrus, 1851.

Saint-Exupéry, Antoine de. *Wind, Sand and Stars.* 1939. Reprint. New York: Harcourt, Brace, 1968. Translated by Lewis Galantière.

Saugnier, F., and Pierre Raymond de Brisson. *Voyages to the Coast of Africa, by Mess. Saugnier and Brisson: Containing an Account of Their Shipwreck On Board Different Vessels, and Subsequent Slavery and Interesting Details of the Manners of the Arabs of the Desert, and of the Slave Trade, as Carried On at Senegal and Galam.* Translated from the French. 1792. Reprint. New York: Negro Universities Press, 1969.

Savage, Robert D. *The Savage Family of Connecticut; Line of William Savage*. Middletown, Conn.: Godfrey Memorial Library, 1978.

Schmidt-Nielsen, Knut et al. "The Question of Water Storage in the Stomach of the Camel." *Mammalia* 20 (1956): 1–15.

Schroeter, Daniel J. *Merchants of Essaouira: Urban Society and Imperialism in Southwestern Morocco, 1844–1886*. Cambridge: Cambridge University Press, 1988.

Scott, Alexander. See Traill, Thomas Stewart.

Sparks, Jared. "Riley's Narrative." *North American Review and Miscellaneous Journal* 5 (1817): 389–409.

Stiles, Henry R., ed. *The History of Ancient Wethersfield*. Vol 2. Facsimile of 1904 ed. Camden, Me.: Picton Press, 1974.

Stofko, Karl P. "The Tale of the White Cat." *East Haddam Mysteries: Part V*. Paper delivered at the meeting of East Haddam Historical Society, Connecticut, November 1995.

Thesiger, Wilfred. *Arabian Sands*. 1959. Reprint. New York: Penguin, 1991.

Thoreau, Henry David. *Cape Cod*. 1865 (written 1855–57). Reprint edited by Joseph J. Moldenhauer. Princeton, N.J.: Princeton University Press, 1988.

Traill, T. S., and W. Lawson. "Account of the Captivity of Alexander Scott, Among the Wandering Arabs of the Great African Desert, for a Period of Nearly Six Years." *Edinburgh Philosophical Journal* IV, no. 7 (January 1821): 38–54, and no. 8 (April 1821): 225–34.

Tyng, Charles. *Before the Wind: The Memoir of an American Sea Captain, 1808–1833*. New York: Viking, 1999.

Vieuchange, Michel. *Smara: The Forbidden City*. 1933. Translated from the French by Edgar Fletcher-Allen. Reprint. New York: Ecco, 1987.

Weed, Thurlow. *Life of Thurlow Weed*. Vol. 1, *Autobiography of Thurlow Weed*, edited by his daughter, Harriet A. Weed. 1883. Reprint. New York: Da Capo Press, 1970.

Wellard, James. *The Great Sahara*. New York: Dutton, 1965.

Westermarck, Edward. *Ritual and Belief in Morocco*. 2 vols. 1926. Reprint. New Hyde Park, N.Y.: University Books, 1968.

Willshire, William. "Mr. Willshire's Narrative of Eight Days' Events at Mogadore." November 1844. Public Record Office, FO 174/49.

Wolf, A. V. *Thirst: Physiology of the Urge to Drink, and Problems of Water Lack*. Springfield, Ill.: Charles C. Thomas, 1958.

～ **Acknowledgments** ～

ᴄᴧ My thanks to everyone at Little, Brown who made the writing of this book possible, especially to Michael Pietsch and Geoff Shandler, whose guidance and insightful readings helped in so many ways.

As always, my wife, Jessica, provided invaluable support. She and friend Charles Slack helped shape the narrative even before it reached Little, Brown. Their editorial comments, inspiration, and many other contributions to this book cannot be measured, nor can my gratitude to them. Likewise, my agent, Jody Rein, provided support and advice, upon which I depend.

John Harland, M.D., author of *Seamanship in the Age of Sail,* lent his invaluable understanding of all matters maritime. Historian emeritus Donald J. Ratcliffe, of the University of Durham, England, generously shared his singular knowledge of the publishing of Captain Riley's memoir and his wisdom on other topics. Mohamed el Mansour, professor of history at Université Mohammed V, in Rabat, Morocco, and Piotr Kostrzewski, director of Cross Cultural Adventures, answered my exhaustive questions about Moroccan and Saharan culture, language, and history with unceasing good cheer. Gus Robbins, a descendant of Archibald Robbins's brother, kindly shared his time and allowed me to see some of the family heirlooms.

My gratitude goes to *National Geographic Adventure* editor Jim Meigs and the editors of that magazine for supporting my research in Africa and for serializing the book in the pages of their magazine. Jim Meigs and my friend Logan Ward both read the manuscript and offered up useful suggestions for fine-tuning. (The Ward family also kindly took in the King family in the aftermath of Hurricane Isabel, allowing work on the book to continue smoothly while all was dark in Richmond.)

My assistant and researcher Alexandra Benwell pursued leads to the far ends of the earth. Others who contributed to the research effort include Kenneth Buckbee, Diane Cameron, Jane Hines, Harlan Jessup, Sarah Raper Larenaudie, Elford Messer, John Morgan, Valérie Rodger, and Nancy Steed.

To the many other scholars and specialists whose knowledge enriches this book, my sincere thanks; they include Tony Hodges, co-author of *Historical Dictionary of Western Sahara;* Daniel Schroeter, professor of history at the University of California, Irvine; Gene DeFoliart, professor emeritus of medical entomology at the University of Wisconsin–Madison; camel expert Ahmed Tibary, assistant professor of theriogenology at Washington State University; Mohammed Sawaie, professor of Arabic, University of Virginia; Barry Cook of the British Museum; Peter Schlegel, M.D., Cornell University medical school; Warner V. Slack, M.D., professor of medicine and psychiatry at Harvard Medical School; Jo Benwell, nutrition lecturer, ret., Farnham College; Maryam and Nancy Abeiderrahmane of the Tiviski camel dairy in Mauritania; Read McGehee III, M.D., of the Virginia Eye Institute; Madia Thomson; Ellsworth Grant; Mark Snow; the Reverend Greg Jones, St. James's Church, Richmond, Virginia; and Pastor Don Hay, Congregational Church of Eastford, Connecticut.

In helping me reconstruct weather and tidal conditions, the following were essentially helpful: Bernard Ducarme of the International Centre for Earth Tides at the Royal Observatory of Belgium; Joseph M. Moran of the American Meteorological Society; Commander John Page, Royal Navy; Malcolm Walker of the Royal Meteorological Society; and Philip Woodworth and David Blackman of the Proudman Oceanographic Laboratory.

Kenneth Wilson of the Science Museum of Virginia helped me

capture astronomical details, and Roger Key of the British Geological Survey shed light on the nature of Saharan terrain.

The staffs of many libraries and historical societies were instrumental in helping me locate books, newspapers, and documents, especially Dave Grabarek at the Library of Virginia. Also, Nancy Milnor and Martha H. Smart of the Connecticut Historical Society; Allison Guiness of the Connecticut River Museum; Stephen Shaw of the Connecticut Society of the Sons of the Revolutionary War; also in Connecticut, Brenda Milkofsky of the Wethersfield Historical Society; Wendy Schnur of the G. W. Blunt White Library at Mystic Seaport; Karl Stofko, municipal historian of East Haddam Historical Society; Terry Crescimanno of Cromwell Belden Public Library.

Elsewhere, Dennis Beiso of the Gibraltar Archives; Robert Henderson of the General Society of the War of 1812; Josh Graml of the Mariner's Museum; Michael T. Moore and Susan Abbott of the National Archives and Records Administration; Paul Adamthwaite, Ph.D., of the Archives and Collections Society; David Clendinning of the Robert Manning Strozier Library of Florida State University; Kevin Windsor of the Lundy's Lane Historical Museum; Nan J. Card of the Rutherford B. Hayes Presidential Center; Habte M. Teclemariam of the Library of Congress; and the staff of the New-York Historical Society, which holds Captain Riley's manuscript.

To my travel companions, camel handlers, and camp hands on the research expedition through Western Sahara — Claudia D'Andrea, Remi Benali, J. P. Kang, Ted Lawrence, Jouwad, Hussein, Ali, Mohammed el Arab, Karim, and Achmed — thanks for your help and your forbearance on an often difficult adventure. Know that you contributed in spirit and body to this telling of Riley's and Robbins's journey. Tech wizards J. P. Kang and Lucas Krost helped me make cool show-and-tell.

Finally, I'd like to thank Little, Brown assistant editor Liz Nagle, who made sure everything got to where it was going, and copyediting pros Peggy Freudenthal, Steve Lamont, and Anne Montague made sure it read well when it came back.

Again, thanks to all.

Dean King

～ Index ～

Note: *Italic* page numbers refer to illustrations.

About the Author

Dean King is the author of ten books, including the acclaimed biography *Patrick O'Brian: A Life Revealed* and the Aubrey-Maturin companion books *A Sea of Words* and *Harbors and High Seas*. He is the series editor for the Heart of Oak Sea Classics, published by Henry Holt, and a contributor to the *Oxford Encyclopedia of Maritime History*. He has written for many publications, including *Men's Journal, Esquire, New York* magazine, and the *New York Times*. He lives with his wife and four daughters in Richmond, Virginia.

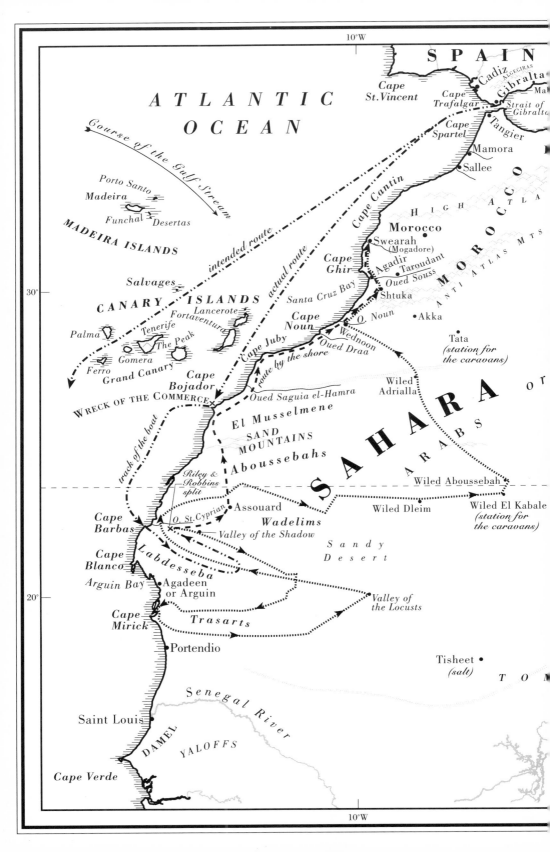